Mastery's End

Travel and Postwar American Poetry

Mastery's End *Jeffrey Gray*

THE UNIVERSITY OF GEORGIA PRESS

ATHENS AND LONDON

© 2005 by the University of Georgia Press

Athens, Georgia 30602

All rights reserved

Designed by Sandra Strother Hudson

Set in Monotype Garamond by Bookcomp

Printed and bound by Thomson-Shore

The paper in this book meets the guidelines for permanence
and durability of the Committee on Production Guidelines for
Book Longevity of the Council on Library Resources.

Printed in the United States of America

09 08 07 06 05 C 5 4 3 2 1

Library of Congress Cataloging-in-Publication Data

Gray, Jeffrey, 1944–

Mastery's end : travel and postwar American poetry / Jeffrey
Gray.

     p. cm.

Includes bibliographical references and index.

ISBN 0-8203-2663-1 (hardcover : alk. paper)

1. American poetry—Foreign influences.   2. American poetry—
20th century—History and criticism.   3. Americans—Foreign
countries—History—20th century.   4. Foreign countries—In
literature.   5. Travelers in literature.   6. Travel in literature.
I. Title.

PS157.G73 2005

811'.040932054—dc22

2004018183

British Library Cataloging-in-Publication Data available

In memory of my parents

David Elmer Gray Jr., 1909–1971

Agnes Olive Tveter Gray, 1912–1949

CONTENTS

The man who finds his homeland sweet is still a tender beginner; he to whom every soil is as his native one is already strong; but he is perfect to whom the entire world is as a foreign land.

HUGH OF ST. VICTOR, *Didascalicon*

Preface
Points on a Personal Compass

The road is a metaphor for most human pursuits as well as for life itself. It is also a figure for memory. One can cast "a backward glance o'er travel'd roads," as Walt Whitman did. Marcel Proust spoke nostalgically of "the paths of childhood." Bruce Chatwin wrote that paths are the *first* of our memories, even before persons or events. Such remarks may suggest roads as recovery, as routes to the past. Literal travel, by contrast, carries one away; roads link to other roads and those in turn to others. This latter narrative—of forking paths rather than of origins—evokes the history of an increasingly large number of people in the world. Americans, particularly in the western United States, see uprootedness as central both to the myth of American inauthenticity and to that of American freedom of choice and self-invention, a cause thus for both regret and celebration. In fact, however, the situation of Americans is now (or has long been) that of hundreds of millions of people around the planet, perhaps of most nationalities in the last half of the twentieth century. One recent formulation of this condition appears in *Éloge de la Créolité* (*In Praise of Creole-ness*), by Patrick Chamoiseau, Raphael Confiant, and Jean Bernabé, where the authors offer the example of the child of a German and a Haitian, born and living in Beijing, who is "caught in the torrential ambiguity of a mosaic identity"(112–13). The future of the world, these authors insist, is Creole.

Given this movement forward and the hybridity it confers, what sort of past is recoverable? We are led to see that the past that most grounds a person may not be his or her ancestry or birthplace, no matter how foundational such sites appear. The personal, ongoing process of drift and digression provides other pasts, other problems and opportunities. For me, five years spent in Central America, six in Asia, two in Europe, two in the South Pacific, and more moves than I can count in the United States have complicated any roots-seeking I might undertake.

In discussing the kind of identity formation suggested by Chamoiseau et al., the word *errancy* may be useful since it retains the *error* but also the drift that more romantic and politically charged categories such as *exile* and *expatriate* do not offer. *Errancy* is also appropriate for a study of poetry, since, as Charles Bernstein writes, "poetics must necessarily involve error. Error in the sense of wandering, errantry, but also error in the sense of mistake, misperception . . . as projection (expression of desire unmediated by rationalized explanation): as slips, slides" (*A Poetics* 153–54). In fact, travel is an expression of that perpetual displacement of meaning that critical theory ascribes to discourse itself in the face of cultural hungers for foundation in ethnicity, nation, or community.

As the following chapters are meant to illustrate, in the Americas after World War II, and particularly from the 1960s onward, the hold of "home" on the traveler becomes less strong. The centrifugal force of desire and the response to the call of the Other become more compelling; the process of substitution and displacement that constitutes identification becomes simultaneously less stable and more energized. Increasingly, we live, inwardly as outwardly, in that "torrential ambiguity" described by Chamoiseau, in a somewhere made up of many elsewheres.

I am grateful to several readers of this book or chapters of it: Lee Altman, Steven Gould Axelrod, Mary Balkun, Martha Carpentier, Emory Elliott, Melissa Fabros, Julia Fiedorczuk, Henry Hart, Lei Jun, Paul Mariani, James McCorkle, Jeanne McNett, Marjorie Perloff, Stanley Plumly, Dermot Quinn, and David Stevens. Emory Elliott first gave me the idea of writing about travel and poetry. Steven Axelrod suggested I write a chapter on Robert Lowell and has been an invaluable help in numberless ways ever since. I thank the poet Stanley Plumly, who kindly recommended the book to the University of Georgia Press, the Brazilian scholar Carmen Oliveira for inspiring talks and valuable information, and Melissa Fabros for her friendship and resourcefulness.

I am also grateful to Frank Bidart, Robert Creeley, and Derek Walcott, three poets who, different as they are from one another, helped me think about poetry's involvement with the journey.

I thank Seton Hall University's Walsh Library, particularly the Interlibrary Loan Division, under the direction of Barbara Ward, for obtaining many necessary texts, and the Special Collections division of the Cornell University library for access to the archives of A. R. Ammons. I am grateful for research support from Seton Hall University Research Council during four summers. I also enjoyed a National Endowment for the Humanities Summer Institute on Caribbean literature and art during six weeks at the University of Puerto Rico, Rios Piedras. I thank the organizer, poet and critic Lowell Fiet, and the participants, especially Herbert Blau, Felipe Smith, and Rafael Escribano.

As regards my own puzzling over questions of travel, I am grateful for a Fulbright Scholar's Award that allowed me to research, teach, and visit in Guatemala at the University of San Carlos in 2000. The Guatemala trip closed an arc so wide I hadn't recognized it as a circle. Beginning in Antigua, Guatemala, twenty-five years ago, the circle included lengthy divagations through Guanajuato, Mexico City, Pago Pago, Honolulu, Tokyo, Osaka, Kichijoji, Kurashiki, Seoul, Songtan, Athens, Crete, Heidelberg, Nuremberg, Haifa, Rome, Venice, Sardinia, Seattle, San Diego, Los Angeles, Riverside, San Francisco, New York City, San Juan, Vieja Havana, Belo Horizonte, Wuhan, Beijing, Shanghai, and South Orange, New Jersey.

I thank my brother and sister, David and Judith, and my cousin Jay and aunt Julia Gray for having stayed where (and who) they are, so that the idea of "home" so often questioned in these pages has not become entirely immaterial. I owe incalculably much to Rebeca Duarte Quiroga. I thank Lei Jun for showing me that love moves irresistibly across history and space. I thank my two children, Pablo and Maira, for their example of grace and hope. "*Caminante, no hay camino—se hace camino al andar.*"[1]

Most of the writing in this book has not been previously published. The section on Guatemala from "Roots and Routes" appeared in my article "Literature, Difference, and the Land of Witness" in the Modern Language Association's *Profession 2002*. A version of the Robert Lowell chapter appeared in *Papers on Language and Literature* (41.1). A few paragraphs of the same chapter appear in my essay on Lowell's *Day by Day* in *Critical Responses to Robert Lowell*, edited by Steven Gould Axelrod. Similarly, a few paragraphs of my chapters on Elizabeth Bishop and John Ashbery appear in *The Explicator* (54.1 and 54.2, respectively). My comments on the work of Nathaniel Mackey in "Travel and Difference" are adapted from my longer essay on his work published in *Callaloo* (23.2). An adaptation of a section of the chapter on Derek Walcott also appears in *Callaloo* (28.1); other parts were presented as papers at the following conferences: Modern Language Association (MLA), Chicago, December 1999; Pacific Ancient and Modern Language Association (PAMLA), Claremont, California, November 1999; PAMLA, San Jose State University, California, November 1997; "Poetry and the Public Sphere," Rutgers University, New Brunswick, New Jersey, April 1997; and Northeast Modern Language Association (NEMLA), Philadelphia, Pennsylvania, April 1997. Key ideas in my chapter on Elizabeth Bishop were also presented at conferences: the American Literature Association (ALA), Cancún, Mexico, December 2003, and, again, ALA, San Francisco, California, May 2004. Some of the introductory chapter was given as a paper for the conference "Signposts: Discourse on Travel" at the Catholic University of America in Washington, D.C., April 2003.

Lyn Hejinian's poems "Chapter Sixty-Three," "Chapter 187," and "Chapter 253" are taken from *Oxota: A Short Russian Novel*, published by The Figures, Great Barrington, Massachusetts, and appear here with permission.

ABBREVIATIONS

ROBERT LOWELL

DD	*Day by Day*
D	*The Dolphin*
LH	*For Lizzie and Harriet*
FUD	*For the Union Dead*
H	*History*
LS	*Life Studies*
N	*Notebook*

JOHN ASHBERY

AG	*April Galleons*
DDS	*The Double Dream of Spring*
FC	*Flow Chart*
HL	*Hotel Lautréamont*
HD	*Houseboat Days*
RM	*Rivers and Mountains*
SP	*Self-Portrait in a Convex Mirror*
ST	*Some Trees*
TP	*Three Poems*

ALLEN GINSBERG

CP	*Collected Poems 1947–1980*

GARY SNYDER

MR	*Mountains and Rivers Without End*

DEREK WALCOTT

AT	*The Arkansas Testament*

AL	*Another Life*
B	*The Bounty*
FT	*The Fortunate Traveler*
GN	*In a Green Night*
M	*Midsummer*
O	*Omeros*
SAK	*The Star-Apple Kingdom*
SG	*Sea Grapes*
TH	*Tiepolo's Hound*

Mastery's End

"But where you are born is a funny thing. . . . All right, you go away. But you will come back. Where you born, man, you born. And the island is a paradise, you will discover."

I said, feeling that he was seeking to drag me back into his world, where he walked with security, "I am not coming back."

v. s. naipaul, *The Mimic Men*

To theorize, one leaves home.

james clifford, "Notes on Travel and Theory"

Roots and Routes
The Trouble with Travel

In the year 2000, I made a return visit to Guatemala, where I had lived for five years in the 1970s. I was prepared for changes in government, in tourism, in the sprawl and blight of Guatemala City, and in the situation of the Indian people. But in the sphere of Guatemalan writing, one thing remained the same: most of the important authors were living *outside* Guatemala. Augusto Monterroso, possibly Guatemala's greatest writer, lives in Mexico City, as does Otto Raul Gonzalez. Dante Liano lives in Milan; Victor Montejo in Davis, California; Arturo Arias in San Francisco; Mario Roberto Morales in Iowa; Franz Galich in Managua; and Rodrigo Rey Rosa in Tangier (and, at this writing, in India). Leaving aside the individual, sometimes political reasons for these re- and dislocations, the situation raises the question of what the category "Guatemalan writer" might mean. It reminds us, moreover, that any effort involving a literary explorer setting out for the *altiplano* to interview the writers of Guatemala is doomed from the start. Better to undertake the kind of venture described in James Clifford's writing—for example, in *Routes*, where he writes,

> [O]nce the representational challenge is seen to be the portrayal and understanding of local/global historical encounters, co-productions, dominations, and resistances, one needs to focus on hybrid cosmopolitan experiences as much as on rooted, native ones. (24)

In other words, on *routes* rather than *roots*. Clifford explains the need to focus on "any culture's farthest range of travel while *also* looking at its centers . . . its intensive fieldsites" (24). "Driving to the interior" is necessarily an illusion, whether in ethnographic accounts or in the poems of Elizabeth Bishop, where that phrase occurs (*Complete* 90).

In writing about travel and poetry, it has sometimes occurred to me that expectations of rootedness no longer exist, that no one expects writers to be native informants, that even nationalities such as Mexican or Canadian, or regional indicators such as Caribbean, can be seen as partial acknowledgements of birthplace, cultural commonality, and language, disguising greater variations within the categories than between them.

But after this reflection comes another. In the academic world, roots *are* still preferred to "routes," sometimes out of a laudable commitment to community, sometimes out of nostalgia for a real or imagined lost ethnicity. Because of this, negative understandings of travel, not just as transience, escape, or tourism, but, more seriously, as betrayal, are current in the humanities—not only in the realms of teaching and writing but also on search committees, where, frequently, nonwhite candidates are expected to represent national or ethnic constituencies.[1] The moral emphasis on home and one's fidelity to it is very much part of contemporary U.S. intellectual life—provided it does not take the form of pro-American hegemony.[2] In this general chapter I examine this struggle between roots and routes in the context of contemporary cultural and literary studies, and I explain my choices of the poets included here.

The Trouble with Travel

Whether in stasis or in transit, humans understand themselves by means of a detour through otherness. This is the act of travel or, in Greek, *metafora* (to carry over). Pathologists investigate deviance to understand and finally to define the normal. Oppositions such as home and abroad, duty and desire, and fidelity and betrayal imply a ground or norm of home against which travel is the figure or aberration. In this book, I entertain the possibility of inverting the latter relationship, suggesting that home, by the early twenty-first century, has become the figure against the ground of travel. Driven by economic, political, and cultural pressures, facilitated by communications and technology, human migrations have never before occurred on the scale now occurring. While the present book examines literary texts rather than demographic movements and the reasons behind them, travel, in the pages that follow, will have to be repeatedly reconceived, and thus home also will require reconception.

Travel and *trouble* suggest a common etymology, but in fact they are linguistic false friends. *Travel*'s root is much stranger than the turbulence that is *trouble*'s cognate. A variant of *travail*, *travel* derives from *tripaliare* (to torment) and *tripalium*, a device of torture consisting of three stakes between which the victim was stretched. When we travel "beyond the pale," that *palus* marks not only the boundary beyond which lies the unknown but also the perimeter of homebred pain.

Travel has come far since that grisly association. In scores of books and articles in the last three decades of the twentieth century, it has been associated with agency and power, whether as exploration, conquest, adventure, or, more recently, tourism. Mary Louise Pratt has argued, for example, that nineteenth-century travel literature worked to bring the foreign site—artistic, geographic, or human—under conceptual control by means of the colonial "gaze."[3]

Throughout this book, I suggest an alternative model, perhaps a return to "travel"'s unsavory roots: a view of travel not as mastery, hegemony, acquisition, penetration, pollution, rapine, and centripetal force, but, instead, as vulnerability, diminution, incoherence, disorientation, and centrifugal force. Travel is destabilizing in crucial and obvious ways. One leaves what is familiar and supportive, if sometimes oppressive—family, community, language, legal system—to immerse oneself in the unfamiliar and unsupportive, in the hope, if the move was voluntary, of achieving a sanctuary, a heightened awareness, a perspective, or a release not available at home.

Pratt's book *Imperial Eyes: Travel Writing and Transculturation* argues that the metropolis blinds itself to the ways in which it is determined by the periphery. But as regards travelers, this observation belongs to another era. Travel writers today, even such popular and conservative literary voyagers as Paul Theroux and V. S. Naipaul, seem keenly aware of the returned gaze and of one's ongoing self-constitution in terms of the Other. This is the explicit subject of travel novels such as Paul Bowles's *The Sheltering Sky* or Naipaul's *In a Free State*, to mention two out of hundreds of titles. Among travelers from the 1960s to the present, the blindness of which Pratt speaks seems improbable. Many traveler-writers of the last half of the twentieth century actually longed to be determined by the periphery, to be "worlded," in Gayatri Spivak's phrase, by those other worlds. Even in the eighteenth and nineteenth centuries, as Ali Behdad points out in *Belated Travelers*, the European traveler's nostalgic desire for the "other" betrayed a critique of European life, a deep split within European discourses of otherness.

Moreover, if travel is the new opium of the people, as David Lodge suggests in *Paradise News*, it is not the opium of all people. The millions who travel by choice are still a minority. Rockwell Gray writes,

> [I]n the total human record, journeys undertaken in desperation for sheer survival bulk indescribably larger than those recorded in the lively, polished accounts of modern travelers in search of adventure and refreshment. For the homeless wanderer, the semantic value of "home" differed profoundly from its connotations for those of us who have the choice to depart and return, enriching our sense of native realm by seeing it from afar. (48)

Desperate mass journeys are particularly important in the period discussed here. The greatest displacement of human populations in recorded history took place during and after World War II: thirty million people were uprooted during Hitler's regime; postwar redistribution of the European population resulted in the migration of another twenty-five million (Kulisher, qtd. in Bammer xi). Movement has not slowed down since then. Mass migration and expulsion are, Angelika Bammer writes, "a numbingly familiar feature of 20th-century domestic and foreign policy, . . . [w]ith an estimated 60–100 million refugees worldwide since 1945" (xi).

This collective aspect of travel always connotes pain. Travel as forced relocation, paradigmatic in the Middle Passage from Africa but reinvoked in the flight of Vietnamese boat people, the dispersion of the Tutsis, and the relocation of Bosnian Serbs, is a duress that the individual traveler also may experience, given the right (or the wrong) coordinates of ethnicity and border politics. The cultural critic bell hooks recounts an incident at an Italian airport where she was strip-searched and asked if she spoke Arabic by officials who feared she might have been given something to carry. Because of this experience, hooks feels that versions of travel as "playful" fail to account for encounters with "terrorism" (174). In fact, however, many who have been verbally and physically abused, jailed, and otherwise mistreated by officials in various countries find that such experiences, far from exceptional, are precisely what "travel" means today (and what it meant in Mungo Park's time also): *travail*, if not *tripaliare*. Hooks's color and gender, while relevant to Italian officials wary of (and certainly profiling) Arab women bearing Arab men's gifts, do not account adequately for the terrorism of the travel experience.

Objecting to the limiting nuances of the word *travel*, and perhaps inflating her own touristic case to the dimensions of the following examples, hooks writes,

> Travel is not a word that can be easily evoked to talk about the Middle Passage, the Trail of Tears, the landing of Chinese immigrants, the forced relocation of Japanese-Americans, the plight of the homeless. Theorizing diverse journeys is crucial to our understanding of any politics of location. (173)

"Travel," however, as James Clifford points out, remains a useful term "precisely because of its historical taintedness, its associations with gendered, racial bodies, class privilege, specific means of conveyance, beaten paths, agents, frontiers, documents, and the like" (*Routes* 39). Clifford prefers it to the more neutral and *au courant* "displacement," which subsumes too much, conflating, among other things, the postcolonial with the postmodern.

Perhaps "the crippling sorrow of homelessness and estrangement" (12) that Trinh Minh-ha associates with exile can apply as well to travelers not associated with mass displacements. Individual griefs, illnesses, losses, and compulsions—economic, political, emotional, biochemical—also can produce the "stunned, traumatized, and mutilated" condition that Trinh attributes to victims of mass expulsions. The examples of South American and East European poet-exiles, if not the mental illness and suicides of the generation of U.S. poets who came to maturity at the midcentury, certainly suggest such an argument.

The Case against Travel

Emerson disapproved of travel on two grounds. First, from a stoic perspective, he thought a person should aspire to the inner voyage, not to outward searches for the truth: "The soul is no traveler; the wise man stays at home" (133). The virtue of staying home consisted, for Emerson, in duty and responsibility as much as in centeredness and mastery. Some kinds of travel may be defensible—for art or study, he allowed—but amusement and cultural or religious longing are not valid reasons. In *The Sun Also Rises*, Jake Barnes echoes Emerson when he advises the romantic Robert Cohn against a trip to South America: "[G]oing to another country doesn't make any difference. I've tried all that. You can't get away from yourself by moving from one place to another" (11). Moreover, travelers betray not only themselves but their place, since places, Emerson argued, become venerable because of people's dedication to them. Jake and Robert, having their conversation in Paris, are already traitors from this standpoint.

But Emerson objected to travel on New World grounds also: for an American, the error of looking elsewhere is compounded by a fawning posture toward things ancient or European. "Insist on yourself," Emerson admonished; "never imitate," and "what is imitation but the traveling of the mind?" (134). One aspect of this New World objection concerns the kind of literary work that results from travel abroad, a question that Emerson addressed in "The Poet" and that numerous U.S. poets and critics have taken up since. William Carlos Williams felt that American poets writing descriptive poems about a desiccated, irrelevant Europe were turning their backs on a new and vibrant America. Charles Olson, thirty years later, wrote that travel poems were just not serious enough; they failed to engage the really pressing matters, such as "the Americanization of the world" (qtd. in von Hallberg, 63). Robert von Hallberg, writing about the midcentury and seeming to share Williams's and Olson's distaste, remarks that the poems of Americans abroad—those, for example, of Richard Wilbur, James Merrill, Anthony Hecht, Randall Jarrell, Adrienne Rich, and John

Hollander—"tend to gather, like pigeons and hawkers, around the sights and monuments" (71).

At the turn of the twenty-first century, the American case against travel continues to be made but from other perspectives. Janet Wolff argues against the travel metaphors used in postcolonial criticism, postmodern theory, and poststructuralism ("nomadic subjects," "cognitive mapping," and the like) because, first, such metaphors frustrate any politics of engagement, and, second, they leave women out. "[T]here is something *intrinsically* masculine about travel . . . therefore there are serious implications in employing travel *metaphors*" (229). She is correct in pointing to travel in the West as traditionally a male prerogative, but is there no choice but to reinscribe this traditionalism? Could not feminism benefit from a critique of stasis? Wolff argues that it cannot. Postmodernism's critique, instead, "undermines the very basis of feminism, itself necessarily a particular narrative" (235).[4]

This version of travel—as counter to a politics of engagement—is echoed in Caren Kaplan's *Questions of Travel,* where the author finds the Elizabeth Bishop poem from which she takes her title guilty of the irresponsibility of modernist exile. For Kaplan, Bishop's question "Should we have stayed at home?" needs to be answered with "a futile but emphatic 'yes' if 'we' are a particular cast of historical agents" (7), and, according to Kaplan, "we" *are* that cast. But while she is suspicious of Bishop's use of the words "we" and "us" as tacitly assuming a transcendental group identity that it is Kaplan's project to demystify and historicize, she does not extend that suspicion (or historicizing) to the "we" that she calls a "particular cast of historical agents," a cast that remains assumed rather than defined.

Kaplan rightly says,

> [F]or many of us there is no possibility of staying at home in the conventional sense—that is, the world has changed to the point that those domestic, national, or marked spaces no longer exist. So I cannot respond to Bishop's more modernist question by "staying put" or fixing my location or promising not to leave my national borders. (3)

Given this crucial concession, it is hard to account for Kaplan's dismissal of Bishop. She offers no coherent alternative to "celebrating the rootless traveler of Bishop's text," a curious remark about a poet who never "celebrated" her unstable position, indeed who, like a great many travelers, never intended to be "rootless" at all. In lieu of celebrating rootlessness, Kaplan offers the following as her project: "I suggest that the fragments and multiplicities of identity in postmodernity can be marked and historically situated" (7).

Yet no situating or marking of Bishop's identity actually takes place. "Situating" Bishop in Brazil *might* have meant what Bishop herself and other poets of her time and circle, most obviously Robert Lowell, *did*: that is, to offer critiques of, and alternatives to, the Cold War ethos of the time, which concerned and sometimes plagued these poets. It might have meant, also, to explore and problematize the touristic persona, as Bishop did in several key poems, including that of Kaplan's title, "Questions of Travel." Bishop's letters and the early drafts of her *Brazil* book reveal her awareness of, and distress at, the political moment she inhabited.

Kaplan argues the need to "deromanticize" tourists, warning that they should not be seen as "postmodern cosmopolitan subject[s] who articulate hybridity" but rather "specifically Euro-American construct[s]" (63). This is a curious complaint since, while travelers may be romanticized, tourists are far more often the objects of derision. More important, one wonders how tourists can be Euro-American constructs when millions of them are Japanese, Korean, Indian, or Latin American. (I am fairly sure that by "American" Kaplan means the United States and that by "European" she means the British, French, and Germans, principally, and *not* the Polish, Ukrainian, Slovakian, Croatian, and so on.) Indeed, the Euro-American tourist is today, in most touristic venues, in the minority. An afternoon at Niagara Falls will confirm this as readily as an afternoon in Heidelberg or Vienna.

Nevertheless, Kaplan does not want to detach tourism from its "colonial legacy" (83). To prevent that detachment, she must reify a particular kind of tourist, specific in nationality as in discursive formation. Is it true that "[t]ourism . . . arises out of the economic disasters of other countries that make them 'affordable'"? (63). Even taking the archetypal 1950s "Ugly American" in France and Italy, a tourist who seldom ventured into Africa or India, what facilitated travel was economic differential, not disaster, unless we are to broaden the sense of the latter term beyond recognition. That differential changed only a few decades later. The number of Europeans touring the United States has for some time outstripped the number of North Americans in Europe.[5] It is not a state of "disaster" that brings this much-encouraged flood of foreign tourists into the United States. Countries genuinely crushed by disease, poverty, and exploitation attract tourists in relatively small numbers, a "disaster" in itself since some of those countries depend on tourism for economic survival.

But Kaplan's insistence on nationality is not unusual. One finds it also in a book on travel writing by Terry Caesar, *Forgiving the Boundaries*, where the author writes, "My point is that any American writer who writes travel is positioned by the very dynamics of the subject *as* an American" (145). One finds it in Virginia Harrison's *Elizabeth Bishop's Poetics of Intimacy*, where Harrison writes of Bishop's time in Brazil, "Bishop was *first* an American, who never abandoned her *primary* literary, political, and personal allegiance to things American" (143, emphasis added). And, most significantly, one finds it in Edward Said's *Orientalism*, which argues for a fixed home and an apparently ineradicable nationality. As the European or American confronts the Orient, Said writes,

> he comes up against [it] as a European or American first, as an individual second. And to be a European or an American in such a situation is by no means an inert fact. It meant and means being aware, however dimly, that one belongs to a power with definite interests in the Orient, and more important, that one belongs to a part of the earth with a definite history of involvement in the Orient almost since the time of Homer. (11)

Said elsewhere calls exile "the unhealable rift forced between a human being and a native place, between the self and its true home: its essential sadness can never be surmounted" ("Reflections" 357).[6] But can we continue to assume such stability in the traveler, the foreigner, even the tourist, and such a "true home" for the self? One of the arguments of the present book is that displacement is *constitutive* of human meaning, not a figure against an unbroken ground of home. A "native place" today exists often only in the literal sense, as the place where one was born. Even thirty or forty years ago, when an American was asked "Where are you from?" the response was "Do you mean where was I born?" as if birthplace were incidental, as if other equally important choices were available from the repertory of homes one accumulates. To say, for example, "Bishop was first an American" poses the same problems as saying she was first a woman, first a white person, first a poet, or first a lesbian. Any of these might take precedence over "American."

The critical bias that argues the primacy of the national would be fruitful to historicize. By the very fact of travel, the supposedly stable orientation these critics refer to is altered. Unquestionably, some travelers appear incapable of examining the premises they have assumed all their lives, but even those premises are often multiple and conflicting. Travel, in any case, often forces such an examination. Some travelers are brought early and harshly to that examination and to unexpected and painful changes in subjectivity, a point developed next and in the chapters that follow.

American Neoteny

Said, Wolff, Kaplan, Caesar, and others—despite the different formulations set out here—share an idea: the continuity of the self (particularly a national self) across linguistic, cultural, geographic, and temporal borders. In the interest of accountability for what one writes, James Clifford says, "To know who you are means knowing where you are. Your world has a center you carry with you" (*Routes* 10). The first of those two clauses suggests that with a change of place one might expect a change of subjectivity, as I argue here; however, the second falls in line with the views I have questioned. Clifford's examples, the Oglala Sioux, suggest rootedness, hallowed places, spiritual, gravitational centers in the land. Neither Clifford nor Said wants to come down too strongly on the side of a fixed identity, but they also fear negating it. Clifford writes,

> I do not accept that anyone is permanently fixed by his or her "identity"; but neither can one shed specific structures of race and culture, class and caste, gender and sexuality, environment and history. (*Routes* 13)

About a third of a century of theory, however, has found the latter "specific structures" far less solid and continuous than they appear. A particularly useful view, in the field of travel theory, is developed in Eric Leed's *The Mind of the Traveler*, which traces numerous shape-shifting travelers, arguing that "identity is done with mirrors" (264). Travel, Leed says, offers the ideal opportunity to see this mirroring, this shaping of the Self through detours in the Other, at work. Passage "supplies information not only about the world but about the 'self' of the passenger, about the lenses, premises, and assumptions through which the traveler views the other" (159). No other means *besides* travel may exist for really examining these lenses and premises.

Travel helps us think about essence and construction. Buckaroo Banzai's maxim warned that wherever you go, there you are. But "wherever" plays a larger part in youth, when "you" is still fluid. With advancing age, it is "you" that overwhelms "wherever" to the point of the latter's irrelevance. There is a continuum of lability, in other words, on which "you" in the course of life takes on greater solidity. It is widely observed that children can quickly adapt to and assimilate a new place—language, culture, ethos—which thereafter, increasingly, constitutes their identity. We know that some, though fewer and usually younger, adults also can make these changes, depending on their makeup and the depth of their investment in and attachment to prior cultures. The retention of juvenile characteristics into adulthood—the evolutionary mechanism called fetalization or neoteny—offers a useful analogy for American modes of cultural change. Identity formation and solidification take place quite early in traditional societies. By contrast, many Americans, by their own self-description, and by the description commonly heard from European and other observers, are childish, naïve, and "unformed" well into adulthood. Or, more positively, they are seen as creative, inventive, and fresh by non-Americans.[7] None of these traits, obviously, are peculiarly American, but Americans, the myth has it, exhibit this malleability, this juvenility, this self-invention, perhaps this lack of a center, in greater numbers than Europeans, Asians, or Africans.

There are strong reasons to treasure roots, but the Americas were founded by, are sustained by, and are still flooded by people in flight. Many Americans are lightly rooted, if rooted at all. Call it postmodern eclecticism—Americans' sampling cultures and religions and countries the way they sample architectural styles and musical genres—or call it American neoteny.

Poststructuralist theory has often suggested that people are prisoners of their discursive formations or communities and that radical differences exist between these. At the same time, these communities of discourse inevitably overlap, and people generally belong to several if not many of them—whether these are communities of language, geography, local economy, sexuality, religion, or profession. Thus, the idea of discourse as a collective enterprise—in early Foucault and in Said, for example—fails to account for the impact the individual makes on discourse. Foucault seemed to struggle against such a limiting idea, searching for possibilities of agency, as did Said also.[8] Dennis Porter, in the preface to *Haunted Journeys*, points to the "coarseness" of current Foucauldian discourse, arguing that the human subject is not "merely a passive reflector of collective speech. We leave our individual mark." Moreover, "not only are the uses of an inherited language invariably overdetermined at the level of the individual, but natural languages themselves provide the resources to loosen the constraints they also impose" (4). Finally, and importantly for the present study, the implication that people have no way out of culture or language becomes highly problematic where the representation of foreign places is concerned. To travel is to shuttle between multiple overlapping and sometimes mutually canceling discursive communities. Both later Foucault (the second and third volumes of *The History of Sexuality*, and "On the Genealogy of Ethics") and later Said (notably "Representing the Colonized: Anthropology's Interlocutors") offer avenues out of this apparent impasse. Indeed, Said concludes the latter article with the statement that "Exile, immigration, and the crossing of boundaries are experiences that can provide us with new narrative forms or, in John Berger's phrase, 'other ways of telling'" (225).

The Case for Travel

If the labile element is the subject, can't one just stay home and change inwardly in response to one's dissatisfaction? In "Questions of Travel," Elizabeth's Bishop's answer to this key question was no, or at least not likely. Going away teaches the lability of the subject, precisely because the object world poses new contexts and models. Ironically, these new contexts also can reinforce subject definitions. Thus, Americans may feel more "American" in Europe, where the burden of national/cultural representation weighs on them in ways unlikely or impossible in the United States. Thucydides observes that the Greeks were not aware of themselves as a collectivity and never used the word *Hellenic* until their contact with the Persians in the Persian wars (Leed 20). "I didn't know I was German until I came to the United States," a German friend says. Conversely, in what way is one "black" if everyone else in the community is also black? Discovery or recognition of identity lives not so much in cultures as in the meeting of cultures. Ethnicity becomes a question of position. National rootedness, as Derrida has noted, is linked to geographic displacement. We are defined by and through the other place.

In this light, it is important to consider that the contemporary discovery and celebration of difference—not in the poststructuralist but in the multicultural sense—has taken place, more than anywhere else, within the state apparatuses of the only global superpower, which, by its own economic self-definition, abhors stasis and demands change and expansion. In the United States at this time in history, origins are sought and valued, or "imagined" in Benedict Anderson's formulation, more than ever before; in origins, one hears, you find "who you are." The *pluribus* of the nation's motto has for the past quarter century taken marked precedence over the *unum*, as many a conservative critic has complained.

But, just as speaking the name comes at the moment of the name's erasure, so origins appear at the moment of their obliteration, that is at the moment one discovers they are lost. Pastoral is the generic example of this cultural irony: it marks the loss of what it celebrates. Theocritus had already lost the pastoral site, living as he did in the urban corruption of third-century Alexandria. In the late twentieth century, V. S. Naipaul's protagonist Salim, in *A Bend in the River*, says, "But home was hardly a place I could return to. Home was something in my head. It was something I had lost" (107). Travel theorist George Van Den Abbeele notes that "home" occurs retroactively, after it has been left behind (*Travel* xix). James Baldwin confirms, in *Giovanni's Room*, "You don't have a home until you leave it and then, when you have left it, you can never go back" (171). Consider, finally, Anthony Appiah's account of U.S. ideas of multiculturalism: Jews, Italian Americans, Chicanos, or African Americans, Appiah suggests, insist on their difference at precisely that time when differences are slipping away (30). Travel, in the sense I have been describing, *produces* ethnicity. Identities are formed not so much out of imagined communities as out of the losses of imagined communities.

According to Emerson, one should not need the artifice of geographic change; one should find inspiration in the near, the lowly, the common. But travelers, for whom the common is uncommon, have an advantage. If the locals take the conventional as natural, foreigners are not similarly handicapped: they can and must perceive freshly. The local culture is not "natural" to the foreigner, whose inner reference to another culture produces contrasts, lacks, and differences. To maintain that sense of difference, however, the foreigner must continue to hold the host culture at arm's length, a difficult and impractical stance since the resulting alienation inhibits agency, not to mention pleasure and involvement, in the new culture. If a foreigner wants difference at all costs, he or she must move. Stasis inhibits defamiliarization. Thus, the exote, one of the ten types of traveler Tzvetan Todorov lists, must stay embedded in the foreign in order always to see afresh, to forestall automatism and enslavement by convention (347).

The traveler as exote lives in an unstable equilibrium between surprise and familiarity, and thus, as Todorov writes, his happiness is fragile: "if he does not know the others well enough, he does not yet understand them; if he knows them too well, he no longer sees them" (347). Claude Lévi-Strauss, traveling in the Amazon, raised the same issue:

> I had only to succeed in guessing what they [the Tupi-Kawahib people of the Amazon] were like for them to be deprived of their strangeness: in which case, I might just have stayed in my village. Or if, as was the case here, they retained their strangeness, I could make no use of it, since I was incapable of even grasping what it consisted of. Between these two extremes, what ambiguous instances provide us with the excuses by which we live? (333)[9]

As soon as the exote is comfortable, his experience becomes stale; as soon as he arrives, he must prepare to leave.

The artistic counterpart to this rule of exoticism is Victor Shklovsky's *ostranenie*, or defamiliarization. Shklovsky located real perception at a mythic "first time" of naïve experience, whose loss to automatism is restored by aesthetic fullness. Defamiliarization is accomplished through effort, delay, perception, and finally presence. The result is a mirage; it resembles "real" perception but is *more* real, better able to offer full/live presence of its object than "real" perception. Importantly, just as for the traveler, the defamiliarized does not stay defamiliarized but must continually be re-defamiliarized.

But ostranenie requires more effort at home than abroad, where one can more consistently count on difference. And if Lévi-Strauss's monoculture has materialized in the coca-colonization of the planet, one motive for Western travel is to see "home" defamiliarized. Pico Iyer writes,

> If the great horror of traveling is that the foreign can come to seem drearily familiar, the happy surprise of traveling is that the familiar can come to seem wondrously exotic. Abroad, we are not ourselves; and as the normal and the novel are transposed, the very things that we might shun at home are touched with the glamour of the exotic. (108)

If travel is a quest for difference, then a native custom or performance in its context may not be as interesting as a Sylvester Stallone movie in Bandar Sri Begawan or a Dunkin' Donuts parlor in Chiang Mai. This is the other way of achieving ostranenie—not by presenting familiar reality in "other" language, but by transporting the whole subject-object system from one cultural and geographic context to another.

Traversing territories, immersing oneself in new object worlds, reconstituting the known as unknown—these have constituted not only modern travel but also modern poetics. The various poetic movements of the twentieth century, from early modernism (in the word's continental sense, to include surrealism, dadaism, futurism, cubism, and other movements) through the 1960s—all those antirealist directives and manifestos—are recipes for defamiliarization, for making a reader see and feel anew. Proust's dismissal of the "mere vain and tedious duplication of what our eyes see" in favor of "that reality which it is very easy for us to die without ever having known and which is, quite simply, our life" is the imperative to overcome stupefying habit in both experience and representation (1013). Frequently, these antirealist directives have been recipes for the derangement of the subject, as in Rimbaud or Baudelaire. Travel, as a mode of derangement by geographic de- and recontextualizing, however, is the most expensive, uncomfortable, and life disrupting of modes. After a night of absinthe, a séance, a session of psychotherapy, or an injection, the voyager can at least take a taxi home.

My treatment of travel in this book is at the individual rather than the collective level, because individuals write poems. However, a topic of much of today's literature—most explicitly, in this study, Derek Walcott's—is that very tension between the flight of individual desire and the counterpull of collective gravity. Freud wrote that "a great part of the pleasure of travel [is] . . . that it is rooted in dissatisfaction with home and family" ("Disturbance" 246–47). Thus, of the various drives behind travel, consider that offered in Derek Walcott's poem "Crusoe's Island":

> We came here for the cure
> Of quiet in the whelk's centre,
> From the fierce, sudden quarrel,
> From kitchens where the mind,
> Like bread, disintegrates in water.
> (*Castaway* 54)

The paradox, as Freud showed in "The Uncanny," is that at the core of the familiar, the *heimlich*, or homelike, lies the unknown, and thus what is most familiar is most strange. Conversely, at the core of the strange lies something quite familiar. American travelers abroad often feel they are traveling from a centerless, deracinated, albeit familiar United States toward a consolidated authenticity, toward the old, the "traditional," the collective—not their collective but someone else's, not their tradition but something they recognize as tradition because they see it from outside. Is that reality the known or the unknown? In that strangeness lies home, deeply remembered comfort and familiarity, just as in "home" lies the *unheimlich*, which the traveler flees. The real familiar is unfamiliarity.

Representative Poets

Apart from very recent studies, most critical books on travel concern earlier times than the twentieth century.[10] Moreover, virtually all travel studies in the past quarter century pertain to narrative genres. The present book proposes shifts in both regards: first, to a different model of travel subjectivity from the mid- to the late twentieth century; and, second, from a focus on narrative, with its promise of access to cultural coherence, to one on the lyric, with its heritage of provisionality and indeterminacy.

Edward Said refers to the novel as "*the* aesthetic object" to be studied if one wishes to understand literature's connections to imperialist societies (*Culture* xii). Jean-Francois Lyotard refers to narrative as "the quintessential form of customary knowledge" before the scientific age and, after it, "the quintessential form of imaginative invention" (19, 60). Frederic Jameson views "story-telling as the supreme function of the human mind" (*Political Unconscious* 123). Given the emphasis of the most influential contemporary critics on narrative, clearing a space for the poem becomes difficult, even atavistic, and therefore necessary. If the poem's connections are not as explicit, if its speaking subject is not as stable, if reference to material history is problematic or absent—if, in short, the time and space of the poem are not those of the novel—these differences constitute provocative reasons to look at travel in the poem and to find other categories of discovery, in this way complementing the large body of work done to date on travel, colonialism, and narrative.

In the following chapters, I suggest that postwar travel, far from producing colonial mastery, has been most often experienced as absence or loss. Travel of any time entails sensitization and, beyond that, an undoing, a coming apart. But travel's dislocation also releases one from the obligations of "home," including the obligation to cohere. Thus the centrifugal, often debilitating movement of travel may effect a subjective and textual liberation. My concern is not only with the psychological shocks and changes to identity, nor even with the "real world" shocks of culture and geography during this period, but particularly with travel as a mode of understanding and composition, a path of *poesis*.

Since many if not most American poets have traveled, my selection of poets requires explanation. I focus on those I see as the most representative and conspicuous of New World anglophone poets since the end of World War II, but "representative" here carries several sometimes overlapping senses, including that of representing one's milieu; that of mimetic representation, faithfulness to the visible world; and that of representing a political, national, or ethnic constituency, whether in the United States or the Caribbean. The relative importance or emphasis of each of these will depend on the poetry in question.

Elizabeth Bishop begins this book because travel is the imaginative domain she, more than any other American poet, staked out as her own. The tourists and travelers who speak in her poems question both themselves and the surroundings that shape them; most importantly, they question the possibility of ever arriving at an unmediated, prelinguistic site, a "virgin mirror / no one's ever looked at / that's never looked back at anyone" (*Complete* 107). The promised interiors for which travelers yearn constantly recede in memory and imagination, text and experience, map and territory.

Bishop's titles would alert a reader to her themes of travel even if one were unacquainted with her life and her poems. Robert Lowell, by contrast, was a reluctant traveler. His center of gravity, whatever his ambivalence toward it, was New England. Bishop, who said she always felt like a guest in her relatives' houses and who was in fact a guest in other countries thereafter, spent her life looking for a home of that kind. For Lowell, travel was a space and not a place—a physically and mentally turbulent condition. The topos of Lowell's later work is the representation of vulnerability— not a pain separate from that representation—of which the dislocating travel experiences he describes are my principal examples. Lowell's poetic departure from *For the Union Dead* onward owes profoundly to Elizabeth Bishop's example.

John Ashbery's position in late-century American literature is comparable to that of Lowell at midcentury. No other contemporary American poet stands in the relation to readers and society in which Lowell stood.[11] The relative critical attention each has received is one indicator. Jerome Mc-Gann writes, "As earlier Lowell became the exegetical focus of high/late New Critical discourse, Ashbery has become the contemporary touchstone for deconstructive analysis" (McGann 257). From *Life Studies* onward, but especially since the spate of books and articles on him in the 1970s and 1980s, Lowell has been seen as a poet who made poetry out of his life. Ashbery has been viewed, with a similar consensus, as a poet of language and indeterminacy. These two poets are "representative" also in the sense that critics now view them as "mainstream," a fatal designation for any American artist and one I have taken up in a separate chapter.

John Ashbery says of his poetry that he hopes it will be "as representative as possible" (qtd. in Shoptaw 1). He has frequently remarked that his work should not be read as personal or confessional, but this goes further: he speaks in one interview of his desire "to democratize all forms of expression, an idea which comes to me from afar, perhaps from Whitman's *Democratic Vistas*" (qtd. in Longenbach, *Modern Poetry* 1). Elsewhere, he says, "What I am trying to get at is a general, all-purpose experience—like those stretch socks that fit all sizes" (Shoptaw 1). John Shoptaw claims that this representativeness is "akin to political representation in which a candidate is selected to fill a position, stand for a segment of society, and represent its interests" (1). In a way no one has satisfactorily explained, Ashbery does seem to speak for a constituency—one that no longer expects poetry to be about personal experience or even to have a subject, in either sense of that word, but that finds language alone, formed of the "sawdust" of a culture, its slogans, idioms, and clichés, sufficient to "carry" the poem.

Ashbery's "real" travels—principally to France, where he lived between 1955 and 1965—are therefore less relevant here, though the literary connection, especially to Raymond Roussel, is important. Travel is for Ashbery something at once liberating and constructed. Tracing these two aspects, I focus, on the one hand, on the poet's "childish geography," to use a phrase (not pejorative) from Ginsberg—that is, on travel as escape, orality, and *ekstasis*; and, on the other, on travel as textuality and simulacrum. These two concerns often reveal themselves in combination.

Robert Lowell, Elizabeth Bishop, and Derek Walcott knew one another and one another's work very well. Lowell and Bishop's long friendship may be traced in their letters and is the subject of numerous books and articles. Lowell visited Walcott in Trinidad, introduced his New York readings, and sometimes asked his advice. For his part, Walcott has often acknowledged his debt to Lowell. In an essay collected in *What the Twilight Says*, Walcott writes about Lowell's behavior toward him in and out of Lowell's manic bouts. Moreover, many of Walcott's poems are decidedly Lowellian, mimicking both the early textural density and the late topos of the anguished, aging self. With Bishop, Walcott shares a fascination with arrivals and departures and the viewpoint of the rootless tourist. But Walcott joins questions of travel to questions of identity and solidarity that are only implicit in Lowell and Bishop.

"Representative" thus has an additional dimension in Walcott, by contrast with these other poets, that of a call to represent a community. Walcott seems often to dismiss that call, but the dismissal also preoccupies him. Shabine, the narrator of "The Schooner *Flight*," proclaims, "Either I'm nobody or I'm a Nation" (*SAK* 4), yet, more often than not, Walcott's speakers flee the native site, geographically, metaphorically, and linguistically; they are uncomfortable with the role of witness. The Oedipal refusal of the traveler in Walcott, important also in Ashbery and Ginsberg, represents a desire for release from family, career, citizenship, and, for the poet, from representation in two key senses of the word—mimetic responsibility to "reality" and political responsibility to community.

Arguably the two most prominent Americans (writing in/from the Americas) writing poetry in English today, Derek Walcott and John Ashbery form an instructive opposition, illustrating the two principal versions of the postmodern in circulation: the poststructuralist postmodern, which erases presence and finds that language writes well enough without the subject intervening; and the multicultural postmodern, which is radical in reconceiving the canon but conservative in its restoration of the author and representation. Rather than endorse this opposition from a particular critical standpoint, I suggest seeing it as a topic under exploration within the poems themselves, most obviously in Walcott's work, which struggles with problems of history, witness, and presence, alternately claiming solidarity with place and people and refusing commitment to representation. Travel, in Walcott's poems, makes clear this painful and unresolved ambivalence.

Ashbery and Walcott are strikingly alike in important regards: first, as poets who refuse to fly from the aesthetic—poets, that is, of *dis*engagement; and second, as masters of diverse rhetorics. Walcott's rhetorics are literary but multiple—often, as with Ashbery, several in a single poem; Ashbery's are sometimes literary but, just as often, commercial, political, devotional, pop, academic, or philosophical. Walcott's movement is always from the historical toward the linguistic, without ever quite escaping history's grip. Ashbery never leaves the linguistic, but, for him, the linguistic includes everything.

Finally, these two poets are similar in their constant conflation of maps and territories. Bishop's "The Map" provides a forecast of this, but in Ashbery and Walcott the mutual conversion of earth and text becomes a near obsession. Streets, beaches, and boulevards almost reflexively become words, pages, and paragraphs. As such passages are too numerous to discuss here, I have listed many in an appendix.

One of the most important senses of "representative" concerns American poetry itself, a poetry often perceived as most American when it is most open-ended, provisional, and inclusive, the kind of poetry Emerson celebrated in Whitman. While this poetics may not suit all the poets here, it readily characterizes the work of Allen Ginsberg, Gary Snyder, John Ashbery, and Robert Creeley. It also, arguably, characterizes the Lowell of the notebooks and of *Day by Day*, much of Bishop if only in the sense that in her best-known poems she refuses choices and frustrates teleology, and much of Walcott, particularly the daybooks *Midsummer* and *The Bounty*.

But, most of all, in this connection, one thinks of Ginsberg. His large poetic structures with their ecstatic catalogues make him the most Whitmanesque of late-twentieth-century poets as does the sense in his work that mind and world cannot stand still but always must be dissolved in movement, that poems do not represent moments of repose but what Emerson calls "the shooting of the gulf" (129). Without the long lines and catalogues, one finds this property also in Creeley, Snyder, and numerous poets under the influence of William Carlos Williams since the 1960s. With Ginsberg, writing out of a romantic and expressivist tradition, biographical travel is important again, as it often is also with Creeley and Snyder. Ginsberg's "childish geography" has much in common with the "innocent, astonished, ravished voice" that Richard Howard early attributed to Ashbery (34), but Ginsberg reports from the "personal" front. His travels were unusually wide and constant; thus his life, like his work, also may be seen as working against repose.

Snyder's poetry, especially the book-length *Mountains and Rivers without End*, offers an unsuspected commonality with a poet such as John Ashbery: in this later work, Snyder's emphasis is on reality as being no less "made"— no less a production of poesis—than the poem. Snyder draws this insight from Buddhism; Ashbery draws it principally from the French surrealists and Raymond Roussel. Thus, in my discussion of Snyder, I turn again to the interplay and frequent collapse of the dreamed, the constructed or "painted," and the physical, geographic journey.

Robert Creeley, like Ginsberg, writes a peculiarly American idiom but in a meter always recognizable as his own. His poems, far quieter than Ginsberg's, are often, like Snyder's, somewhat orientalist. His poems from Latin America, the Mediterranean, and Asia bring us back to a concern that runs through this book: the conflict between accountability and pleasure. In Creeley's work we see these divided into content and form, respectively. Creeley's famous early remark, quoted by Charles Olson, that "form is never more than an extension of content" is contradicted in his travel poems, where pleasure, sensuousness, and defamiliarization play on the surface, while large, nagging moral questions lie just underneath (Olson 16).

My final chapter, "Travel and Difference," revisits the linguistic and expressivist poles of American poetry, focusing on the former category, particularly on Lyn Hejinian's *Oxota: A Short Russian Novel*, a book of poems about traveling in Russia, and on the long poem "Song of the Andoumboulou" by Nathaniel Mackey. Mackey's poem explores the relation between ethnicity, music, and geographic movement. His narrators are techno-travelers who long for a mythical, aboriginal site, where they would understand themselves and their origins, but whose very technology of travel and information precludes such a mission. Indeed, as in Ashbery, the travelers frequently realize that they have not moved, that their journey has been imagined. In the subjective and geographic drift of this poem, travel and displacement become the norm, revealing the stability of home to be an aberration.

Lyn Hejinian's *Oxota* (the Russian title translates as "hunt") concerns the hunt for a language. Among many instances of linguistic confusion between English and Russian, the poems explore how both linguistic and affective pressures of travel alter or condition the process of representation. Hejinian's book provides perhaps the most vivid contemporary example of the breakdown and shape-changing of the self as it travels across a linguistically unfamiliar terrain. Experience and the grammar of experience are everywhere conflated. Again, travel enhances an observation that ideally can be made in any place, at any time: that reality moves in and out of language, newly defamiliarized with each transition.

In the context of what may be seen as a contemporary aesthetic of decenteredness in the West, Mackey's and Hejinian's tracing of journeys without maps of the self are more believable scenarios than are the familiar models of an empowered subject, so much so that readers today may find it difficult to credit any other kind of journey.

A principal concern of this book is the dialogue between accountability and solidarity, on the one hand, and flight, escape, and ekstasis on the other. Dennis Porter offers one formulation of this opposition in *Haunted Journeys*: "[F]or a long time much of the tension experienced by male travelers, at least, tends to be focused on reconciling the call to pleasure in a foreign land with the demands of duty emanating from home" (10). This is a split noticed by other writers on travel. I have mentioned earlier, for example, Ali Behdad's understanding of European nostalgia for the "other" as an implicit critique of Europe, a split within Europe's own discourses of otherness. Behdad points out that the search of some commentators (e.g., Diderot on Bougainville) for a universal moral code derived from nature is really the urge to conflate this opposition, to make a duty of desire (10–11). Probably no single theory can negotiate this duality. We may instead, to use Richard Rorty's terms from his autobiographical essay "Trotsky and Wild Orchids," require one theory for orchids, another for Trotsky, that is, one for art, another for politics.[12] Antitravelers—whether Emerson or contemporary critics such as Kaplan, Wolff, and Caesar—argue the necessity for solidarity with home. The theory that might underpin and accommodate their view cannot simultaneously support a view of poetry as transgression. I can only plead, as does the narrator of Walcott's "Sea Grapes," on seeing Ulysses' sail on the horizon, that

> the ancient war
> between obsession and responsibility
> will never finish and has been the same
>
> for the sea-wanderer or the one on shore.
> (3)

I hate traveling and explorers. Yet here I am pro-

posing to tell the story of my expeditions.

CLAUDE LÉVI-STRAUSS, *Tristes Tropiques*

Falling off the Round, Turning World
Elizabeth Bishop's *Tristes Tropiques*

Elizabeth Bishop is the United States' principal travel poet, one might say its *only* real travel poet, were it not for Hart Crane. Like Crane's, Bishop's axis for travel was north and south, as the title of her first book (*North and South*) announced, not the east-west axis that has traditionally defined the journeys of American writers.[1] Though she visited Europe on occasion, her principal travels and her longest residencies were within the Americas, what José Martí called "Nuestra América."

That America's chief poet of travel is a woman refutes the received wisdom that travel is a male prerogative, as it does John Donne's domestic metaphor of woman as fixed foot of a moving compass. This is not to say, however, that Bishop's poetry calls on us to reconceive woman (or traveling woman) as empowered. Bishop herself did not feel empowered in or by travel, her longest residence abroad, nearly twenty years in Brazil, having been dictated not by plan but by accident.[2] ("I'm afraid in my life everything has just *happened*," she remarked in an interview [Spires 77].) Rather, it is to say that this shy and private poet, who disliked being photographed, who refused to allow her poetry to be published in anthologies of women's poetry, and who once remarked to Frank Bidart, in regard to her private life, "I believe in closets and more closets" (qtd. in Fountain and Brazeau 327), nevertheless chose travel as a defining activity of her life—travel, that mode of being in the world that is most likely, in reconfiguring the self, to strip and destabilize it.

Driving to the Interior

Postcolonial studies and the New Historicism have concentrated, during the past twenty-five years, on the metanarratives of empire, principally the narrative of bringing light—cultural, Christian, scientific—to a benighted world, and the forms of subjugation that depended on that narrative to explain and justify themselves. But the Columbian or Conradian models of penetration and mastery must be so thoroughly revised as to be unrecognizable in approaching a poet of travel such as Elizabeth Bishop. The subjectivity of the quizzical and vulnerable tourist configured in her poems is not that of Alexander von Humboldt or Kurtz or even of V. S. Naipaul. Instead, Bishop helps us understand travel in postmodernity—neither as conquest, nor as pilgrimage, nor even as immersion in societies necessarily less spoiled and more grounded than one's own but rather as decentered, travel in which neither the traveling subject nor the visited site are stable entities. For this reason, Elizabeth Bishop is celebrated as the poet who, like Wallace Stevens's poet of the blackbird, is involved in what she sees, who describes the scene before her and the subjectivity viewing it. John Ashbery, early in his career, identified Bishop's "great subject" as "the continually renewed sense of discovering the strangeness, the unreality of our reality at the very moment of becoming conscious of it *as* reality" and praised her ability to help us grasp "our coming to know ourselves as the necessarily inaccurate transcribers of the life that is always on the point of coming into being" ("Second" 10). Virginia Harrison has remarked Bishop's concern with the "situatedness of speakers and subjects throughout her writing on

Brazil" and with "the dynamics that bind and distance" those speakers and subjects (143). James Longenbach writes that the poem "Brazil, January 1, 1502" is "more than an unveiling of Portuguese colonialism; it is also a recognition of the possibility of Bishop's—or anyone's—complicity in the continuing imposition of those values" ("Elizabeth" 482). The hesitant voice in these poems argues the value in recognizing the lenses one wears, the baggage one carries, and the forms—linguistic, rhetorical, poetic— one uses to mediate experience. Memory is one of those forms, as suspect as any: "Of course, I may be remembering it all wrong" ("Santarém" 185).[3]

The subjectivity and poetic approach I am describing may remind one also of well-known views of Bishop's reticence: the idea of her work as "descriptive," as withholding emotion, and of the poet as content to receive impressions but not to assume mastery of the alien world before her.[4] In some criticism, this reticence is read as repression, particularly of the erotic. To regard Bishop as "withholding emotion," however, may give too much credence to the belief, common in the United States, that reticence or politeness masks unexpressed emotion, usually id driven and "negative." American travels abroad, like American international politics, have been frequently conducted under such assumptions. Bishop's were not, and her diffidence served her well in her roles as traveler and as poet.

Asking questions, for example, is laudable touristic behavior, preferable, at least, to making pronouncements. Questions suggest the perceiver's incompleteness, her need for supplement. The following reflections are organized around a particular question, the most fundamental of this poet's many "questions of travel," repeated several times in the poem of that title: "Should we have stayed at home . . . ?" (93). It is a question that, like Bishop's structuralist inquiries in "Brazil, January 1, 1502," seems to rise out of anthropological writing, particularly out of Claude Lévi-Strauss, who asks it often in *Tristes Tropiques*, a book that Bishop read while in Brazil and that I refer to often in this chapter:

> He [the anthropologist] has in front of him and available for study a given society—his own; why does he decide to spurn it and to reserve for other societies—which are among the most remote and the most alien—a patience and a devotion which his choice of vocation has deflected from his fellow-citizens? (383)

Lévi-Strauss describes anthropologists as travelers who, while often critical of the cultural forms of the West, nevertheless accept and praise the cultural forms that they discover in the other place—even those involving cruelties and injustices they would deplore at home. Similarly, the differences that Bishop's narrators experience both excite them and help them shape a critique of home. The implicit answer to the anxious "Should we have stayed at home?" then, is no; the last half of "Questions of Travel," as we will see, explains why. But from this question others branch, perhaps the most telling of which is the one Bishop's traveler jots in her notebook at the end of the poem: " '*Is it lack of imagination that makes us come / to imagined places, not just stay at home?*' "[5] This is the view of travel as supplement, of defamiliarization as the energizer of stale minds. The question suggests that Emerson's diagnosis of travel as "a symptom of deeper unsoundness" (160), with its implicit recommendation to *stay home*, may have something to it. But Bishop's is still a question, not an answer, and I will take up an alternative possibility in a later discussion of this poem. In the meantime, that Emersonian objection to "lack of imagination" must be faced.

As much as she prized "truth," Bishop felt limited by literalism. In a long letter to Lowell (April 4, 1962), Bishop comments on the imaginative richness of *For the Union Dead* and notes, by contrast, her own "George Washington handicap": "I can't tell a lie even for art, apparently; it takes an awful effort or a sudden jolt to make me alter facts" (*One Art* 408). Discussing the genesis of "Santarém," she writes to Jerome Mazarro, " 'Santarém' *happened* just like that, a real evening & a real place, and a real Mr. Swan who said that—it is not a composite at all" (621). She gives a similar account of the writing of "The Burglar of Babylon": "The story of Micuçús true"; she watched the pursuit of the burglar from her balcony, and "the rest of the story is taken, often word for word, from the daily papers" (qtd. in Harrison 162). In general, "The settings, or descriptions, of my poems are almost invariably just plain facts—or as close to facts as I can write them" (*One Art* 621). The "plain facts" account may seem naïve to readers today, accustomed to regard memory and observation as every bit as textual as other accounts, but Bishop's comments reveal deep ambivalence: on the one hand, palpable pride in truth telling; on the other, implicit equation of the literal with the trivial, conveying the sense, as Lowell did in his poem "Epilogue," that what is valuable in poetry is not the remembered but the imagined.

Bishop's own poems, however, belie her self-image as literalist. "The Map"—the first poem she wrote after leaving Vassar ("My first poem in my first book" [A. Johnson 24–25])—demonstrates that, despite diffidence, humility, and literalism (the humility precluding, it might be thought, alteration of the perceived), perception is impossible *without* construction. "The Map" provides both a plan for that construction and an account of how it takes place. It points to the concerns Bishop was to take up in the writing career that lay ahead—the conflation of map and territory, the aesthetic delight in pattern, and the mutual implication of perceiver and perceived. Placed as it is at the beginning of both *North and South* and *The Complete Poems*, "The Map" has come to be regarded as paradigmatic of all of Bishop's poetry. Particularly, critics have seen the poem's unusual last line—"More delicate than the historians' are the map-makers' colors"— as prefiguring the later work, though Thomas Travisano argues that "the poem is really poised ambivalently *between* the attractions of the abstracting, fiction-making functions of the map-maker and the more matter-of-fact observation and judgment of the historian" (40; emphasis added). Travisano argues, further, that the later poetry shifts the balance away from map making and toward history. But Bishop, as traveler and poet, is attracted to an undetermined history, a field in which, to quote Myra Jehlen in a different context, " 'the fact'—how things will turn out—has not yet emerged and for that reason is being described the more believably" (190). Elizabeth Bishop was engaged not so much in maps, which make the world cohere, as she was in map *making*, the poesis of maps, a sensuous and digressive enterprise.

For example, "The Map" opens with what could be construed as a picture, confirming the view that began with Randall Jarrell and continues in the work of Bonnie Costello, which sees Bishop as principally a visual poet. Indeed, "The Map" is an ekphrastic poem in that—like "Large Bad Picture," "The Monument," and "Over 2,000 Illustrations and a Complete Concordance"—it describes a visual artwork. But the first lines already mark the conflation of the three concentric worlds of language, map, and territory, with the linguistic world absorbing even while it elucidates the others:

Land lies in water; it is shadowed green.
Shadows, or are they shallows, at its edges

showing the line of long sea-weeded ledges
where weeds hang to the simple blue from green.
Or does the land lean down to lift the sea from under,
drawing it unperturbed around itself?
Along the fine tan sandy shelf
is the land tugging at the sea from under?
(3)

The shadows/shallows uncertainty is linguistic, seemingly a mis*hearing* (as when Bishop's Crusoe mistakes a "baby goat" for a "baby's throat" [165]) as much as a misreading. And yet, on a map, shallows *are* depicted as shadows. "Shadow" is both index and icon of "shallow," according to C. S. Peirce's classification of signs—that is, it is both metonymy and metaphor: a "shadow" on the map both points to a "shallow" and resembles it. In parallel manner, the "edges" of the land are also "ledges." The thick mix of sense and semiotics, based on aural as well as semantic overlap, is never again so thoroughgoing in Bishop's work as it is in this early poem.

This first verse paragraph employs an end-rhyme scheme that is really a word scheme (as in the French *rimes riches*) and that Bishop uses in another poem from the same collection, "Cirque d'Hiver." Beyond that, it is full of repetitions and inner rhymes. The echo of "weeds"; the sibilance of "shadowed," "shadows," "shallows," and "showing"; and the multiple consonance of "land lies," "line of long . . . ledges," and "land lean . . . lift" are only the most obvious of the patterns Bishop uses in a poem whose title points to an inert and abstract object. Importantly for the work that followed, the first stanza begins with a confusion and ends with a question. Is the land overcome by the sea, or is it the other way round?

This ordered first verse paragraph, with its thematic emphasis on construction, is identical in design to the third and last one, down to the extra foot in the fifth line and missing foot in the seventh. But the second, longer verse paragraph is allowed to fall apart in all of these respects. It has no end rhymes and no regular meter. In spite of this more "natural" structure, it is clearly a map rather than a territory that the speaker caresses here: "We can stroke these lovely bays, / under a glass as if they were expected to blossom, / or as if to provide a clean cage for invisible fish" (3). The movement of "The Map," at this midpoint, is toward the representation under discussion—literally, the map-as-text that Bishop is studying alone in an apartment in Greenwich Village on New Year's Eve of 1935. The lines that follow—"The names of the seashore towns run out to sea, / the names of cities cross the neighboring mountains"—are, on the one hand, unproblematically literal: on maps, one sees these names crowded together in populous spots, stretching far into the ocean if the names are long, or, when they are short and important, spaced and spread over whole provinces and continents. "Mapped waters are more quiet than the land is," Bishop writes in the third verse paragraph, because they are not covered with names to the extent the human-settled areas are. On the other hand, such lines resemble those we find in John Ashbery's map-and-territory poems, where the traveling subject may be fingering "the dog-eared coasts" and where a reader is much less certain as to the relation between material geography and representation.[6] Bishop's names overrun and exceed what they name—or rather the simulacra of what they name, since they name a signified at a second remove (territory—map—name). The map is an icon but also a symbol. That is, it resembles metaphorically what it represents but also offers an arbitrary, symbolic relation to its referent. The "shadow" of this section's first line—"The shadow of Newfoundland lies flat and still"—suggests that the map is the shadow of the territory, in the sense of the *shade* (the ghost) of the territory, as well as its double. The shadow "lies," we note, as the land lies in the poem's first line, at once inert, passive, and deceptive.

The last verse paragraph continues the childlike questions begun in the first: "Are they assigned, or can the countries pick their colors?" ("Labrador's yellow," the speaker observes earlier.) Here, as in the second section, we have childlike readings: "Norway's hare," like Italy's boot or Central America's waist, offers a surfeit of interpretation, as do the "profiles" of various peninsulas and coastlines, which seem to "investigate the sea." As with the map's colors, so with its shapes: beyond the questions of toponymy and cartography, we have a heightened play at the level of the map as fiction. Denotation, the function of the map as an aggregate of knowledge, is cast aside; instead, it becomes a Rorschach or a game like that of children naming passing clouds.

"The Map," then, questions a sign's relation to its object and sets the tone of questioning that will characterize the poems to come. In its emphasis on the aesthetic rather than the historical, on the arbitrariness of the sign rather than on its referentiality, the poem prefigures the moment in Bishop's poetry roughly thirty years later when, referring to a spherical rather than a plane map, the panic-stricken girl "Elizabeth" cries out her age, "saying it to stop / the sensation of falling off / the round, turning world / into cold, blue-black space" (160). In response to psychological vertigo, "Elizabeth" reaches out for reference points, locating herself by date, by town, and by historical event: "The War was on. Outside, / in Worcester, Massachusetts, / were night and slush and cold, / and it was still the fifth / of February, 1918" (161).

If "The Map" refuses to confront reality, as Thomas Travisano has suggested (41), then the much later "In the Waiting Room" retrospectively suggests the price of that refusal. The former poem's final preference for the aesthetic over the historical arises out of a resistance to the epistemological closure the map implies. It is not so much an aesthete's as a traveler's preference, one that Bishop maintained in her later travels and the poems that emerged from them. Thus, "The Map," written in 1935, opens the way to reading the more mature poems written when Bishop had begun her travels in earnest.

Bishop's second book, *A Cold Spring*, offers a second map-reading poem.[7] "Over 2,000 Illustrations and a Complete Concordance," while it concerns a close reading of an archaic text, stands between the early, somewhat New Critical poem that examines an inert map and the explicit travel poems of *Questions of Travel* and *Geography III*. The poem splits itself in two, comparing textual travel to the poet's own geographic travel, then returning to the text. But the split is not even, either formally or thematically: the return to the text at the end reflects Bishop's uncertainty about the value of her "actual" nontextual travel with its fearful incoherence. The scenes are organized according to categories of the familiar and the foreign, as they will be also in "In the Waiting Room" and "Brazil, January 1, 1502." The poem begins,

Thus should have been our travels:
serious, engravable.
The Seven Wonders of the World are tired
and a touch familiar, but the other scenes,
innumerable, though equally sad and still,

are foreign. Often the squatting Arab,
or group of Arabs, plotting, probably,
against our Christian Empire,
while one apart, with outstretched arm and hand
points to the Tomb, the Pit, the Sepulcher.

(57)

In "The Map," the speaker refused to be, or was too innocent to be, intimidated by the map's imperial authority. In "Over 2,000 Illustrations," however, the text exists to intimidate—by its serious canonical precedence and by its coherence, which the poet contrasts to her own (as she sees them) belated, trivial, and incoherent moments of travel. And yet the unreliable narrator often guides the reader away rather than toward canonical authority. The poem begins humorously, in its "found" title, an advertisement for an illustrated Bible, and in its description of stereotypical Arabs "plotting . . . against our Christian Empire." Moreover, the purported sanctity of the textual engravings the poem offers in its first verse paragraph is undermined, first, as Anne Colwell points out, by the second meaning of "engravable"—to be "able to be put in a grave" (103)—and, more important, by the same strong misreadings we saw in "The Map." Just as in the latter poem, where the worlds of representation and geographic reality (respectively, "shadows" and "shallows") are indistinguishable, so, here, we are never sure whether we are on the "real" geographic journey or on the textual, "engravable" one. The date palm branches "look like files," the courtyard is "like a diagram," and "[a]lways the silence, the gesture, the specks of birds / suspended on invisible threads above the Site, / or the smoke rising solemnly, pulled by threads" (57).

This interweaving of landscape and language also characterizes "Brazil, January 1, 1502," where the landscape, as that poem's epigraph warns us, is seen as an embroidered, tapestried "web" or "backing," a trope of nature-as-text that becomes hypertrophied in Bishop's admirers John Ashbery and Derek Walcott. The supposedly solemn and sacred site in the present poem is, on the poet's own close reading, a Wizard of Oz setup: artificial, constructed, operated from behind or above. At this point the language becomes intensely textual, no longer concentrating on the referentiality of the scenes but on their minute design, as if the focus had become magnified.[8]

Granted a page alone or a page made up
of several scenes arranged in cattycornered rectangles
or circles set on stippled grey,
granted a grim lunette,
caught in the toils of an initial letter,
when dwelt upon, they all resolve themselves.
The eye drops, weighted, through the lines
the burin made, the lines that move apart
like ripples above sand,
dispersing storms, God's spreading fingerprint,
and painfully, finally, that ignite
in watery prismatic white-and-blue.
(57)

These lines trace the act of reading more than they do any prior content. The first half-dozen lines suggest that even these features of design "resolve themselves," yield up meaning, when looked at carefully enough. Here is the same close ekphrastic detail we see in "The Map." After the parallel "granted" phrases, which grant the incoherence resulting from this collapse of scenes into their constituent atoms, the main clause comes back to the point of their coherence: they *do*, "when dwelt upon . . . resolve themselves." The lines that follow explain the dynamics of that resolution. The eye itself, dropping like a plumb through the lines—reading between the lines—sets the lines in motion. The burin engraved those lines in some hallowed, canonical past, but the eye ripples them apart, "dispersing storms." The engraving technique that creates shadow by curving equidistant lines—the very technique used to indicate map contours—produces the whorls characteristic of fingerprints. The question remains whether "God's spreading fingerprint" stands in apposition to those storms, as it may seem, or to the moving apart of the lines, which is the movement toward coherence. After all, the second occurrence of the noun "lines" controls the rest of the sentence's syntax. It is the "lines" that "painfully, finally . . . ignite." While the lines, seen from a distance, merely serve to form larger figures, they are, in this rainbowlike, magnified textual chaos, excited and kindled, freed from their role as components of a larger figure.

These two rather theoretical sentences contrast with the homely descriptions of illustrations with which the poem opens. The former provide a testimony to the power of the images, as well as a theory of how meaning is produced by the reader, who is lying on the floor thumbing through the big concordance as she did twenty years earlier with a world map. Both poems waver between the aesthetic (lines, lunettes, circles, colors, in the case of the illustrated Bible) and the historical (the archaic and sacred reference), a movement of equivocation characteristic of Bishop, who demonstrates it in poems as varied as "In the Waiting Room," "Questions of Travel," and "Brazil, January 1, 1502." Such movement reveals that same ambivalent attitude toward literalism discussed earlier. That is, the poet criticizes the literal as limited, as insufficiently imagined or transformed. And yet the speaker in "Over 2,000 Illustrations," out of her insecurity, embraces the literal, the known, the dead.

The second verse paragraph consists of a series of vibrant vignettes of the traveler's career, spanning a much wider geographic range than that of the biblical illustrations. Newfoundland, Italy, Mexico, Morocco, Ireland, England, Morocco again—the places, and the brief, beautiful but frightening events recounted—are presented either without transition or with only the transition of addition: "And at St Peter's," "And at Volubilis," "And in the brothels of Marrakesh." As the poet's famous commentary indicates— "Everything only connected by 'and' and 'and'"—the phrases alone hardly seem enough to make these moments either serious or engravable. Or, if serious, the moments are too mobile and too imbued with uncertainties to be engraved. The goats' bleating, the robed collegians who resemble black ants, the Mexican corpse, the volcanoes that glisten like lilies, the jukebox's incongruous pathos, the poppies of the dead, the pockmarked prostitutes, and, "what frightened me most of all" (suggesting that these moments dotted across the years were *all* frightening), the empty grave— these images complement and underscore the journey's emphasis on mortality. This world of dying creatures is so serious as to be unrepresentable, *un*engravable. And of the two dreads, death and incoherence, the latter is most terrifying. As Robert Pinsky notes, "the nightmare of the dust-filled grave is not merely of death, nor even of nothingness, but rather of meaninglessness, accumulated particles, casually tangent" (63). Mere witness is not enough to provide connection; sight itself—unless "the eye drops, weighted, through the lines"—is without agency:

Open the heavy book. Why couldn't we have seen
this old Nativity while we were at it?

—the dark ajar, the rocks breaking with light,
an undisturbed, unbreathing flame,
colorless, sparkless, freely fed on straw,
and, lulled within, a family with pets,
—and looked and looked our infant sight away.

(58–59)

Sight is mute, as the Latin *infantia* (speechless) suggests; indeed, Bishop, in an earlier draft, had written "silent" for "infant" (Kalstone, *Becoming* 130). The poem ends with a question, disguised by the syntax: "Why couldn't we have . . . looked our infant sight away?" What had we missed by failing to see this primal, sacral mystery on the bestial floor, the Nativity scene itself controlled by the image of the grave, "the dark ajar"?

But a poem that presents itself as a doubt if not a rejection of the speaker's own travel in favor of a legendary and coercively meaningful text ends by stressing the wonder of the personal perception, the disconnected seeing of travel. The great heavy book with its gilt-edged pages, which "pollinate the fingertips," is a marvel, but the subjects of its engravings, despite the sense of belatedness they inspire, are hackneyed—*unless* they are transformed by a gaze that extends beyond reading as decoding, that forces the images to reveal their subliteral designs.

Is this not the meaning of looking one's "infant sight away"? A visual equivalent of Tennyson's reciting his name until it dissolved into abstraction, the phrase suggests looking until one's sight is gone, until one can no longer look in the customary way. Depending where the emphasis is placed, the phrase suggests also the idea that *infant* sight, a nonparticipatory, mute sight, needs to be looked *away*, that is, exhausted in favor of a more involved mode of vision. The last sense, not exclusive of the others, involves reading "away" to describe people doing something to their hearts' content, without moral or temporal limit: "There they were—just dancing away."

By contrast to the engraved "Wonders . . . tired / and a touch familiar," the beauty and terror of one's own disconnected life are unanswerable. To be sure, one may wish to turn away from that life, but even in turning away and commanding "Open the book," Bishop turns toward a Nativity not yet seen but vividly imagined, a place unvisited, a place where one *meant* to travel, as the poet would say later in "One Art." This, the still unseen future site, as opposed to the past text, is the always-receding travel prospect. Indeed, this association of place with future, and of text with past, is central to several of Bishop's later travel poems, notably "Santarém."

In Bishop's 1965 volume *Questions of Travel*, travel sites are specific and developed, rather than dispersed and miscellaneous, as in the two previous travel poems. "Brazil, January 1, 1502" is the second poem in the volume, standing between "Arrival at Santos" and the title poem. In the commonality of their themes, and in that all three concern arrivals, the poems constitute a suite. But it is instructive to look at this second poem first, since, in comparing one moment of arrival with another, "Brazil" replicates the structure of "Over 2,000 Illustrations and a Complete Concordance."[9] Only the order is changed: in "Over 2,000 Illustrations," Bishop presented historical travel followed by contemporary, personal travel. In "Brazil," present-day touristic travel—almost entirely description of flora and fauna—comes first, followed by the historical moment of the Portuguese "discovery" of Brazil. The struggle to make sense of the comparison and to examine the cargo brought by both tourist and conquistador to the would-be colony constitutes the poem's action.

In other words, the poem itself—like its subject of the racially and culturally hybridized Brazil—is a hybrid, not only for the reason Dale Parker has offered, that it relies on no historical account but instead chooses whatever best represents Brazil's colonial fate (94), but also because of its joining of two experiences of discovery: the classical moment of the conquistador and the modern arrival of the tourist. The juxtaposition is offered without delay, as it was in "Over 2,000 Illustrations," in the opening two lines:

Januaries, Nature greets our eyes
exactly as she must have greeted theirs.
(91)

Missing, though, is the value judgment of "Thus should have been our travels"; here, the two arrivals—of the sixteenth-century Portuguese and the twentieth-century Americans—are "exactly" equated, as if "Nature," existing outside of historical time, had not changed in the intervening four and a half centuries.

Several "Januaries" are at work: the January of the Portuguese discovery; January 1952, when Bishop first arrived in Brazil; January 1959, when, for New Year's Day, she mailed this poem to Robert Lowell; and the January of the river's name: Rio de Janeiro the discovery site (though not mentioned in the poem). This *rio* is, in fact, not a river at all, but an enclosed bay. Like Columbus's "Indian," the misnomer tells us more about the traveler's expectations than it does about empirical reality. Rivers lead us, in the literature of exploration, to dark, fecund, and dangerous interiors, not a possibility with this "river." For tourists, interiors are where one finds the *real* France, the real Brazil. Bishop herself was not above using this generic trope in her Time-*Life* book *Brazil*, where she equates, as do most travel books, geographic otherness with temporal otherness, backlands with backwardness in time and the interior with authenticity:

> Men from two, three or more eras of European history live simultaneously in Brazil today. The coastal cities . . . are filled with 20th-century men. . . . Then in the surrounding countryside is a rural or semi rural population who lead lives at least half a century behind the times. . . . And for the people of the fishing villages . . . all the backlands people—time seems to have stopped in the 17th century. Then if one ventures even a little farther on, one enters the really timeless, prehistoric world of the Indians. (12)

The site of the "really timeless" world of homogeneity, silence, and purity is the heart of the country. The coast is the outside, the place of modernity, heterogeneity, and contamination. Postcolonial theory has devoted itself to interrogating this kind of discourse. Perhaps it is difficult *not* to reinscribe Conrad: "Going up that river was like traveling back to the earliest beginnings of the world" (102).

In her poetry, Bishop problematized this question of interiors, emphasizing their deferral and fictiveness. In "Cape Breton," the road, or perhaps the entire landscape, appears to have been abandoned: "unless the road is holding it back, in the interior, / where we cannot see, / where deep lakes are reputed to be"(67). The depths, the mysteries, the attractions are always beyond, or, rather, we think them to be. And for both explorer and tourist, as at the end of "Arrival at Santos," that elusive "interior" has a double meaning, since voyages are notoriously journeys within oneself. In "Brazil, January 1, 1502," rather than sailing up a river with its nominal promise of a beginning, the explorers find themselves trapped in a bay. The elusive interior—whether as subjective inaccessibility or geographic or human Other—is a controlling topos in Bishop's Brazilian poems. This poem, in fact, ends on that elusiveness: the "maddening little women" whom the Christian men chase through the jungle's "hanging fabric" keep on "retreating, always retreating behind it" (92).

The poem's epigraph from Sir Kenneth Clark—"embroidered nature . . . tapestried landscape"—predisposes us to see the jungle, during the subsequent catalogues of plants, rocks, and birds, as something artfully and *densely*, even impenetrably, constructed: a canvas or a tapestry, "fresh as if just finished / and taken off the frame," not a Nature with interstices. The striking feature of the "Nature [that] greets our eyes" is this density, "every square inch filling in with foliage," with emphasis on the large: "monster ferns" and "giant water lilies" (91). ("Questions of Travel" continues this theme of disturbing abundance: "too many waterfalls," "crowded streams," "so many clouds.") Though the language is ambivalent—"solid but airy"— the sense is that one wants room to move. The fullness oppresses and restricts the dreams brought to the toured or colonized land.

In the second verse paragraph, the narrator's eyes lift to see "blue-white sky," then lower to see that "in the foreground there is Sin," in the form of five lizards "near some massy rocks." The "Sin" is evidently sexual: all the male lizards are breathlessly watching the female's "wicked tail . . . red as a red-hot wire" (92). The scene is both present and past, this being "exactly" what the Portuguese also projected onto the landscape, allegorizing nature in the yes-no vines and the licentious lizards, domesticating the new by seeing it in terms of the old. Nature greeted them, as it does the tourists, according to their lights.

The third and last section seems at first to fulfill the us-them, now-then comparison set up in the opening two lines. That is, having finished the present description of "Nature," we are ready to turn to that of the Portuguese discoverers: "Just so," thinks the contemplative tourist, "the Christians . . . came and found it all." But, following as it does the irruption of sex and "Sin" in the form of mythicized lizards ("sooty dragons"), "Just so" also must be read as introducing a comparison with what has "just" been described: like the lizards, so the Christians. The suggestion extends to the poem's end, with its image of the conquistadors' pursuit of native women. The poem is thus grounded, albeit ambiguously, in the rhetorical model of the epic simile, in the form of "just as . . . , so . . ." (unlike "Over 2,000 Illustrations" with its emphasis on the difference between the two worlds and epochs).

The Christians "came and found it all, not unfamiliar," the passage continues, "corresponding . . . to an old dream of wealth and luxury / already out of style when they left home—" (92).[10] The "old dream" is important to Bishop's theme of travel projection; to apprehend is also to obscure and to lose, just as the trope's function is both to reveal and conceal. Because the Portuguese are primed with Edenic texts and dreams, they find Brazil "not unfamiliar." Bishop acknowledges this particular history in her book *Brazil*, writing that "a land called 'Brasil' was a legend in Europe at least as early as the Ninth Century" (25).

We get, from the "now-as-then" beginning of the poem, not only the touristic reprise of the conquest but also the travel-brochure promise of a voyage back in time. Tourism is the pursuit of archaism—in aesthetic, cultural, and even economic terms (if the dollar is strong, as it was in Bishop's time, against local currencies). The Portuguese, too, were exploring an old myth of "Brasil" before that myth materialized in the geographic Brazil.

But now, at the end, in addition to the dream of "wealth and luxury," Brazil offers "a brand-new pleasure," one that ties together the tapestry theme of the epigraph and first section and the Sin-and-lizards theme of the second section. The new pleasure consists in the Christians', after Mass, "ripp[ing] away into the hanging fabric, / each out to catch an Indian for himself—" (92). The pursuit is not successful. The densely woven *textus* of Nature provides inexhaustible paths of recession for the native women, paths the Christian predators find hard to follow. Bishop grafts the idea of native as object onto the familiar idea of woman as object—here, as object of prey. But insofar as woman (replacing the earlier figure of "Nature") is a trope of the "interior"—in this travel poem as well as in ethnographic narratives—she is "maddening" because she is uncatchable.

Of the two touristic poems that bracket "Brazil, January 1, 1502," the first, written eight years earlier, begins *Questions of Travel* and is appropriately a poem of debarkation. In "Arrival at Santos," Santos is, like Rio de Janeiro, a port—the port of Sao Paulo. While the poem does not compare earlier journeys or texts, it addresses, as does "Brazil," the impossibility of finding that "different world" unconstructed by and uninvolved with ourselves. The poem introduces us to a somewhat unreliable tourist narrator, who is nevertheless reflective enough to know that her "demands" on the new country are unrealistic and "immodest." Flatly and unsympathetically, the tourist begins by describing the harbor, echoing the children's rhyme "Here is the Church, Here is the Steeple," as Costello (*Questions* 139) and Colwell (131) have both noted:

Here is a coast; here is a harbor;
here, after a meager diet of horizon, is some scenery:
impractically shaped and—who knows?—self-pitying mountains,
sad and harsh beneath their frivolous greenery.
(89)

The tourist reduces landscape not only to utility ("impractically shaped" mountains) but also to sustenance ("a meager diet of horizon"). If this tourist and her cohorts belong to that army of semioticians that Dean Mac-Cannell describes in *The Tourist* as predisposed to find signs everywhere of authenticity—in this case, the "real" Brazil—what she sees is disappointing: not only the "self-pitying mountains" and the "frivolous greenery" but, in the next stanza, a "little church," "warehouses . . . painted a feeble pink," and "uncertain palms." Something more *essential* would have better answered her purpose.

As the tender approaches, she spies a flag: "I somehow never thought of there *being* a flag, // but of course there was, all along. And coins, I presume." (89) The "I presume" supplies the imperialist touch: ignorance dressed up as omniscience, the landscape coerced into conformity with expectation. She had imagined a country anterior to such properties as flags and coins, since these, after all, belong not to "countries" but to "nations." Disappointed, she is now in the process of adjusting map to territory or vice versa. Thus, her readings of the othered landscape or native are not "strong," but rather vulnerable and open to revision. The speaker in "Arrival at Santos" debarks in the hope that the customs officials will speak English and that her bourbon and cigarettes won't be confiscated. "Ports are necessities," she fairly sighs, but she has already had enough of the harbor. In the last two lines, she sketches her itinerary for the rest of the book, her intention to penetrate beyond the touristic, beyond mere coasts: "We leave Santos at once; / we are driving to the interior" (90).

The play on "interior," as I have noted of "Brazil, January 1, 1502," is important to all travel writing that sees itself as both discovery of the Other and of the Self. But Bishop's poems distrust and disturb the nostalgia for interiors of either kind. In this opening sequence of three poems, the last word of "Arrival at Santos" functions as a connection to the next poem, "Brazil, January 1, 1502," where, as we have seen, vain attempts to locate an interior plague both tourists and conquistadors.

The same sense of disjunction between expectation and reality, along with the same querulous touristic voice heard in "Arrival at Santos," opens "Questions of Travel":

> There are too many waterfalls here; the crowded streams
> hurry too rapidly down to the sea,
> and the pressure of so many clouds on the mountaintops
> makes them spill over the sides in soft slow-motion.
>
> (93)

The disappointment here is not, as it was in "Arrival at Santos," at the flatness of coast, harbor, and "some scenery" but at the fullness of presence familiar from the opening of "Brazil, January 1, 1502," where Nature is oppressively replete, all "fill[ed] in" with "big leaves," "giant leaves," "monster ferns," and "giant water lilies." This unaccustomed fullness alienates and nauseates more than it excites by its difference and strangeness. Along with this outward unfamiliarity is something new, not developed in the first two poems of this triptych: an inner disturbance at the increasingly dubious ethics of travel itself, which had only *begun* to trouble the tourist of "Santos": "Is it right to be watching strangers in a play / in this strangest of theatres? (93)

Clayton Eshleman reads Bishop's phrase "watching strangers in a play" as implying a view from the tower of wealth, privilege, and geographic mobility (75). While not irrelevant, this kind of reading not only assumes an unproblematic identity of author and speaker but also ignores the critique inherent in Bishop's poem. I have mentioned the *economic* archaism—the favorable exchange rate, which can make travelers feel they are traveling in time—that characterized midcentury American tourism. That exchange rate did indeed make even the least privileged of Americans at home quite privileged abroad, though Bishop, with her modest patrimony, was not among the least privileged of Americans. But the disturbance in the touristic voice of these poems rises precisely out of the awkwardness derived from the capacity for travel—the awkwardness of being outside, anthropologically, as it were, looking in.

After the questions that occupy most of the first half of "Questions of Travel," the speaker recites a catalogue of all she would have missed had the trip not been taken. This catalogue, more unified and coherent than the potpourri of travel events in "Over 2,000 Illustrations," offers the alternative view toward which the poem is weighted: the idea that Pascal (along with Emerson) was wrong, that the trouble of the world is *not* caused by failing to stay in one's room. "Questions of Travel" counts the losses of staying home, the living and seeing one would not have done. "Not to have seen," "not to have heard," and "Never to have studied" introduce these potentially missed connections, much like Pound's retrospective view at the end of Canto LXXXI, where "error is all in the not done, / all in the diffidence that faltered." And what would have been missed? The list begins with "trees along this road, / really exaggerated in their beauty, / . . . gesturing / like noble pantomimists, robed in pink" and ends with rain like "two hours of unrelenting oratory / and then a golden silence" (94). But the images most developed here are two, one aural and the other visual, set into a comparison that elicits a Lévi-Straussian commentary on the problems of monoculture. The first image is the sound of

> the sad, two-noted, wooden tune
> of disparate wooden clogs
> carelessly clacking over
> a grease-stained filling-station floor.
> (In another country the clogs would all be tested.
> Each pair there would have identical pitch.)
> (94)

The second image starts with the song of the "fat brown bird / who sings above the broken gasoline pump" (94) but quickly moves from the birdsong to the bird's cage. The memory of the cage leads to the following reflection:

> —Yes, a pity not to have pondered,
> blurr'dly and inconclusively,
> on what connection can exist for centuries
> between the crudest wooden footwear
> and, careful and finicky,
> the whittled fantasies of wooden cages.
> —Never to have studied history in
> the weak calligraphy of wooden cages.
> (94)

The connection, as Bishop suggests, is worth pondering. "In another country"—in a modern, technological, "efficient" country—those clogs would have been manufactured so as to make their materials and construction (and therefore their sounds) identical.[11] That sameness—in the absence both of cheap labor and of traditional artisans—is the *only* possible outcome. In industrial societies, *difference*, not sameness, is the difficult and costly thing to achieve. But here, in rural Brazil, no one bothered to devote the care to these practical everyday implements that would result in that sameness. Or, if one had desired that sameness, the technology was lacking. Sameness, uniformity, utilitarianism, and Lévi-Strauss's "monoculture"— these are the horrors from which many first-world travelers fled at the midcentury and from which many continue to flee. By contrast with the shoes, something as frivolous and unnecessary as a birdcage is painstakingly carved into the form of "a bamboo church of Jesuit baroque: three towers, five silver crosses" (94). What is the "connection" that has "exist[ed] for centuries" between these two productions? It is a question not only of travel but also of value: on what activities or productions does a culture place importance?

Derek Walcott has discussed the Caribbean carnival mentality, which "solemnly dedicates itself to the concept of waste, of ephemera, of built-in obsolescence. . . . Last year's intricate sculptures are discarded as immediately valueless when it is midnight on Shrove Tuesday, last year's songs cannot be sung this year, nor last year's tunes" ("Caribbean" 9–10). Walcott's remarks suggest part of an answer. The shoes' perfection and longevity were not goals for the maker, nor, apparently, did consumers prize them much. But a house for birdsong is another matter. A society that encodes history in the calligraphy of its birdcages while turning out crude wooden shoes with relative carelessness is a society that prizes frivolity, transcendence, and *poetry* more than efficiency.

These are reasons for travel. Only through travel can such observations be made, and only in this way can travelers be brought to examine their own imported values and to see their less-than-"natural" place in a larger scheme. Culture and ethnicity, like language, must always be contrastive to be understood. One does not discover interiors; one uncovers qualities in the dynamism of juxtapositions. If the catalogue of sights and sounds in this poem offers persuasive reasons for travel, the last two italicized sections, especially the very last, return us to questions of the self:

Continent, city, country, society:
the choice is never wide and never free.

And here, or there . . . No. Should we have stayed at home,
wherever that may be?

(94)

The ages of discovery, as Lévi-Strauss observes, revealed that we (whoever "we" may be) need the Other to understand the self. But the problem is not only the self's identification or disidentification with the other ("here, or there"); it is also the text's intervention in that process. The gesture of this poem is not to answer but to inhibit the questions posed by and to the traveler. Is "no" really an answer to the question of "And here, or there"? It is, rather, one of those facetious answers to questions deliberately misunderstood: "Do you want to go or stay?" "Yes." Since home is finally impossible to locate, Bishop's response is a rejection of the choice and of the pressure to make that choice.

The touristic perspective of the three opening "Brazil" poems illustrates the irony of the quest for Eden by forms of consciousness that inherently defeat that ideal. The ideal itself denies separate identity to the world encountered and thus must be abandoned, as it is in "Brazil, January 1, 1502" and "Questions of Travel." Bishop's tourist is not the passionate Lawrentian pilgrim of *Sea and Sardinia*. She is not consumed with the search for sexual or spiritual foundation; her effort is to stretch the traveler's purview, to immerse the traveler in the Other, to blur the boundaries between past and present, home and abroad. Her way of seeing, "blurr'dly and inconclusively"—with lenses not unclouded but complicated by an awareness of their own occlusion—is key to both the ethos and the appeal of Bishop's work at this stage of her life.

Uncanny Places

Bishop's fourth collection of poems was titled *Geography III*—a title that, as John Hollander points out, recasts *North and South* and *Questions of Travel* as *Geography I* and *Geography II*, respectively. The book opens with Bishop's most controversial poem, "In the Waiting Room." This rather long, prose-like narrative poem concerns a six-year-old girl who, while waiting in a dentist's office for her aunt, experiences an identity crisis, brought on in part by what she sees in the pages of *National Geographic*. Critics (Cucullu, Edelman, Costello, and others) have read the poem as a text of connectedness, an account of the development of a child's feeling of solidarity along gender lines. With its juxtaposition of the tropical travel text and the northern home, its positioning of the naïve subject as floating between two frightening othernesses, one domestic but strange and the other foreign but familiar, "In the Waiting Room" is a poem at the heart of Bishop's poetics of travel. Written later than the other poems discussed here (with the exception of "Santarém"), it retrospectively comments on those poems while placing them in a context provided by the young traveler *before* her travels. The poem thus looks backward to childhood and, from that vantage, forward to Bishop's subsequent travels.

"In the Waiting Room" illuminates a particular anthropological challenge more clearly than any of Bishop's poems of elusive interiors: that of finding the juncture between nature and culture, of separating universals from particulars. Lévi-Strauss summed up the impetus to locate such a site when he remarked, "I had been looking for a society reduced to its simplest expression" (317), believing as he did that the study of a "simple" society would reveal the underpinnings of more complex societies. "In the Waiting Room" puzzles over the site where nature and culture seem to part, while it also traces the interpellation of the young protagonist as poet and traveler.

Robert Dale Parker, commenting on this poem, notes that "The *National Geographic* trades on an unwitting sense of specialness in western culture. Westerners look; others are looked at, and nakedly, as if absolutely" (139). Only the knower has the problem of selfhood; the native is inert, a given, a ground for knowledge.[12] And yet the magazine also involves the assumption that, underneath our clothes, humans are all alike, that a presocial human nature of the kind Lévi-Strauss hoped to locate exists. Bishop's speaker finally wonders which is stranger—sameness or otherness.

That issue of *National Geographic* holds several shocks for the six-year-old Nova Scotian girl, but the principal shock is the sight of

black, naked women with necks
wound round and round with wire
like the necks of light bulbs.
Their breasts were horrifying.[13]
(59)

The young reader tries to get her bearings by repeatedly returning to the magazine's date and yellow margins—as if to keep herself from slipping at once out of history. At this vertiginous point, she hears "from inside" a sharp "*oh*! of pain." She assumes it comes from her Aunt Consuelo, a "foolish, timid woman," but then discovers it came from herself. Just as Bishop's "interior" in "Arrival at Santos" suggests more than one meaning, so here the poet puns on "inside." Inside the dentist's office, we think at first, until we realize as the speaker does, that "inside" means inside her own body. The uncontrollable cry erupts, like the volcano she had seen in the magazine.

This poem has been read as a coming-of-age by means of "a guerilla attack of the alien" (Vendler 87), but two crises rather than one occur. One, the most obvious, is the shock of identity with the human race—both with the distant figures in the magazine and with the equally alien neighbors in the waiting room, whose disembodied knees, hands, skirts, and boots the girl glimpses as she glances up from her magazine. To be individuated or embodied—as anything—is strange: "Why should I be my aunt, / or me, or anyone? What similarities . . . held us all together . . . ?" (159).

But Lévi-Strauss's question was also the question of what, in a culture, is universal and therefore not of the culture but of nature. (Jacques Derrida's essay "Structure, Sign, and Play" deconstructs just this opposition in Lévi-Strauss.) Lévi-Strauss's Nambikwara (now a vanished people) are walking artifacts; their face painting is their only art. When they die, that art dies. This is the other crisis or threshold in "In the Waiting Room": "Elizabeth" experiences body as art when she reads the *National Geographic*. The women's necks are long because they are "wound . . . with wire." Their babies have "pointed heads." While these attributes have been read as gender-specific constraints—the wire neckpiece cutting off woman's speech—they also must be seen as art. Of course, they *are* seen as art in the culture in question, which, like the Nambikwara (as if they had listened to Nietzsche), transforms humans into art objects, willing culture out of nature. Similarly, too, the supposedly familiar humans in the waiting room with her are variously perceived as "knees" and "hands" and "trousers" and "skirts," estranged and synecdochical, a mixture of biology and artifice.

"Elizabeth's" terror and vertigo continue, in the frame not only of the *National Geographic* but also of the waiting room, now saturated with strangeness. The child knows "that nothing stranger / had ever happened, that nothing / stranger could ever happen" (160). But, in the final stanza, after the trauma and the unanswered questions ("Why should I be . . .

anyone?"; "How had I come to be here . . . ?"), "Elizabeth" is "back in it." The "it" is the world grounded and framed by that magazine cover: history, reinforced by a date:

> The War was on. Outside,
> in Worcester, Massachusetts,
> were night and slush and cold,
> and it was still the fifth
> of February, 1918.
> (161)

The poem's question of travel is complex. Is it culture or nature that frightens "Elizabeth"? Is it the body ("the awful hanging breasts") or the artifice written on the body? Is the family voice "natural" or "cultural"? And, to return to the first threshold mentioned, which is more frightening, sameness or difference? Marlow in *Heart of Darkness* offered the colonialist response to the shock of otherness:

> Well, you know, that was the worst of it—this suspicion of their not being inhuman. It would come slowly to one. They howled and leaped, and spun, and made horrid faces; but what thrilled you was just the thought of their humanity—like yours—the thought of your remote kinship with this wild and passionate uproar. Ugly. (Conrad 37–38)

But "Elizabeth" confronts this shock of sameness from a perspective different from Marlow's. Marlow does not see, as the girl does, that difference occurs at both extremes. A sharper formulation of the question might be, Is the foreign or the domestic the most frightening, and which of the two nudges the girl into the consciousness of her embodiment in the world and her connectedness to others? Freud's essay "The 'Uncanny'" explored the fear that lies at both sources: first, the unfamiliar that exists within the familiar and, second, the familiar that exists within the unfamiliar. On the one hand, Aunt Consuelo and the fragmented bodies of the locals in the waiting room are all dramatically alien; and, on the other, the images of hunters in Africa and of African women strangely familiar, people with whom the young girl feels a hint of Marlow's "thrill" of identity.

Though she is "back in it" at the end, she is not the same person she was before her nausea and vertigo. "Foreign" and "domestic" have lost definition. The uncanny "similarities" that "held us all together" are mostly *here* at this point:

> boots, hands, the family voice
> I felt in my throat, or *even*
> the *National Geographic*
> and those awful hanging breasts—
> (161; emphasis added)

I emphasize "even" to note that principally the local sensations—boots, hands, voice (the latter *inside* her, intensely local)—form the answer to her question of what holds us all together and makes us "all just one"; the distant and strange are added on, as if they were less likely ("even / the *National Geographic*") to have given rise to the trauma or the epiphany. The held book with its foreign images, and dated cover, like, in earlier poems, the map and the illustrated Bible or gazeteer (opened to substitute for the open grave the traveler sees), grounds her, providing a measure for understanding her own existence. "There" provides "here" with a counter-point, not a choice. As in "Santarém," the binary oppositions of "life/death, right/wrong, male/female" are refused; and, as at the end of "Questions of Travel," the choice of going or staying is refused, so here the alternatives of "here" or "there" are refused. "In the Waiting Room" reveals a childhood precedent, perhaps even a genesis, of this refusal.

Arguably, Bishop's most sensitized and certainly her quirkiest traveler is the late-twentieth-century-sounding Crusoe, who examines himself and his "adventure" with extraordinary candor. "Crusoe in England" ("Crusoe at Home" was an earlier title) is the longest poem of Bishop's career, following "In the Waiting Room" as the second poem in *Geography III*. It is, like "Santarém," a poem of retrospect, looking back on a departure. In this, it contrasts with the poems of arrival examined earlier in this chapter and with "In the Waiting Room," which, given its youthful subject, is more a poem of prospect than of retrospect.

But, as in "Over 2,000 Illustrations and a Complete Concordance," "In the Waiting Room," "The Map," and "Brazil, January 1, 1502," a text pre-dates the poem. In this case, it is Daniel Defoe's novel. Bishop, when asked how the Crusoe poem originated, told George Starbuck,

I reread the book and discovered how really awful *Robinson Crusoe* was, which I hadn't realized. I hadn't read it for a long time. . . . I had forgotten it was so moral. All that Christianity. So I think I wanted to re-see it with all that left out. (Starbuck 319)[14]

This imperative to "re-see" Crusoe and his island appears in the first verse paragraph of the poem, where Crusoe complains, "None of the books has ever got it right." The revising process begins, immediately following that complaint, with the locale, substituting the Caribbean island of Aruba for the Juan Fernández islands off Chile where Alexander Selkirk, the real-life prototype of Crusoe, had been marooned.[15] In the same interview, Bishop remarks, "And then I was remembering a visit to Aruba—long before it was a developed 'resort.' I took a trip across the island and it's true that there are small volcanoes all over the place" (319). In a letter to Robert Lowell, on April 26, 1962, Bishop writes, "nothing could be worse than Aruba." Indeed, the description of Crusoe's island is even more dyslogistic than the "meager," "sad," and "harsh" landscape described by the jaded tourist of "Arrival at Santos." This island "smell[s] of goat and guano"; the sky is always overcast; the volcanoes are "miserable, small . . . dead as ash heaps"; the "beaches [are] all lava"; and the monotony is practically paralyzing:

The sun set in the sea; the same odd sun
rose from the sea,
and there was one of it and one of me.
(163)

This is neither the lush, beckoning jungle of the conquistador's imagination nor the white sand, sun, and sexual promise of the travel posters. "Crusoe" (he has no first name) is similarly reseen, a far cry from the optimistic and enterprising young hero of Defoe's novel. In fact, the inadequate, impoverished, and incoherent island is a metonymy for the speaker, who regards himself in much the same terms. That connection is spelled out when, for a moment, Crusoe expresses a certain proprietary pleasure in "my poor old island" and then immediately qualifies it, turning to what he sees as his own inadequacy:

I felt a deep affection for
the smallest of my island industries.

No, not exactly, since the smallest was
a miserable philosophy.

Because I didn't know enough.
Why didn't I know enough of something?
Greek drama or astronomy? The books
I'd read were full of blanks;
the poems—well, I tried
reciting to my iris-beds,
"They flash upon that inward eye,
which is the bliss . . ." The bliss of what?
(164)

The blanks, of course, are not in the books but in the speaker's memory. Wordsworth's "I wandered lonely as a cloud," incompletely remembered, locates the source of consolation and inspiration in the memory of natural images. But not only is the passage incomplete—Crusoe having forgotten the very word necessary to describe his own condition—but also the line's application in this context is misunderstood. The memory of the "iris-beds" themselves—actually snail shells in Crusoe's world, daffodils in Wordsworth's poem—is meant to be the "bliss of solitude." Crusoe has matters turned around: he recites the lines about solitude (missing that key word) *to* the supposed iris beds, which should have been his inspiration, at the giving, not the receiving, end of the poetic process as Wordsworth saw it. Bishop's Crusoe is a cross between an absent-minded professor—classifying and experimenting with local flora and fauna—and a self-deprecatory stand-up comic playing to a well-read house. A version of Crusoe as dark comic, in fact, provides us an alternative to current readings of the poem as a text of repression. But those readings first require comment.

Critics often have seen Crusoe as Bishop, just as it is easy to see the tourist in "Arrival at Santos" or the "Elizabeth" of "In the Waiting Room" as the poet herself. Is Crusoe's feeling of inadequacy also Bishop's? And, more important for recent critics, is his reticence about Friday a match for Bishop's own concerning her private life? Is "Crusoe in England," in other words, a late instance of the famous "withholding of emotion," in this case an instance of repression of homoerotic desire?

Recall the line in the first verse: "None of the books has ever got it right."

One misrepresentation that bothers Crusoe concerns Friday, about whom "Accounts . . . have everything all wrong" (165). But the version he would substitute for those erroneous accounts is sketchy. Several readers (Diehl, Goldensohn, and Merrill) find Crusoe's description of Friday flat and impoverished. Goldensohn writes that the "muted, deadened, and repetitive baby speech ['Friday was nice . . . Friday was nice . . . pretty . . . pretty . . . Friday, my dear Friday'] signals a helpless burden of unacknowledgeable feeling that swells somewhere blackly behind the voice, choking it" (77). Goldensohn also suggests that the poem is really Bishop's numbed reaction to the death of her companion, Lota de Macedo Soares, an idea other critics have since adopted (e.g., Millier and Curry).

Yet the "feeling" is not really "unacknowledgeable," unless in the sense that all our feelings for loved ones are finally unacknowledgeable. In fact, with reference to homoerotic desire—not the only component, in the affection of Crusoe for Friday—the feeling *is* acknowledged: "If only he had been a woman! / I wanted to propagate my kind, / and so did he, I think, poor boy" (165). It would be improbable—particularly considering the place of Defoe's novel in the history of literary realism—for Crusoe to say, or for the poet to have him say, more than this. Sexuality and desire are acknowledged, as is physical attraction: "—Pretty to watch; he had a pretty body" (166).

If, however, the "unacknowledgeable" feeling is that of the bond of (nonhomoerotic) friends, then the sentiments Bishop gives to Crusoe are highly expressive, exactly the kind one would expect from this voice as it has established itself over the first four pages of the poem: "Friday was nice. / Friday was nice, and we were friends" (165). True, "we were friends" does not remove the silence surrounding their day-to-day life together, yet Bishop gives no indication of a master-servant relation or of a Christian-heathen opposition, both of which we find in Defoe. This expressiveness through rhetorical restraint or even apparent ineptitude is also, of course, typical of Elizabeth Bishop, in her combination of indirectness and childlike conversation, the same kind of writing one finds in "Santarém": "I liked the place" (185).

Before publishing the poem, Bishop seriously considered James Merrill's suggestion to her that she include more on Friday. In a letter to Merrill, she explained that earlier drafts *had* included more lines but that she had dropped them along with other material, thinking the poem too long.

I might be able to put back a few lines about Friday. I still like "poor boy"—because he was a lot younger; and because they *couldn't* communicate (ghastly word) much. Crusoe guesses at Friday's feelings—but I think you are right and I'll try to restore or add a few lines there before the piece gets to a book. In fact, now that I think of it, I can almost remember 2 or 3 lines after "we were friends"—that's where something is needed, probably. (*One Art* 584)

An alternative emphasis to that of repressed content "swell[ing] . . . blackly" would be to see "Crusoe in England" as a comic elegy. In the many readings of this poem, it is surprising to find Crusoe's wry, self-deprecating humor virtually overlooked.[16] The tone is that of a speaker who, despite deprivation and admitted self-pity (a subject he is decidedly comic about), has learned to live with his fate; who loves anomaly and cherishes memory; who, while on his island, drunkenly danced and played his flute; and who now looks back over his life and that of Friday with a disenchanted but still absorbed curiosity.

Consider Crusoe's time-killing activities, which include painting a goat red and playing with words. "I'd time enough to play with names," he comments (165). He christens one of his volcanoes "*Mont d'Espoir* or *Mount Despair*," names that are phonetic cognates but semantic opposites. In one of his frequent nightmares, a verbal slippage of this kind involves the transition from an act of survival, butchering a "baby goat," to infanticide, slitting a "baby's throat." This dreadful misreading or mishearing, like the joining of despair and hope in the homophonic slippage of the volcano's names, suggests the doubleness of the poem, its nature as both elegiac and comic. It is not a mock elegy, not a parody, but an elegy that mourns genuinely while maintaining a casual, deliberately *un*inflated and often comic tone. (Indeed, the reticence that critics so often point to in Bishop is a condition of the dryness of the humor.) The doubleness of the volcano's names brings to mind "The Bight," whose last lines seem to sum up Crusoe's view of the island, as Bishop suggested they might sum up her own life, with the last three words as epitaph: "All the untidy activity continues, / awful but cheerful" (61). Both of these apparently polar elements pervade "Crusoe in England": on the one hand, monotony, deprivation, sorrow, and grief; on the other, light and self-mocking irony. Much of the poem seems quipped by a philosopher–Woody Allen: "My island seemed to be / a sort of cloud-dump"; "What's wrong about self-pity, anyway? . . . 'Pity should begin at home'"; the goats and gulls "thought / I was a goat, too, or a gull"; "*baa, baa, baa* and *shriek, shriek, shriek* . . . got on my nerves"; and so on (162, 163, 164).

An elegy is always a poem of retrospect, spoken from a sadder place than that it mourns. This is Crusoe *afterward*. The transition from "there" (the tropical island) to "here" (England) is abrupt: "And then one day they came and took us off" (166). Crusoe has no more choice in leaving the island than he did in arriving. The abrupt announcement returns us to the frame of England where the poem begins. As bad as Crusoe's situation on the tropical island may have been, his perspective now—"Old" and "bored" and "petered out"—is one from which he can only look back, not forward. Crusoe's elegy is as much for his own lost self as it is for Friday. In this regard, the reseeing of Crusoe is really an extending of the Defoe character: the practical, resourceful, enterprising young man now sadder and wiser. Crusoe's present melancholy is not the result of a desiccated life in England but rather of that tropical island where his adult identity was forged, a severely constrained island that had only "one kind of everything" (including gender). If Crusoe is stunted, he is thus in harmony with the island's cruel limitations, its flora and fauna, as well as its absences. His drunken bouts, poetry recitals, and practices of defamiliarization such as goat painting and word games were vain efforts to exceed those limitations. Like the magus in Eliot's "Journey of the Magi," Crusoe's "home" in England can only be alien now:

> I'm old,
> I'm bored, too, drinking my real tea,
> surrounded by uninteresting lumber.
> (166)

Crusoe's "alien people" (his own) are mentioned only at the poem's end: "The local museum's asked me to / leave everything to them . . . How can anyone want such things?" (166). Tedious as island life was, the accretion of experience there imbued objects with both value and vitality:

> The knife there on the shelf—
> it reeked of meaning, like a crucifix.
> It lived. . . .
> Now it won't look at me at all.

The living soul has dribbled away.
My eyes rest on it and pass on.
(166; ellipsis added)

Only a museum values such desacralized artifacts. Crusoe briefly remembers and mourns them, then concludes his meditation with one of the few unrelievedly gloomy endings in Bishop's poetry: "—And Friday, my dear Friday, died of measles / seventeen years ago come March" (166).

These final lines remind us that the poem has been an elegy all along, though a more formally conventional elegy might have begun rather than ended with these lines. As elegies do, the poem questions its own elegiac tradition while it carries on Freud's "work of mourning" ("Mourning and Melancholia" 257). One convention of an elegy is the finding of consolation in the face of grief; another, paradoxically, is the refusal to accept consolation, especially the consolation of poetry. In Bishop's poem, the "re-seeing," the "getting it right," is a way of settling accounts, thus, in Freud's thinking, decathecting from the object of mourning. And yet no consolation is found in this re-membering. There are other elegiac elements (leaving aside the figure of Crusoe as pastoral flutist). One is Crusoe's ambivalence over what he mourns; another is the juxtaposition of peace and trauma, a hallmark of the genre, as Peter Sacks has demonstrated. Crusoe mourns Friday, who has died of a European disease; he mourns the island life and the years lost there; and he mourns the loss of immanence emblematic in the objects that are the only proof he ever lived on the island and that are now drained of their "living soul." Finally, most poignantly for Bishop, he mourns the impossibility of representation, of ever "getting it right." The peace that accompanies this work of mourning springs from Crusoe's ability, through humor as much as through a ruthless aesthetic of honesty and literalism, to face a kind of suffering he can do nothing about.

"I want to go back to the Amazon; I dream dreams every night," Bishop wrote to Robert Lowell in 1960 (One Art 383). "Santarém" is an effort to go back in memory, and in poetry, to the Amazon. Written in Boston in 1978, a year before the poet died, "Santarém" is, like "Crusoe in England," a poem of retrospect, but rather than looking back on monotony and deprivation, it remembers a time and place infused with the marvelous, a version of the Golden Age of both classical and romantic nostalgia. The poem begins,

Of course I may be remembering it all wrong
after, after—how many years?

That golden evening I really wanted to go no farther;
more than anything else I wanted to stay awhile
in that conflux of two great rivers, Tapajós, Amazon,
grandly, silently flowing, flowing east.
(185)

Leaving aside for a moment the first two lines, the recollection here is of both an arrival and a departure, and since the ship arrives at sunset, the allusion to a Golden Age is appropriate: "That golden evening," the narrative begins, followed soon by "everything gilded, burnished along one side, / and everything bright" and, in the second stanza, blue or yellow buildings and flamboyants "like pans of embers." "The street was deep in dark-gold river sand," "the people's feet waded in golden sand, / dampered by golden sand" (185–86). In addition to this visionary language, Bishop uses value words completely unlike those of her familiar travel poems of dissatisfaction—the "meager" and "sad" of "Arrival at Santos," the "small" and "miserable" of "Crusoe in England"—here, instead, we have "gorgeous," "bright, cheerful, casual," "dazzling," and more.[17] She also makes, almost excessively, blunt declarations of "I really wanted to go no farther," "I liked the place; I liked the idea of the place," and, later, "I admired it so much" (185–86).

What are the sources of the unqualified pleasure recounted in this poem? Several answers suggest themselves. The first two are obviously touristic and aesthetic: first, the sunset suffusion of color that has painted the entire "golden evening"—no negligible matter when we consider the poignancy of sunsets, especially for travelers, and in this case the visual and sensuous pleasure that is vanishing as the traveler arrives. Second, the charm of the local flora, fauna, and human culture: the glowing flamboyants, the "*azulejos*, buttercup yellow," the exotic teams of blue zebus pulling carts, the cathedral, the river schooner, and so on—all of this is bathed in the golden light of a tourist's Platonic postcard.

But two other, paradoxical answers suggest themselves. One source of pleasure is the activity on the river and *of* the river: the hybrid teeming of riverboats, nuns, and cattle and the vision of the two great rivers converging. The poet is part of this fluid activity, since "Santarém" begins with a disembarkation and ends with a reluctant reembarkation. All of this "crazy shipping," as she describes it, has something in common: like the two great rivers, everything is not just in flux but in "conflux."

> I liked the place; I liked the idea of the place.
> Two rivers. Hadn't two rivers sprung
> from the Garden of Eden? No, that was four
> and they'd diverged. Here only two
> and coming together.
> (185)

The "idea of the place" is convergence. Its opposite, the Edenic branching of originary sources, imported from Western mythologies, is, as this traveler sees it, less attractive—either irrelevant or, worse, a symbol of division, of the Fall. The hustle and bustle, in contrast, are pleasurable, in part because all of it, carried by the currents, is merging. Races and cultures are part of this merging, as the poet notes in parentheses:

> (After the Civil War some Southern families
> came here; here they could still own slaves.
> They left occasional blue eyes, English names,
> and *oars*. . . .)
> (186)

The hybridity of the rivers, two becoming one, is repeated in the human activity on the river, first in the "mongrel riverboats" and then in the native faces that reveal the blue eyes and English names of nineteenth-century American slave owners, whose descendants, by mating with former slaves, dissolved that binarism too.[18]

This merging provides the other pleasure described in the poem: while the rivers join around her, the speaker finds momentary joy in the sensation of calm amid intense, "flowing" activity: "I wanted to stay awhile." The two great rivers are "grandly, silently flowing, flowing east"; the activity is all "bright, cheerful, casual"; and, beside the river, despite the busy scene, "almost the only sounds / were creaks and *shush, shush, shush*" (185–86).

This traveler, however suffused with pleasure, is nevertheless the familiar Bishop tourist, if anything more diffident than ever. At the beginning of

"The Map," the young poet stops to wonder if she has got it right: "Shad-ows, or are they shallows . . . ?" (3), the first of several questions in that poem. Here, near the end of her poetic career, doubts come sooner and graver: the doubtful introspection of the perceiver frames the vision of the town and its converging rivers, even before we know what the poem concerns, what "it" is: "Of course I may be remembering it all wrong / after, after—how many years?" (185). Not merely a doubt, this doubt is folded inside a doubt. As with "Crusoe in England," the burden of faith-fulness to literal fact—as if the event still existed somewhere outside the speaker's memory—pesters the speaker, not only here at the beginning but throughout the poem, in phrases such as "Or so it looked" and "Hadn't two rivers sprung / from the Garden of Eden? No, that was four" (185). But at this point in Bishop's career, one might see this gesture as a reflex or a stylism. Anyone who begins a story by saying, "Of course I may have got this all wrong," always follows that phrase with "but" and proceeds to tell the story. "Or so it looked" identifies the quizzical tourist we have come to know; it is also a way of saying, "This is going to have to do."

The familiar indefiniteness characterizes not only inner states such as memory but also outward choices. The pleasure of "Santarém" is the peace of an immersion in hybridity and, with it, the rejection of binary oppositions. The poet is theoretically explicit about the latter, having built into the poem its own treatment of literary criticism:

> Even if one were tempted
> to literary interpretations
> such as: life/death, right/wrong, male/female
> —such notions would have resolved, dissolved, straight off
> in that watery, dazzling dialectic.
> (185)

It is characteristic of this alluvial dialectic of Bishop's that resolution comes not through making sense of things but through the opposite, the dissolu-tion of conflicting terms; that clarity and focus come through liquidity, not solidity. This passage elaborates on the succinct "*And here, or there . . . No*" (94) of "Questions of Travel." It also informs current gender readings of Bishop in that it includes in its oppositions that of "male/female."

But, consider again, in this connection, the first three narrative lines of "Santarém" condensing the poem's theme and sentiment: "I really wanted to go no farther; / more than anything else I wanted to stay awhile / in that conflux of two great rivers" (185). These lines now may be seen in the context of the other poems that ponder over binary choices. To "stay awhile" is a choice, but the tourist knows she will leave the very same evening. The freedom to change one's mind, as these "crazy" people do, which is at least vicariously a pleasure for the speaker, is denied her, since, according to the rules of her world, her path is determined: "my ship's whistle blew. I couldn't stay" (187). The poem seems to end with that concession to binaries that, within the poem, is strenuously rejected. And, yet, no choice has been made: the town of Santarém was not a personal choice but a stop on a tour; the speaker had no idea of the pleasure it was to give her. Similarly out of her hands is her departure. And, after all, she did stay "awhile." Choices—even the choice of making choices—have been avoided.

The golden, sunlit, and comforting evening of "Santarém," where opposites and differences dissolve dazzlingly, is a "childish geography" of the kind I discuss further in the poems of Ashbery and Ginsberg. The desire *not* to have to choose—like the rapprochement pattern of the infant who crawls away from its mother, then cries to be taken back—can be seen as a failure of accountability (and is seen as such by Caren Kaplan). But this is the necessary if costly failure of all travel. Bishop, like virtually all the poets discussed in this book, was not free of the guilt of departures. "Here" and "there" were agonizing choices in the last fifteen years of her life, particularly following the death of Lota de Macedo Soares. Some of Lota's friends held Bishop responsible for her death, since Bishop's leaving to the United States had prompted Lota's anxiety and depression. But leaving to South America *from* the United States was also the occasion of guilt, as it has been for many American travelers. In Key West, in 1941, just three weeks after the Pearl Harbor attack, Bishop wrote to Marianne Moore about trips she was considering: "I haven't given up the idea of South America. I'm not a bit sure of the ethics of it all—what do you think?" (*One Art* 105).

"Home" has a chance to reply to Bishop's "exotic" exploits in the last verse paragraph of "Santarém," which acts as an epilogue. A local pharmacist graciously presents her with "an empty wasps' nest" she had admired (echoing "my gray wasps' nest . . . glued with spit" of more than thirty years before in "Jerónimo's House" [34]). When she carries the nest on board the ship, she places her whole conception of beauty and value in home's context, the context of "Mr. Swan, / Dutch, the retiring head of Philips Electric, / really a very nice old man, / who wanted to see the Amazon before he died, / [and who] asked, 'What's that ugly thing?'" (187).

Mr. Swan's opinion of the wasps' nest makes the poet's pleasure in the transgressive more transgressive still, reviving the "here"-versus-"there" opposition she has assiduously avoided. To Mr. Swan, this "mongrel," seedy river town may be ugly as well. To Bishop, its mongrel quality is part of its fluidity and ephemerality and thus its allure. But "home" is the arbiter of beauty as it is of the oppositions set out by Bishop. From the standpoint of "home," avoiding the "right/wrong" opposition is unforgivable. Yet "home" makes mistakes; this one about the wasps' nest is trivial; others may be disastrous. Home is not only the place of choices; it also is the place of custom, conformity, and prejudice.

As Bonnie Costello has suggested, travel in Bishop's poems is not so much a quest as it is a condition and "a means to free ourselves from a parochial view of the world, to heighten sensation and invention" (*Elizabeth* 128). The remark seems to refer to an early letter to Marianne Moore (May 14, 1942) in which Bishop referred to "that uneasy heightening of sensation that I think is really essential to travel" (*One Art* 108). In Bishop's poetry, even at its most "descriptive" and "reticent," we find no rest, no safe harbor. In "Large Bad Picture," ships are decried for reaching their destinations. In "The Imaginary Iceberg," the explorer will trade everything for wider, deeper experience, "although it meant the end of travel" (4). The sea, in "At the Fishhouses," is "like what we imagine knowledge to be: / dark, salt, clear, moving, utterly free" (66). Poems such as "Questions of Travel," "Over 2,000 Illustrations and a Complete Concordance," and "Santarém" offer no possibilities for settling.

When James Longenbach suggests mapping postmodern poetry in the United States on Bishop's career and not on Lowell's, he is thinking of Lowell's "apocalyptic fervor" ("Elizabeth" 484), whether in *Lord Weary's Castle* or *Life Studies*.[19] If, in the usual account, Lowell's career maps a "break-through," Bishop's does not. The apocalyptic, the grand, the global—these elements are absent in Bishop, whose emphasis on a proliferation of small narratives rather than on larger historical metanarratives, along with her mode of composition and her almost exaggerated awareness of subjectivity, might also identify her as a postmodern.

The mixed pleasures of "vulnerable" travel—desire, unpredictability, hybridity—fuse in "Santarém" into a sublime moment. Bishop's comment that she saw herself as a "minor female Wordsworth" is appropriate here. The traveler's sensations at Santarém are Bishop's equivalent, equally golden, of Wordsworth's daffodils, which now, after many years, "flash upon [her] inward eye." But Bishop's poems of travel are not catalogues of sensation, any more than they are "entropological" elegies for lost interiors—or lost opportunities—in the manner of Lévi-Strauss. The vulnerable traveler/poet is involved at this point not in the desire to find what is common to differing cultures, or even what is useful, but in the immersion in difference, in an effort to surrender the self. This is not to suggest that Bishop spent her time going native; to the contrary, she was a privileged visitor in Brazil, owing largely to her association with Lota de Macedo Soares and the artistic and political circles of which Lota was a part. But the questions of travel that Bishop explored in her poems entail fitting the Other, or the Other Place, into one's world (or what is left of it), not by reducing the Other to a known datum but by juxtaposing experiences and subjectivities in what Hans-Georg Gadamer calls a "fusion of horizons" (289–90). Perhaps Bishop's traveling subjectivity evolved out of her lifelong sense of herself as a guest wherever she lived, of not having a home. Perhaps it stemmed, as Steven Gould Axelrod suggests in speaking of Bishop and the Cold War, from her being "born into a civilization . . . in which surveillance and conformity take the place of adventure" ("Heterotropic" 64). Possibly for both of these reasons, Bishop created poems as provisional homes, as traces of their own activity, as "wasps' nests." In such light, unfurnished structures, one can—as Bishop wrote in "The End of March" of her "proto-dream-house"—"retire there and do *nothing*, / or nothing much, forever" (179). If such passages suggest escapism, Bishop's was an escape from a hegemonic subjectivity, an undesired mastery. Travel and its poesis allowed that escape and the performance of a subtler subjectivity, one that involves, as the poem "Santarém" demonstrates, dissolution more than synthesis, perplexity more than power, dialectic more than domination.

Postscript: Ouro Preto

Conseilhero street, blacktop now, carries heavy traffic. Approaching it on foot from Ouro Preto, you are just as likely to take Rua Chico Rei, really a walking path and a steep half-mile of steps. Once you are up on the Conseilhero, no sign indicates Bishop's former house. The plaque that reads "Aqui Viveu Elizabeth Bishop" is mounted inside the wall that encloses house and garden. Linda Nemer, Bishop's onetime companion, owns the house, which is vacant most of the time, except when Ms. Nemer visits it from her usual home in Belo Horizonte. Inside the wall, by the garden, a huge, lame, and docile German Shepherd sleeps, cared for by Lolo, the housekeeper who lives nearby. The garden, all flowers, descends in tiers along the hillside. The house itself is bigger than I imagined. It has four bedrooms, two of them quite large and most with the same beautiful view that the living and dining room have, a panorama of Ouro Preto below with its dozen baroque churches and green surrounding hills.

The large living room features what looks like an abstract collage of old wood, string, wire, and plaster but is actually the innards of the wall that had been cracked and exposed. Bishop had decided to place a frame around it. Touches like these, along with the view and the general fine taste, earned the house an opulent spread in *Arquitetura e Constucao*, Brazil's glossy architecture and design magazine, which lies with some other books beside the fireplace. I take some photos, including some of Zenith Inacio, who came with Lolo's son to open the house for me. She owns the posada nearby (which she seems anxious to sell) and worked as a maid for Bishop forty years ago. According to Zenith, Bishop helped her with money and gifts when Zenith was twenty-three, pregnant, and married to a heavy drinker. She describes how she once found Bishop drunk on the floor of her room, her face beet red, and how she nursed her back to health.

It is the end of April, and the "Tiradentes" festival is in full swing—honoring the Brazilian patriot, nicknamed "Tooth-puller," whose head was displayed on a pole in the plaza in 1797 as a warning to troublemakers. Dignitaries and soldiers give speeches by day, and thousands of teenagers gather by night to hear the rock bands play on a large stage. Huge speakers are stacked in towers near the monument. *Capoeira* dancers perform every night in the street and in front of the church by my hotel. I try to visit Bishop's old friend and drinking partner Lili Correa de Araujo, but I have waited too long for this trip: she is a hundred years old now and cannot receive visitors.

Walking the streets, asking directions to the Bishop house, I remember the time I visited Julio Fausto Aguilera in a poor and dusty pueblo on the outskirts of Guatemala City. I asked a young woman directions to Aguilera's home; she said, "A poet lives *here?*" Nobody in Ouro Preto had heard of Elizabeth Bishop.

Rudderless, I was driven like a plank . . .

ARTHUR RIMBAUD, "The Drunken Boat,"

trans. Robert Lowell, *Imitations*

Travelers and Tourists

From Bishop to Lowell

If Elizabeth Bishop's poetic stock is higher now than Robert Lowell's, it is in part, as David Laskin writes, because "her limitations now recommend her to us. Her cool, skeptical restraint accords better with our played-out anti-idealistic sensibility. We have become fed up with large gestures" (398). Yet Bishop's star was not quick in rising, and even after it had risen, books on American poetry that dealt with both poets customarily began with a chapter on Lowell. Lowell himself was ahead of his time in seeing Bishop's importance, particularly to his own work. Reading her poems in the 1950s, he said, "suggested a way of breaking through the shell of my old manner" (*Collected Prose* 227).[1]

But it was not only Bishop's poetic style that Lowell admired; it was also her life. When Lowell was visiting Amsterdam with Elizabeth Hardwick in the early 1950s, he wrote to Bishop, "You always make me feel that I have a rather obvious breezy, impersonal liking for the great and obvious, in contrast with your adult feeling for the odd and genuine" (qtd. in Mariani 213), and, comparing his recent travel to Bishop's, he remarked that, for oddity and authenticity, even she could not match Amsterdam. But his European trip did not bring about the hoped-for new way of writing. On the contrary, as he confided to William Carlos Williams, he found himself more than ever immured in his mannered style, the more so now that it was laden with "travel impressions" (Mariani 211).

Five years later, after seeing Bishop and Lota de Macedo Soares off at the Bangor, Maine, airport, he returned to Castine and tried his hand at a travel poem to Bishop.[2] More than a dozen versions of the poem exist, usually titled "Flying Down to Rio," but the first published, in *Notebook*, "Flying from Bangor to Rio 1957," reads in part as follows:

> North & south
> from Halifax to Rio the same Atlantic—
> you can never settle on where to be,
> lashed by your giant memory to the globe.
> (234)

In *History*, this became:

> *North & South*, Yarmouth to Rio, one Atlantic—
> you'd never found another place to live,
> bound by your giant memory to one known longitude.[3]
> (197)

The *Notebook* version is more concise and also rings truer than the *History* version, in that Bishop could "never settle on where to be" but did find "another place to live." More significant, "lashed . . . to the globe"—especially by memory—foreshadows Bishop's "In the Waiting Room" and Lowell's "Dropping South: Brazil," providing a figure for the literalism, the need to be grounded by observation and memory, which both poets worried about.

Two years later, *Life Studies* appeared, a book Lowell had begun immediately after Bishop's visit to Maine and that marked his "breakthrough" into a new style and a new subject. But leaving aside the more-or-less symbolic journey from religious Rome to secular Paris in "Beyond the Alps," all but one of the journeys (and that connected to death) in that volume are within the U.S. Northeast: Boston to Cambridge, Cambridge to Maine, Boston . to Beverly Farms, Manhattan subway rides, New England Sunday spins, and visits to family burial grounds. Also, while psychological vulnerability appeared as a trope in these poems, it had not yet been exacerbated, as it soon would be, by international travel.

Americans began traveling abroad in unprecedented numbers in what Lowell called the "tranquilized fifties." The dollar was strong against European and other currencies, and commercial airlines, displacing the luxury liners that crossed to Europe between the wars, offered affordable fares. "One shouldn't gloat over a good exchange rate," Bishop says in a letter, pleased nevertheless at how easily she could get by in Brazil. The first edition of *Europe on Five Dollars a Day* came out in 1957; the wherewithal of the U.S. middle class to take vacations in Europe was but one index of the strength of American economic interests, which, following World War II, moved into markets formerly controlled by French and British corporations. In this context, Robert von Hallberg argues that American poets in Europe, far from opposing political expansion, were as caught up as other Americans in the proliferation of American interests. Indeed, he suggests, they carried out the poetic counterpart of that expansion—the establishment of an American cultural hegemony. Thus Allen Tate could write to the U.S. State Department in 1959: "Mr. Lowell is the kind of a man I think we should send abroad more and more in order to eliminate some false impressions that foreigners seem to have about the qualifications of Americans to participate in international cultural life on equal terms with them" (von Hallberg 72).[4]

Tate may have been hasty in his judgment. Did the United States really want to send its most celebrated literary manic-depressive to foreign nations so that he could insult its officials, rave about the Bomb, and have to be sedated and packed home? The notion of Lowell as corporate or government spokesman, promoting U.S. interests abroad, does not sit easily with Lowell's abundantly documented instability. Moreover, even had Lowell wanted to aid U.S. political and cultural expansion—not unthinkable, despite his own left-liberal political affiliations and activism—how would he have done so?[5] Whatever small power American poets wielded at the midcentury—certainly more than they wield today—they occupied a space still well below the horizon of the average person or the average head of state.

For present purposes, the European trip von Hallberg alludes to (when Lowell lectured as part of the Salzburg Seminar in American Civilization), a trip that resulted in a manic episode followed by hospitalization, is not as germane as two subsequent and still more traumatic periods in Lowell's poetic career: when, under the auspices of the Congress of Cultural Freedom, he traveled to South America and Mexico and when, toward the end of his life, having left Elizabeth Hardwick for Caroline Blackwood, he made numerous flights between England and the United States. It was during these years, rather than during the earlier European trip, that Lowell's travels persistently became subject matter for the poems.

the true shark, the shadow of departure.

ROBERT LOWELL, "Flight to New York," *The Dolphin*

Fear of Flying

Robert Lowell and the Trope of Vulnerability

Near the middle of Robert Lowell's *For the Union Dead*, a new trope emerges, one that will continue in several successive books, particularly those whose poems are often presented as daily notes: *Notebook 1967–68*, *Notebook*, *History*, *For Lizzie and Harriet*, and *The Dolphin*. Among the poems of optical, epidermal, and neural sensitivity—"Night Sweat," "The Lesson," "The Neo-Classical Urn," and "Eye and Tooth"—poems of travel appear, with journeys as figures for that sensitization. Poems such as "Going To and Fro," "Buenos Aires," and "Dropping South: Brazil" present the strained, introspective speaker of Lowell's "breakthrough" phase, introduced in *Life Studies*, as increasingly vulnerable to and destabilized by the duress of travel.[1] The rhetoric is murkier and the speaker more disoriented as he moves from his center of gravity in New England. In Lowell, the disorientation of travel becomes a metaphor for, and often a cause of, the disorientation of psychological illness. From this phase till the end of Lowell's life, travel served as a texture out of which he crafted fractured narratives of the troubled traveler's ego.

Falling, Falling: The North-South Axis

Unlike Elizabeth Bishop, Lowell was a reluctant internationalist who seemed to know little about contemporary poetry outside of the European tradition.[2] In late 1961, he had caught a glimpse of Latin America on a ten-day vacation to Puerto Rico with Elizabeth Hardwick and their daughter Harriet, loving the "millionaire hotel world" and "shaken" by the beauty of Puerto Rico and by "all the creeping Puerto Rican life, which is all around us here on the West Side, but which is revealed there in greater purity" (letter to Edmund Wilson, 31 March 1962, qtd. in Mariani). It was a vibrant life, he thought, that would outlast his own culture. In early 1962, the CIA-funded Congress of Cultural Freedom gave him the opportunity, in the form of a reading tour of several South American countries, to accept Bishop's long-standing invitation to visit Brazil.

This trip, with its CIA auspices and the likelihood that Lowell's presence was meant to counteract the influence of leftist writers such as Pablo Neruda, might have lent credence to Robert von Hallberg's assessment of American poets' complicity with U.S. expansionism, were it not for what followed. As soon as he arrived in Buenos Aires, Lowell threw away his medication and had a full manic bout. Taken to a reception at the presidential palace, he downed several martinis, announced he was "Caesar of Argentina," and gave a speech extolling Hitler. He then went out, stripped naked, and mounted an equestrian statue in one of the city's main squares. After several days of this behavior, including spending binges in which he charged all purchases to the Congress, he had to be fought to the ground, straitjacketed, Thorazined, and sent home for treatment (Hamilton 300–303; Saunders 348).

"Dropping South: Brazil" and "Buenos Aires" were written during this trip, though only the latter is clearly autobiographical. One cannot read "Cattle furnished my new clothes: / my coat of limp, chestnut-colored suede" ("Buenos Aires," *FUD* 60) without remembering that Lowell's

Argentine sprees included the purchase of costly leather jackets for himself and his friends.[3] Three of the eight quatrains deal with statuary—"Literal commemorative busts" and "a hundred marble goddesses," with whom the poet "found rest / by cupping a soft palm to each hard breast" (61)—reminding one of Lowell's statue-hugging rampage.

"Dropping South: Brazil" is less descriptive but richer in its treatment of the traveler. Travel in this poem is at once mythic and surreal: "Walking and walking in a mothy robe . . . / I crossed the reading room and met my soul, / hunched, spinning downward on the colored globe" (62). The vertigo of "spinning downward," anticipatory of the vertigo in Bishop's "In the Waiting Room," is emphasized even in the title, since this is not traveling nor even flying but "dropping" south, the motion of an object without agency. Later in the poem, "falling" is introduced as a way of describing travel that then appears in other poems, such as "No Messiah" (*The Dolphin*) and the *Notebook* version of "Mexico." What follows in the poem is enriched with notes from the real Brazil and, possibly, from conversations with Elizabeth Bishop. The "old Atlantic" that the poet knew from Massachusetts (note the echo of "one Atlantic" and the "same Atlantic" in the versions of "Flying from Bangor to Rio 1957") is revised not only by the new geographic perspective but also by magic—literally, by the Afro-Brazilian rites and dances of macumba:

> The ocean was the old Atlantic still,
> always the swell greened in, rushed white, and fell,
> now warmer than the air. However, there
> red flags forbade our swimming. No one swam.
> A lawless gentleness. The Latin blonde,
> two strips of ribbon, ripened in the sun,
> sleeping alone and pillowed on one arm.
> No competition. Only rings of boys
> butted a ball to keep it in the air,
> while inland, people starved, and struck, and died—
> unhappy Americas, ah *tristes tropiques*!—
> and nightly in the gouges by the tide,
> *macumba* candles courted *Yemanjá*,
> tall, white, the fish-tailed Virgin of the sea,
> corpselike with calla lilies, walking

the water in her white gown. "I am falling.
Santa Maria, pray for me, I want to stop,
but I have lost my foothold on the map,
now falling, falling, bent, intense, my feet
breaking my clap of thunder on the street."
(62)

The speaker may be in a "reading room," as he says, walking to and fro in his "mothy robe," but the disorientation is global. In the final lines, the "I" who, at the beginning of the poem, met (past tense) his soul "spinning downward" over the planet, or over a colored model globe, is now falling (present tense), having "lost my foothold on the map."

The "old Atlantic" of earlier poems is also distanced and defamiliarized here by "red flags" forbidding swimming, whether because of riptide or because of pollution (at this writing, no one swims at Ipanema and few at Copacabana, though the beaches are full of sunbathers). The "lawless gentleness" characterizes the sea but also Lowell's own view, not pejorative, of Rio, of Brazil, and perhaps of Latin America in general. In the beach scene, human activity is minimal, a norm if not a cliché of the *tristes tropiques* with their sleepy inhabitants. No one bothers the sleeping blonde woman. The unseen reality behind this tranquil view is the starvation, strikes, and death in the Brazilian backlands and favelas. Following Lowell's chain of scenes, arranged in order of increasing Otherness—private room, to beach, to suffering inland regions, to "Americas" as a whole—we arrive at another, more Other still: the macumba ceremonies, which, like voodoo, or *lucumí*, are New World versions of Yoruba celebrations. Though the vision of the Yoruba god Yemanjá, "corpselike with calla lilies," seems to come out of Brazilian *carnaval* (and Afro-Caribbean music and Santería), the language takes us to the west coast of Africa. When, then, we come to "I am falling," with its abrupt change from past to present tense, we see this bookish, "mothy"-robed poet, who had spun out of his orbit in leaving New England, as threatened by a wider and wider spin. (The structural echo of the poem's first line—"Walking and walking in a mothy robe"—is Yeats's "Turning and turning in a widening gyre.") The quotation marks are a distancing device, but they may also paraphrase a conversation with Bishop, who, a decade later, attributed a similar speech to the young girl named "Elizabeth" in "In the Waiting Room":

I was saying it to stop
the sensation of falling off
the round, turning world
into cold, blue-black space.
(*Complete* 160)

The poem "Going To and Fro," which appears earlier in *For the Union Dead*, also concludes with a falling off the world. Here, however, the fatal experience is displaced onto another traveler, the Symbolist poet Gerard de Nerval. (An earlier draft was titled "For Nerval or Someone.") The poem's title alludes to the book of Job, where God inquires of Satan, "Whence camest thou?" and Satan replies, "From going to and fro in the earth, and from walking up and down in it" (1:6). Twice in Lowell's poem, the devil is mentioned and, at one point, the phrase "he and you," suggesting perhaps that Nerval and the devil colluded in making art: they "dug it all out of the dark / unconscious bowels of the nerves" (30). The poem begins vaguely, "It's authentic perhaps / to have been there," but, by the second stanza, the location is alternately Nerval's France and Lowell's America:

the hot-dog and coca cola bar,
the Versailles steps,
the Puritan statue—
if you could get through the Central Park
by counting . . .
(29)

The last "if" clause suggests what the next lines confirm, that the locales are practically unendurable: "But the intestines shiver, / the ferry saloon thugs with your pain." What redeems the misery is, in Nerval's case and perhaps in Lowell's, the erotic promise of travel:

how often you wanted your fling
with those French girls, Mediterranean
luminaries, Mary, Myrtho, Isis—
as far out as the sphynx!
The love that moves the stars

moved you!
It set you going to and fro

and up and down—
If you could get loose
from the earth by counting
your steps to the noose . . .
(30)

The latter lines evoke Nerval's own suicide by hanging while they remind us that Nerval undertook his travel willingly; the French poet was moved, as Lowell has it, by love, by fantasy (Myrtho was a goddess he invented), and by an aversion to stasis, as if the motion of travel would somehow deter or postpone death, as in Zeno's paradox where one can never arrive at a destination as long as the distance between here and there is endlessly measured and divided. (An earlier draft of the poem reads "Nerval got loose from the dark / By counting his steps to the noose."[4]) Counting is characteristic of obsessive neurosis. What would one count to "get through"—not just to traverse but to endure—the Central Park? Although counting steps to the noose may divert a condemned man's mind from his fate, the image applies more broadly to perceiving the nearness of death at moments of extreme anxiety. This anxiety returns in "Flight to New York," where the poet admits "my bleak habit of counting off minutes on my fingers, / like pages of an unrequested manuscript" (D 75).

The four "if" clauses that structure "Going To and Fro" gain in substance and coherence:

> if now
> you could loll on the ledge for a moment
> . . . .
> if you could for a moment . . . [stanza 1]
>
> if you could get through the Central Park
> by counting . . . [stanza 2]
>
> If you could get loose
> from the earth by counting
> your steps to the noose . . . [stanza 5]
> (29–30)

This latter "if" represents the most fully articulated wish, whose full force has only gradually become utterable—though even this, like the previous "if" clauses, ends in an ellipsis, as though more "if"s lay in abeyance. The counting in the park was not, as it turns out, merely a counting of numbers or sheep, a whistling in the dark. Nor were the "One step, two steps, three steps" at the beginning of the same stanza merely steps from one location to the next. These are, rather, the steps counted toward death, a final "get[ting] loose from the earth," candidly suicidal in Nerval but fraught with terror in Lowell. The wish to "get loose / from the earth" contrasts with "Dropping South: Brazil" and its *fear* of losing one's "foothold on the map," its "falling," and the idea, from "Flying from Bangor to Rio 1957," of being "lashed by . . . memory to the globe" (*N* 237).

After attending a second and less catastrophic Congress of Cultural Freedom in Caracas, in December of 1967, where he met Ivan Illich, Lowell flew to Cuernavaca to visit Father Illich's Center for Intercultural Development. There he met and became romantically involved with one of Illich's assistants, twenty-two-year-old Mary Keelan, an Irishwoman employed by the Monastery of Emmaus. He wrote the sonnet sequence "Mexico" as a result of this romance, including it first in *Notebook 1967–68*, then in *Notebook*, and finally, in the version I discuss here, in *For Lizzie and Harriet*. "Mexico" is the first poetic sequence where extended travel provides a matrix for Lowell's narratives of vulnerability. The poet folds his ongoing personal concerns into notes on local history, customs, flora, and fauna, which exist chiefly to nourish those concerns and give them shape.

"Mexico" is also an instructive example of the way in which travel functions as a mode of composition. It would be next to impossible to puzzle out the hundreds of changes Lowell made, with Frank Bidart's help, in the poems or parts of poems they moved, filtered, and regrouped from *Notebook 1967–68* to *Notebook* and then to *For Lizzie and Harriet*, *History*, and *The Dolphin*. Some of the changes are miniscule, but many are large and structural. The process took the form of shuttling the historical poems— on, say, Verlaine, DeGaulle, and Stalin—into the book *History* and away from the "personal" books *For Lizzie and Harriet* and *The Dolphin*. While the original "Mexico" sequence in *Notebook 1967–68* and *Notebook* had twelve poems, the entire sequence is dropped from *History*, and of the ten "Mexico" poems appearing in *For Lizzie and Harriet*, several are made up of recombined parts of earlier poems.[5]

Overall, the Mexican sonnets seem part of the "waste-marble" that

Lowell had intended to cut from *Notebook* but that nonetheless found its way into subsequent volumes. But—bracketing, if possible, the question of aesthetic value—"Mexico" exemplifies the kind of poem and the kind of combinatory process of composition the poet was developing out of his travels. The poems of "Mexico" may be unevocative of that country— Mexico is a mere backdrop, as Octavio Paz noted with disappointment— but they were probably never intended to be "place" poems such as those of D. H. Lawrence or even those of Bishop. They are, as was "Dropping South: Brazil," principally concerned with the centrifugal and fragmenting psychological processes within the speaker. While all ten sonnets of the "Mexico" sequence are "love" poems, I will address only those that bear on the anxieties associated with geographic displacement, poems whose "love" interest stands in vexed relation to that displacement.

The first six lines of the first poem deal with familiar material—the aging and famous poet, "fifty, humbled . . . / dead laurel grizzling my back," beside his new young lover, "some sweet, uncertain age, say twenty-seven" (*LH* 30)—before a version of Mexico makes its entrance:

> What help then? Not the sun, the scarlet blossom,
> and the high fever of this seventh day,
> the predestined diarrhea of the pilgrim,
> the multiple mosquito spots, round as pesos.
> Hope not for God here, or even for the gods;
> the Aztecs knew the sun, the source of life,
> will die, unless we feed it human blood—
> we two are clocks, and only count in time . . .
> the hand a knife-edge pressed against the future.
> (30)

This sequence of images—from the sun's heat on Sunday to the traveler's physical discomfort and vulnerability to bacteria and insects to God, the gods, and thence to the Aztecs (and back to the sun)—is a loop with a kind of logic. The sun's fever is also the traveler's, and the mosquito draws blood as the Aztec gods did; the one set of terms, centered around the sun, depends on the other, centered around human blood. Having closed this elemental very Pazian cycle, however, the poet returns to the initial impetus of the poem, independent of the "Mexican" reflections. "We two are clocks," he says, the one having ticked off more hours than the other. We two "count" in the sense that, like any organisms, we register and measure the passage of time; but we also "count" as Nerval counts steps to the noose in "Going To and Fro," as a way of surviving; and, finally, we "count" in the sense that we *matter*.

The anxiety about age remains static in the poem, undeveloped by the dystopian portrait of a Mexican town with its baking sun, diarrhea, fever, and mosquitoes, elements forming an ironic frame for a cross-generational declaration of love. Only the last line, where the clock metaphor is abruptly dropped for an image that ties the speaker to the Aztec sacrifices, forges a link between the lovers and "Mexico." The hand, agent both of life and craft, as *The Dolphin* makes clear ("My eyes have seen what my hand did"), is now the edge of a knife, which can, and must, cut in order to keep the sun shining, the clock ticking, and the poems coming. This hand is "pressed against the future" in the sense that it—the poet's actions and poems—will determine what is to come.

The Mexican lizard of the third poem of the series recalls the lizards of Bishop's "Brazil, January 1, 1502" from a few years before. Bishop's lizards "scarcely breathe"; Lowell's "does nothing for days but puff his throat / for oxygen" (*LH* 31). Bishop's male lizards eye the female lizard. Lowell's, too, "loves only identical rusty lizards panting" (31). In Bishop's poem the lizards' lust (or "Sin") is juxtaposed with the lust of the conquistadors. Here, in parallel fashion, the attention returns to the topic of the couple in love. But, rather than lust, the poem evokes the passing of time, the two lovers' measure of it dwarfed by longer arcs: "The Toltec temples pass to dust in the dusk— / the clock dial of the rising moon, dust out of time" (31). The lovers are seen as two clocks again, as in the first poem, but now "two clocks set back to Montezuma's fate," as if partaking of the violence of that time ("when they took a city, they murdered everything" [31]).

Love and death, the passing of time, carpe diem—all this would be poetic convention were it not for the complication of geographic displacement. The poems of this sequence emerge out of Lowell's conflict between his desire to locate the playground for love that travel seems to offer and his inability to grasp or realize the foreign place. The effort of realization may take the form of remembering the Toltecs or the Aztecs or of describing the fountains, the sunsets, or the body with its mosquito bites and diarrhea, but the instability, certainly as much imported as native, is always underscored

("I've lived too long without sense," he writes in the seventh sonnet [33]).

The beginning of the fourth sonnet turns like a compass needle toward home, the present place achieving relevance only to what has been left behind: "South of Boston, south of Washington, / south of any bearing . . . I walk the glazed moonlight" (31).[6] To have or take "any bearing" means to maintain a reference point in the North. To drift "south of any bearing" is to travel beyond the pale. Why travel at all, with such a reluctance to reorient oneself? The answer is, as it is in "Going To and Fro," for "love":

drawn on by my unlimited desire.

(31)

The undertow of obsession—like the counting in "Going To and Fro," the walking to and fro in "Dropping South: Brazil" and the monotony of the bull and cow going "up road and down" in the fourth sonnet—is palpable in the fifth sonnet also, in the walking past the same site "twenty times," as if it were a way of numbing oneself, as Proust warns, to one's surroundings. The fifth sonnet, however, suggests a struggle against this automatism, introducing a figure of Heraclitean flux—"The stream will not flow back, not once, not twice" (32)—which warns against monotony, reminding one of the singularity and irrevocability of every movement, however repetitive it may appear.

The next to last "Mexico" poem opens on the "Next to last day" with a sublime vista of valley, volcano, and a world on fire: the lovers are "baking" on the veranda, the brown rock is "roasting," the grass is "smoking," and "the breath / of the world" rises like smoke (34). This intensity is parallel to another: "the hours / of shivering, ache and burning, when we charged / so far beyond our courage—altitude . . ." (34). If these lines describe love-making, they also refer to mountain climbing, since the vertical metaphor, to emerge in the two poems titled "Eight Months Later," is suggested by the literal "cleavage dropping miles to the valley's body," by the mention of the volcano, and, after the passage about "the hours / of shivering," by the single word "altitude" outside of syntax.

Toward the end of this poem, the poet characterizes his lover:

No artist perhaps, you see the backs of phrases,
a girl too simple to lose herself in words—
I fall back in the end on honest speech;

infirmity's a food the flesh must swallow,
feeding our minds . . . the mind which is also flesh.
(34)

That the "girl" (later a "poor child") is presented as simple, unartistic, and nonverbal may be connected to the poet's Wordsworthian claim to "fall back . . . on honest speech," a claim Lowell, in prizing imagination over "fact," was ordinarily suspicious about.[7] But here we must compare the *Notebook* version, since the vertigo entailed in the project of speaking honestly has been elided from *For Lizzie and Harriet*; in the earlier version, "altitude" and "falling" back on honest speech are connected. The idiom of "falling back on," in the sense of relying on, is conflated with the frightening sense of "falling" or "falling backward," echoed in "Dropping South: Brazil," where the traveler is "falling, falling, bent, intense." Thus, in *Notebook*: "we'd charged / so far beyond our courage—altitudes, / then the falling . . . falling back on honest speech" (105–6).

"Mexico" began with the phrase "The difficulties, the impossibilities," followed by what seems the object of those terms: "I, fifty . . . you, some sweet, uncertain age, say twenty-seven" (*LH* 30). But other "difficulties" and "impossibilities" are at stake: getting the mind to clear, to focus and compose, is certainly one of them. While this sequence traces a short period, it provides a matrix and a set of reference points for Lowell to continue composing around the concerns that animate all of his poetry of this period, irrespective of place: what the past demands of us; how we are to treat others; and what to do with life and life's "notes." The "impossibilities" and "difficulties" concern the latter—poesis—as much as anything else.

The two sonnets that form a coda to the "Mexico" sequence, together titled "Eight Months Later" (individually titled "Eight Months Later" and "Die Gold Orangen"), represent moments of retrospect and nostalgia for the poet's Mexico days and for "[t]he flower I took away" (*LH* 35). The memory draws on the imagery of the ninth "Mexico" poem: "we burned the grass, the grass still fumes," as the poet compares himself first to Lucifer, who "sank to sleep on the tumuli of Lilith" and then to God. His dissatisfaction with home—"Midsummer Manhattan," where "everything is stacked . . . half Europe / in half a mile" (35; ellipsis added)—leads to familiar travel sentiments.

> I wish we were elsewhere:
> Mexico . . . Mexico? Where is Mexico?
> Who will live the year back, cat on the ladder?
> (35)

The invocation of "Mexico" gives rise to the double question "Mexico? Where is Mexico?"—as much a questioning of the subject's own mental processes as a recognition that Mexico is not retrievable. The cat climbs the ladder without trepidation since it does not look back; coming down is another matter.

The ladder metaphor works in several ways. The vertigo is disorienting, the rungs look fragile, and one doubts one's capacity to negotiate the passage. Moreover, the lost time and the lost lover are irretrievable. The alternate metaphor from the fifth sonnet, "The stream will not flow back to hand" (32), shows this ongoing concern. But with the ladder figure, the element of *height* is crucial. What causes the fear is not that one cannot go back, since, if the road were lateral, one could try, but that the only direction is *down*. Again, the speaker's anxiety and enervation concern the chasm below. The way up is by climbing, the way down by falling.

"Die Gold Orangen"—alluding to Mignon's song *Kennst du das Land* in Goethe (or to "Delfica," Nerval's imitation of it)—coheres through its entire fourteen lines by means of landscape description and the conventional reflection that everything described is past—"I see it; it's behind us, love, behind us—" (35). The sentiments are familiar and rhetorical: "What have I done with us, and what was done?" (35), but the poem is overtaken in its last five lines by yet another metaphor of height and dropping, echoing the volcano and the altitude sickness of "Mexico":

> And the mountain, El Volcan, a climber of clouds?
> The mule-man lost his footing in the cloud,
> seed of the dragon coupled in that cave. . . .
> The cliff drops; over it, the water drops,
> and steams out the footprints that led us on.
> (35)

I have made much of "dropping" and "falling" in the travel poems of *For the Union Dead* and *For Lizzie and Harriet*. "Mexico" describes a vertiginous "cleavage dropping miles to the valley's body," and here, at the end of *For*

Lizzie and Harriet, "the cliff drops; over it, the water drops." Just as the speaker fears he has "lost my foothold on the map" in "Dropping South: Brazil," so here the mule-man has "lost his footing in the cloud." If a map is a tenuous place to gain a foothold, a cloud is even more so. Despite William Carlos Williams's poem "The Descent," the descent beckons only in the most terrifying way: as the cat cannot get *down* the ladder but stops, paralyzed, at the top, so, here, tropical waterfalls have "steam[ed] out the footprints that led us on," preventing us from returning. It is not only one of several of Lowell's metaphors for the impossibility of turning around on a path—the theme of transience and unrecoverability that runs through the "Mexico" sequence—but it is also one of the proliferating figures of height and dizziness, of the vulnerability of this queasy, disoriented traveler.

Turbulence: The East-West Axis

Air travel is the norm in both Lowell's poems and those of Derek Walcott. For Walcott, however, the plane is a metaphor not so much of psychic turbulence and insecurity as of privilege, a detached perspective, and the guilt associated with both. For both poets, "flight"—as in Walcott's "The Schooner *Flight*" or Lowell's "Flight to New York"—means running away as much as it means air travel. Walcott, viewing his islands from the plane window, uses these perspectives as opportunities to meditate on identity. Lowell chooses an aisle seat; his travel poems do not concern places so much as they do inner conflicts played out in historical or literary terms. The experience of travel, while it sensitizes, also enervates and disturbs.

Travelers often fall ill because the depletion caused by travel occurs below the threshold of consciousness. Certainly, Lowell's frequent travels by air toward the end of his life were ill-advised. Consider the movements of his last three years: He flew back to Boston from Mexico in 1974; two months later he flew to Spoleto, Italy, for the arts festival, then flew back to Boston to teach, and then, following a collapse in 1975, flew to London for hospitalization. He returned to New York in 1976 for an opening of *The Old Glory*, then flew to Boston again, after another severe attack, to stay with his third wife, Caroline Blackwood, and the children; he flew to England again for Christmas and to work on the *Eumenides*. In January 1977 he returned to Boston, where, staying with Frank Bidart, he awoke in the night with congestive heart failure and was rushed to the hospital. Later that month, he flew to Dublin, returning first to Cambridge after only ten days to give readings at Harvard, then to the University of Tennessee for a reading, and finally to Moscow in July with Elizabeth Hardwick as part of the U.S. delegation to the Union of Soviet Writers. Next he went to Dublin again to see Caroline and his son Sheridan, though his friend Blair Clark told him his going would be a "fatal mistake"; finally, after a frightening night locked up in the mansion at Castletown, Caroline having left despondent for London, he managed the trip to the London airport to catch his last plane to New York. In the taxi from Kennedy airport to West 67th Street, he died of heart failure.

Telescoped in this way, perhaps these travels of Lowell's last three years seem more extraordinary than they were; certainly they were epiphenomenal to the heartbreak that partly caused them. The devastating cumulative effect is as visible in the poems written on the east-west Atlantic axis as it is in the north-south poems. Consider first, to briefly link these two axes, a poem written before the Caroline Blackwood period: "Flight in the Rain," from *Notebook*, which conflates a past north-south flight with a present east-west flight. A poem of personal trauma, it did not survive the sifting process into the subsequent books:

—Why does he say, I'm not afraid of flying?
—His imagination has lost the word for dying.
—It must be worse, if you have imagination . . .
That night: the wing-tilt, air-bounce upright, lighted
Long Island mainstreets flashed like dice on the window;
the raindrop; gut troutlines wriggling on the window;
the landings, not landing; the long low flight at snailspace
exhausting a world of suburban similars . . .
The sick stomach says, *You were*. Says, *Pray*—
this mismanaged life incorrigible . . .
Prayer lives longer than God—God, the déjà vu,
He sees the sparrow fall, heard years from here
in Rio, one propeller clunking off,
our *Deo Gracias* on the puking runway.

(*N* 94)

The memory evoked by Lowell's turbulent flight is that of an earlier, equally turbulent landing at Rio, when passengers said a prayer of thanks as the plane, one prop dead, hit "the puking runway." Because of this pairing of present and past, we have "landings, not landing," the memory of multiple reverberating traumas. The "déjà vu" is this recognition of an ominous parallelism. God, the micromanager according to Christian tradition, counts the hairs of our heads and knows when every sparrow falls. *This* sparrow, the plane, had fallen—in Lowell's sense of "falling"—before and now would again, or so the "sick stomach says." As usual, Lowell is less concerned with what lies out the window—the Long Island suburban streets flashing by—than with the nausea that speaks to him of mortality.

This poem of flight is more specific than most of the poems of vulnerability that spread out from *Notebook* into *History, For Lizzie and Harriet,* and *The Dolphin.* For travel experiences along the east-west axis, I consider only the latter volume in what follows.

The travel theme is largely submerged in the poems of babies, householding, and hospitals that occupy the bulk of *The Dolphin.* But the six-poem sequence "Leaving America for England" introduces a subliminal charge that ignites in the longer sequence "Flight to New York." The former begins, in "America," with a reference to "My lifelong taste for reworking the same water—" (66), reminding one of "the old Atlantic still" and "the same Atlantic" that he contemplated in "Dropping South: Brazil" and "Flying from Bangor to Rio 1957," respectively. This first poem of the sequence emphasizes sameness, stasis, and unwillingness to experience anew. He is content with

> puzzles repeated
> and remembered, games repeated and remembered,
> the runner trimming on his mud-smooth path,
> the gamefish fattening in its narrow channel.
> (66)

The "narrow channel" and the "mud-smooth path" evoke the numbing, back-and-forth routine that figured in the "Mexico" poems and the "going to and fro" of *For the Union Dead.* That Lowell did not see himself as a born traveler is suggested in the middle of this poem, where he declares, paraphrasing Horace, "Change I earth or sky I am the same"—an aged dog, he suggests, well past the age of learning new tricks, and "deaf to the lure of personality" (66). The line suggests, again, Lowell's relative imperviousness—

a protective measure against the trauma of disorientation—to the psychic shaping that can result from travel to other places, amid other cultures and languages.

While the six poems of "Leaving America for England" move from this embrace of the familiar to ruminations on the poet's marriages and to questions about the place of the personal in poetry, the "Flight to New York" sequence stands as an intense linear representation of air travel, moving from preflight jitters to departure to the "Purgatory" of flight and finally to arrival. More than half of the twelve poems define the traveler as not only in transit but also in *flight* in both senses of the word. The experience of planes, airports, tickets, fear, and apprehension is palpable, as suggested by the first lines of the first poem, "Plane-Ticket": "A virus and its hash of knobby aches— / more than ever flying seems too lofty, / the season unlucky for visiting New York" (72). The apprehension plays on the literal "loft" and "aloft" of flying, but "lofty" 's usual figurative sense as "high" is also apt, in that both poet and traveler wished to avoid loftiness, being up off the ground (just as, conversely, "falling" and "falling back on honest speech" were connected in *Notebook*). Despite these apprehensions, the poem depicts the traveler in his honeymoon period, still in the elation of "rock in the leaf" and "green sap" in "arid rind" (the first phrase from "Mexico," the others from the present series):

> I have my round-trip ticket. . . .
> After fifty so much joy has come,
> I hardly want to hide my nakedness—
> the shine and stiffness of a new suit, a feeling,
> not wholly happy, of having been reborn.
> (72)

Lowell's psychological and somatic need for the familiar, however, shadows the elation: to be "reborn," to wear this "new suit" like a boy on his first trip, and to experience "so much joy" are, after all, not "wholly happy" feelings. Happiness is, rather, a worn path.

The following poem, "With Caroline at the Air-Terminal," consists largely of a cut-up letter from Caroline describing desperate love and domestic details—the grey color scheme of the house (and of her mood), the dining room converted to a nursery. She also wonders not, as he does, whether he will arrive in New York, but whether the promise of the round-trip will be fulfilled: "I feel unsafe, uncertain you'll get back"(*D* 72). Only the final five lines are not quotation: he describes the plane, as its "great white umbilical ingress bangs in place," and adds, forebodingly, "The flight is certain" (72). Only one other thing in life is as certain. We may think of the British "terminal" as bearing the semantic weight it does in "Terminal Days at Beverly Farms," the more so since the traveler has just wondered, in "Plane-Ticket," whether the book of life offers "a choice of endings" (72). His question of travel is the simplest possible: will I *arrive*?

In the fourth poem, "Flight," the vertical themes are underscored by the aerial view of New York City with its vertiginous scaffolds and walls "flying like Feininger's skyscraper yachts" (73) as the clouds clear toward the runway. Once the speaker is *in* New York, in the sixth poem, "No Messiah," the topos of travel becomes inextricable from the problems of the poet's existence, both domestic and literary. On the one hand, he "can find no lodging for my two lives," and, on the other, the ability to "write the truth" about matters has been "lost in passage" (74). He shows up on Lizzie and Harriet's doorstep, once his own, "planesick on New York food" and feeling "the old / Subway reverberate through our apartment floor" (74). He stops in the middle of the room, hearing

> my *Nolo*, the non-Messianic man—
> drop, drop in silence, then a louder drop
> echoed elsewhere by a louder drop.
>
> (74)

The drops reverberating rhythmically along these lines continue the echo through Lowell's poetry from the time of "Dropping South: Brazil." The drop here is postflight, as is the reverberation felt under the room, a phantom effect of an experience supposedly completed. The man who refuses, Lowell's Bartleby, has dropped from the sky, though "non-Messianic," at Christmas—but what is that louder drop (since the first was silent) followed by the echo of a louder drop still? Deconstruction's term "dispersed subject" seems designed to describe the dispersal traced in this poem, where, along with allegiances, subjectivity itself has been spread over several sites and time zones. The poet has landed in New York and come to a familiar hearth, but he is still in England and still on the plane. Home has been, through the traveler's own inner divisions and compulsions, de-based. The silent descent of the alienated "Nolo" is displaced by a disembodied echo, which, in a chain of deferral, creates still another echo "elsewhere."

In the last pair of poems of the series, the prospects of distance and of imminent departure come into focus. The poet sees the living-room Christmas tree "fallen out with nature, shedding to a naked cone of triggered wiring" (77), a *Doll's House*–like stage symbol of the poet's and his family's condition. But this deterioration conceals a life force—continuing the metaphor of renewed sexual vigor in age that pervades the poems about Caroline Blackwood (and the "rock in leaf" in "Mexico")—all the more certain of itself for recognizing its instability:

> This worst time is not unhappy, green sap
> still floods the arid rind, the thorny needles
> catch the drafts, as if alive—I too,
> because I waver, am counted with the living.
>
> (77)

Where, at the beginning of this sequence, being "reborn," because of its frightening newness, was "not wholly happy," now "[t]his worst time," because it is familiar, "is not unhappy." Turbulence may mean pathology—sensitization, indecision, and trauma, the last thing the poet needs—but he recognizes that it is life. In making a case for a qualified happiness, the two metaphors for fertility and vigor protest too much and, perhaps inadvertently, suggest a line from "My Last Duchess": "There she stands *as if alive*," implying that the person in question is not alive but simulating life; that he or she is—as in the case of the Browning monologue—a plausible imitation, an artwork; and finally, that the comfort and security of the "mud-smooth path" and "narrow channel" have been overrated.

The last poem of the "Flight to New York" series, "Christmas," is, but for its closing lines, a poem of almost trivial comfort, "the tedium and déjà-vu of home" (77). But if the speaker feared arrival, he fears departure still more, the promise of the round-trip ticket with which the sequence began. Fear of birth or renewal is eclipsed by fear of death. The trip over was rough; even after landing, the traveler's digestion rumbled, and his body trembled, as did the ground beneath, shaken by subways. But now that comfort has come at last, in the warmth of love and gift giving and the reestablishing of familiar writing habits, the traveler must return. Departure will of course be by airplane; its shadow already swims *under* the family, its menace spreading metonymically:

> We are at home and warm,
> as if we had escaped the gaping jaws—
> underneath us like a submarine,
> nuclear and protective like a mother,
> swims the true shark, the shadow of departure.
>
> (77)

The shadow of departure resembles a shark, which in turn resembles both a submarine and a mother. The adjectives respective to these latter two— "nuclear" and "protective"—are instead arrogated only to one, the mother, whose devastating power of protection seems at least as threatening as a shark. The fear instilled by this mother has seeped over from that warmth and comfort, which, at the moment they are so prized, are also impelling the inevitable departure. The threats from beneath were sensed earlier (in "No Messiah") in the rumbling of the subway under the floor. If the airplane is the real threat, it is presaged by something closer to home but similar in shape (subway, submarine, airplane—all metal cylinders). The real fear, as Freud knew and as Bishop's "Elizabeth" finds out in "In the Waiting Room," is always from "inside." The rumble under the floor and the shadow beneath us are the *unheimlich* within the *heimlich*, the uncanny within the familiar.

Shadows and rumblings portend the repressed return, the other half of the round-trip. As with the cat atop the ladder and the vanished footprints in the snow that had once mapped a safe return, the descent is difficult to face. The ominous shadow may be the prospect of England, of Caroline, of a wound reopening, but it is most immediately the prospect of being high off the earth, turbulent, sick, and terrorized again.

Fragility and the "Mud-Smooth Path"

"Flight in the Rain," with its two nauseating landings; "Summer between Terms," where the poet is reduced to "eat[ing] my toad[s] hourly" (*D* 28); "Leaving America for England," which underlines his penchant for comfort, the familiar, and the routine; and "Flight to New York," where the shadow of departure looms like a shark and vibrates like a subway—these poems and others suggest that Lowell experienced travel viscerally and might have wished not to experience it at all. Even in "My Last Afternoon with Uncle Devereux Winslow," the child Lowell, wishing for a homelike home, says, "I won't go. . . . I want to stay" (*LS* 59; ellipsis added). But life demanded movement, not comfortably to and fro on a "mud-smooth path" but across oceans, wrenched out of time and comfort zones. Lowell's travel had less to do with nationalities, differences, or cultures, less with otherness than with the monoculture of airports, bad food, and psychic disequilibrium. The experiences in the poems are similar: turbulence, with the plane's fragility as a trope for that of the traveler. If Lowell did not always seem interested in things or places around him, as Lota de Macedo Soares suggested, travel itself nevertheless operated profoundly on him, at levels below the cognitive.[8]

The disorientation of travel may in the end have unhinged time-space relations for Lowell. In the poem "Fragility" (from the "Caroline" section of *The Dolphin*), the poet attempts to impose the grid of time on the chaos of space, a habit that finally became a therapy in his last book, *Day by Day*. "Fragility" constitutes the effort of a man emerging from trauma to gain perspective:

> One foot in last year, one in last July,
> the motionless month, the day that lasts a month.
> We reach mid-journey, you lag by fifteen summers,
> half a year more than Harriet's whole life.
> The clock looks over my shoulder crazily.
> (12)

One could do the math here, computing Lowell's, Caroline's, and Harriet's ages at the time of writing ("mid-journey" in Dante would be thirty-five), but perhaps more interesting is that time is conflated or confused with space and that, while the clocks in "Mexico" were metaphors for the discrepant biological ages of the poet and his young lover, here an externalized clock, like a mad superego, watches over the poet's shoulder, monitoring the time remaining. The poet has, like Billy Pilgrim in Kurt Vonnegut's *Slaughterhouse Five*, come "unstuck in time."

Yeats said that we make rhetoric out of our argument with others, poetry out of our argument with ourselves. The movement from rhetoric to poetry in Lowell—as the poetry becomes more "personal"—corresponds to another movement, from roots to rootlessness, the heimlich to the horrifying. In "During a Transatlantic Call," he wrote, "I've closed my mind / so long, I want to keep it closed, perhaps—" (*D* 47). Indeed the psychic and poetic energy expended on resisting the change, as with a white-knuckled passenger on a turbulent flight, taxed and probably shortened Lowell's life.

Lowell's was a different talent than Bishop's—large, prolific, allusive, historical, and rhetorical—one that was part of New England soil; he was not a "guest" there as Bishop felt she was. Perhaps we need to revisit the adage that "wherever you go, there you are." The "you" in Bishop was relatively malleable, given not only to doubt but also to change; its vulnerability lay in its capacity to lose itself in places, despite its frequent trope of touristic conventionality—sometimes *because* of it, insofar as that touristic persona was self-effacing. Lowell's "you," in contrast, along with the passionate necessity to comprehend his life, went everywhere with him.

Bishop's last published words to him, in her elegy "North Haven," observe that his relentless revising of poems will now have to stop: "You can't derange, or re-arrange / your poems again" (*Complete* 188). But from the question of words that, because they are stopped now, will never change, she moves without transition to the question of a self, similarly stopped and therefore unchanging:

The words won't change again. Sad friend, you cannot change.
(189)

Everyone's tired of my turmoil.

ROBERT LOWELL, "Eye and Tooth," *For the Union Dead*

We need all the escapism we can get and even that
isn't going to be enough.

JOHN ASHBERY, Interview with Sue Gangel, *American
Poetry Observed*

INTERLUDE

Dandies and Flaneurs
American Poetry and the Center-Margin Debate

Travel is political. From home's perspective, travel stands accused of privilege, disengagement, or dereliction of duty. The charges originate from
the immediate home as much as from the nation that claims your taxes
and urges your vote. How might such charges operate within discussions
of American poetry, itself historically an "escape" genre—"imaginative,"
"subjective," "irrational"—when compared to expository or narrative
prose? As rebellious and lyrical sites, the margins may be prized; as sites of
disengagement and evasion, they may be deplored. In such a context, what
might it mean to say that John Ashbery is a (or the) mainstream poet of
the end of the twentieth century as Lowell was of the midcentury?

Characterizations of social centers and margins often take as their defining terms economy (rich vs. poor), accessibility to an audience (mainstream vs. avant-garde), advocacy (aesthetic, mandarin, patrician vs. engaged, committed, populist), and language (intellectual, erudite, "poetic" vs. demotic, street-wise, "poetic"). As any pop band or pop fan knows, these distinctions are increasingly difficult to make, since today's alternative song is tomorrow's (or this afternoon's) mainstream. When, in advanced capitalism, dissent and struggle are not repressed but organized and channeled, all arts aspire to the condition of Muzak—or, one might say, Muzak waits for them. The lag between subversive musical genre heard "underground" and ambient elevator music is every day reduced. Indeed, this speed of co-optation preoccupies the current academy just as it does popular music artists, a number of whom have spoken on the subject.

Viewing the U.S. poetry scene from the perspective of the Caribbean, Derek Walcott remarks that

> the [U.S.] poet is almost crying out for the society to be hostile to him—or her, I mean both him and her—to repress him, to take notice, to imprison him, to pay attention in a sense. But what happens is suddenly or quietly there is a very wide blandness that occurs, in which the poet is subtly absorbed and given a name and a trade *separate* from the society, maybe because of that naming. (Montenegro 213)

This blandness, whether seen as appropriation or inclusiveness, by which American culture absorbs any radical gesture so that it is first conventionalized and then institutionalized—is problematic for those who invest in the authenticity of the margins. It took Thoreau's face a hundred and Malcolm X's thirty years to arrive on postage stamps: that margin-to-center transition is accelerating. In literary criticism it happens within a few years; in popular music, within months or weeks.

New Critical Dandies

North American poets as a group—compared to, say, Czechs or Chileans—have not been noted for engaging global politics in their poems, however politically engaged they otherwise may be.[1] By America's standard, Robert Lowell comes off well. We are reminded, in *Life Studies*, of his early days as a "fire-breathing Catholic C.O.," making his "manic statement" against the state (82). As evidence of a move from the personal to the global, "July in Washington" translates the pain of the tissue, evoked throughout *For the Union Dead*, from a body to a society and thence to the world. "The stiff spokes" that "touch the sore spots of the earth," in the poem's first sentence, are the rays of power emanating from the nation's capital, which irritate distant vulnerabilities over the face of the planet (58).

Some of the more lucid poems of *Notebook 1967–68* concern political involvement. In "The March I," set in the shadow of the Washington Obelisk, Lowell as protester tells how "our green army staggered out on the miles-long green fields, / met by the other army, the Martian, the ape, the hero, / his new-fangled rifle, his green new steel helmet" (54). Indeed, for an index of political immersion if not activism, one can look to the "Dates" section at the end of *Notebook*, which lists the events from 1967 to 1970 that figure in the poems: the Vietnam War, the Arab-Israeli Six Days' War, the black riots in Newark, Che Guevara's death, the march on the Pentagon, Eugene McCarthy's and Robert Kennedy's campaigns for the Democratic nomination, Martin Luther King's murder, Robert Kennedy's murder, the Russian occupation of Czechoslovakia, and others.

Lowell was often on the road during the writing of the *Notebooks*. He speaks of "a fear of moving," and in "America from Oxford," writing from England where he had suffered a collapse, he worries over his absence from the U.S. political scene:

> at home, the colleges are closed for summer,
> the students march . . . Brassman lances Cambodia,
> he has lost his pen, the sword folds in his hand like felt—
> Is truth here with you, if I sleep well,
> Bystander? The peacock spins, the Revolution
> hasn't involved us . . . a heat that moves
> air so estranged and hot I might be home . . .
> We have climbed above the wind to breathe.
> (*N* 237)

Reading of the students' reaction to the U.S. invasion of Cambodia, Lowell here frets over his own estrangement. Does the poet have the right to sleep well, to join the bystanders, unengaged, on the other side of the ocean?

But after the *Notebook* volumes, politics get sifted out. When "America from Oxford" is revised for *The Dolphin*, a book that explores the guilt associated with a divorce, new marriage, and a different estrangement—that from his former wife (Elizabeth Hardwick) and child—history takes a back seat to domestic themes. The line about locating truth is changed to read "Is truth here with us, if I sleep well?—" and the two lines (starting from "Bystander") about the "Revolution" not involving "us" are replaced by "*the ten or twelve years my coeval gives himself / for the new bubble of his divorce . . . ten or twelve years—*" (17). The revisions are consistent with the overall project of separating the political from the personal, transforming the former into the latter, or writing *over* the political. The result was the three separate books (*History, For Lizzie and Harriet,* and *The Dolphin*) that followed the two *Notebook* volumes. Indeed the separation is threefold: one book for politics and history, another for the poet's former personal life, and a third for his future personal life. Nevertheless, the political filtering is not pure. The line "the students march . . . Brassman [Nixon] lances Cambodia" remains in both poems, and the question remains, in both books, of whether truth is with "us" when we sleep through these invasions and protests.

Interestingly, estrangement, in both versions, has to do with home, not abroad: the "air [is] so estranged" that it feels as if the poet were home. To the extent that Lowell saw his native land as a place of estrangement, he had become an expatriate. Nevertheless, his travel anxiety is travel guilt at not participating in home's struggles and problems. Voices other than his own remind him of obligation, as in "The Revolution," where a poet and former student (Richard Tillinghast), fully engaged in the political scene at Berkeley, writes Lowell at the height of the campus demonstrations against the war in Vietnam:

'We're in a prerevolutionary situation
at Berkeley, an incredible, refreshing relief
from the rather hot-house, good prep-school sanctum at Harvard.
. . . .
Anyway, *you should be in on it.* Only
in imagination can we lose the battle.'
(*N* 220–21; emphasis added)

Consider that, less than ten years ago, the same Richard Tillinghast, echoing other critics, writes that Lowell "as a historical poet, has few rivals among modern writers" (122). Even more recently, Paul Mariani, in his biography of Lowell, remarks, "If anyone, Lowell is *the* poet-historian of our time, aware, like Nathaniel Hawthorne and Henry Adams, of our history judging us even as he undertakes to judge it" (10). And,

> With Lowell's death, the United States lost the last of its influential public poets, poets in the tradition of Emerson, Frost, and Eliot. . . . Can the question of who speaks for America still have meaning? (10)

David Laskin writes, "[W]e must turn to Lowell for the confluence of the significant and American, as Bishop pointed out" (399). And Vernon Shetley: "Robert Lowell may have been the last poet who was felt to be required reading for people with a serious interest in literature" (3).

The past tense is important in most of these encomia. In the late 1970s, Donald Hall predicted, with surprising accuracy, that "In twenty years . . . [t]here will be reaction against Lowell, and it will be severe, unfair, and sheep-like" ("Robert," 11). Hall's article, while it praises much of Lowell's work, is titled "Robert Lowell and the Literature Industry," a forecast of the criticism to come, which would see Lowell as the establishment against which the new culture wars must be waged. Both on the public and personal counts, each term serving as old guard according to the critical contexts, Lowell is frequently treated as the losing, or lost, half of a binary opposition. I first consider two instances where these oppositions are developed at length before turning to some surprisingly parallel cases regarding John Ashbery.

The title of Jed Rasula's *The American Poetry Wax Museum* makes his thesis unmistakable. In the space of a page, he inveighs against the "idolators of the high sublime," the "culture brokers," "(white) America," "cultural watchdogs," and "the Great Tradition" (2–3); dozens more such phrases occur throughout the book. How Lowell figures here is easy to guess. Supported by respectable New York publishing houses, born into privilege, and sanctioned by patrician critical precincts, Lowell *is* the Eastern "establishment," against which Rasula's entire book points like a weapon. In a chapter called "The Age of Lowell" (with an under-erasure line through the words *The Age of*), Rasula compares the achievements of Charles Olson and Lowell, writing that "Lowell's work is compulsively fascinating precisely because it takes on the waxwork character of the freak show, the exhibit of a human life assuming monstrous proportions" (256). He adds, "To *person* in Lowell it's necessary to contrast *polis* in Olson" (256). With this opposition, one recognizes the claim of collectivity as authenticity and a corresponding dismissal of the "personal" as bourgeois, irrelevant, and even, paradoxically, New Critical. Lowell's *History* brings with it "a reminder that myth for Americans is individual, and at its most ferocious may even be private. . . . It's not 'history' at all, of course, but a purely formal exercise of the pretense of history as it's referred to as being *made*, behind the scenes, under the table, and private" (267–68). Lowell's sense of history is confined, Rasula says, to "references to Renaissance Florence, Periclean Athens, or Hannibal crossing the Alps—in short, set pieces suitable to 19th century kitsch genre painting" (289).

This personal-collective opposition, even when presented from more or less the same academic "side"—that is, the side of engaged poetry scholars against apolitical, New Critical atavists—can be strangely reversed. In *The Dark End of the Street*, Maria Damon compares Lowell to some Boston "street" poets, "three unknown teenage women writing from the D Street Housing Projects of South Boston" (77), to argue that "[Lowell's] poetry and personal conduct" should be viewed as *"social* practice—privileged white male poet(ry) in crisis, as it were" (122). Indeed, the other poets' authenticity, by contrast, lies in their personalism. Damon feels no compunction about reciting biographical details about Lowell since these simply "provide poignant anecdotes of teaching-anthology head notes," while "analogous revelations about the girls . . . may luridly reinscribe them as stereotypical objects" (122). Lowell identifies with "official textbook history and the personalizing of institutional discourse" (123). He saw his task as "mediating and witnessing history." Even his personal troubles, mental illness or marital strife, "become, in his work, public matter" (78).

Lowell, then, is too historical for Damon, whereas for Rasula he is not historical enough. But, though Lowell's characterization as historical prepares us for such an opposition, Damon presents no "personal" poetry to compare. The girls demonstrate very little subjectivity: any sense they have of it is "inextricably bound up with economic and sexual subjection" (8). Nor do they write for publication (the very reason for writing that makes Lowell "social" in this account). Their poetry is "the generic, mass-produced poetry of rock lyrics and newspaper verse. . . . We know, for example, that not all of the poems are autobiographical" (78). (Lowell's are not, either, as Damon demonstrates at length.)

So "the perfectly neat contrast" that Damon offers to set out, between "mass culture" and "high art," does not emerge. In fact Damon seems, out of her own caution about binary oppositions, to inhibit its emergence, acknowledging that "Recent critical tendency has fostered a healthy mistrust of neat dichotomies, especially those arranged in hierarchy" (80). But consider the following apparent caveat, where the object of Damon's caution—what she purportedly does *not* want to say—is developed at such length that it is finally the only thing one can take away from the passage:

> Useful as Lowell may be to set off against a valorization of mass and popular art, or as an example of the reified "author" whose hegemonic control over the representation of Bostonian culture is intermittently threatened or broken through by outbursts from the undifferentiated female (or feminized) masses on the other side of town, this division would obscure some of the more interesting questions about the poetry. (80)

In this sentence, the long introductory subordinating material overwhelms the tiny main clause that mentions "interesting questions about the poetry." The sentences that follow do downplay the repressed opposition by declaring a sameness ("the wounded child cries out in Lowell's work as the violated girl does in the South Boston poems" [80]). But were this commonality really the point, there would be no reason for the unmistakable valorizing of the "street" over the "academy," the redskin-paleface dichotomy of yore: "Supremely privileged, preeminently public . . . Lowell serves as a powerful case study of the pathos of failed liberalism" (123). Strangely, as I indicate earlier, the "street" is presented as social and public and so is the academy or the cloister or whatever "street" 's opposite is meant to be.

Consider, too, that the Boston girls' poems resemble—and why shouldn't they?—poems adolescents write all over America: "Courage is to smile when no one smiles, / to be able to laugh when no one laughs," writes "Cheryl" in "The Epitome of Courage," a poem one might find in any middle or high school classroom, and a poem having nothing inherently "Boston" or "street" about it (81). Few readers would label this poetry "postmodern," according to working definitions of that term, and yet Damon invites us to do so, again by contrast with Lowell:

[T]here is nothing remotely postmodern about Lowell's opus. His work is drenched in personal emotion at the same time as it is highly wrought, aspiring consciously to take its place among the best that has been written, said, and done. Lowell does not engage a sense of play, distance himself, or radically question selfhood and authority. (122)

I do not think Damon could with conscience argue that the teenage girls from Boston are radically questioning selfhood and authority. But her silence regarding how "postmodern" might apply to them invites us to assume they stand on the other side of the street from Lowell in this as in other regards.

Postmodern Bards and Dandies

The metaphor of center and margin still thrives, even when framed in the old Rahvian terms. Consider this sentence from a review of a recent book of poems by Maggie Jaffe: "Although the dandies of the mainstream write as if history has indeed ended, as if the bloodbath . . . never happened, the best poets and writers and painters have never had that luxury" (McIrwin 31). On a more sophisticated level, look at almost any prose Charles Bernstein has written in the past twenty years on "official verse culture" or "dominant verse culture." Consider Diane Wakowski on Apollonian (bad) and Dionysian (good) poets. Or consider a review in *Poetry* where Bruce Murphy praises the raw vigor of Les Murray, concluding, "After him it's hard to go back to our tenured bards" ("Verse" 285).

Who *are* the mainstream bards and dandies? Among them would have to be Louise Glück, Jorie Graham, Rita Dove, Robert Pinsky, Galway Kinnell, W. S. Merwin, Robert Hass, anyone published by Farrar, Straus and Giroux, and hundreds more if it is to be a *main*stream. The list would have to include populist Maya Angelou, populist Philip Levine, and the many anthologized in *Norton* or given awards or published in the *New Yorker*, that scourge of the margins. And yet Robert Creeley seems an unlikely mainstream dandy, as does Adrienne Rich or A. R. Ammons or Gary Snyder or any number of other Pulitzer-prize or National Book Award winners. And then there is John Ashbery, winner of the National Book Award, the National Book Critics' Circle Award, and the Pulitzer prize—all for the same book: *Self-Portrait in a Convex Mirror*. Does he not write about paintings? Does he not use French and Latin? Does he not write sestinas and pantoums? Most of all, does he not sell books? A strange mainstream, but if one demands a center to which one can feel peripheral, Ashbery may be the only one we have left.

Jerome McGann's comment, quoted in this book's first chapter, that "[a]s earlier Lowell became the exegetical focus of high/late New Critical discourse, Ashbery has become the contemporary touchstone for deconstructive analysis" (257), suggests both Ashbery's centrality and the Ashbery-Lowell parallel in American critical reception. So does John Koethe's reference to "the celebrity that [Ashbery's] work has achieved since the midseventies, a period in which he has displaced Robert Lowell as the paradigmatic poetic figure of the day" (85). The importance and popularity of Ashbery's poetry stand in somewhat paradoxical relation to widespread discomfort about that poetry's incoherence, indeterminacy, and irreferentiality. Still, the commentaries that follow, widely varying in approach, view Ashbery's work as mainstream, comfortable, establishment, and even "personal." (With the exception of James Longenbach, I leave out here the many critics for whom Ashbery's engagement or lack of it is not an issue.) All of the critiques come from engaged critics, whether, on the one hand, postcolonial theorists, new historicists, East European protorealists, or others who look to literature for a social text, a reflection of and engagement with the material and economic world; or, on the other hand, the more linguistically oriented critics who examine poetry more often than narrative, a group that includes the "language" poet-critics and that also demands social engagement, though not in realist modes. Critiques arise, finally, from the new formalists, whose objections are not only formal but also mimetic and are thus often aligned with, and just as engaged as, the sociotextual or language critics. These various perspectives, however divergent, present a consensus about disengagement in Ashbery. For most, this disengagement is a bad thing.

Since postcolonial critics and new historicists are almost completely silent regarding poetry, some of what I quote does not directly address Ashbery, whose name would simply not come up in a discussion, much less a syllabus, of witness or advocacy.[2] This absence itself constitutes an important critique: such critics no doubt have heard of Ashbery but have not found him relevant to their work. The generic omission of poetry is also worth noting, since it is based on the same trends; narrative has been the preferred genre for several decades; the study of poetry receded with the New Criticism that once thought it central.[3]

Czeslaw Milosz, in *The Witness of Poetry*, bemoans the estrangement of poetry from the human family, offering in its place an archaic theory of language, that of the correspondence between words and things:

> The very act of naming things presupposes a faith in their existence and thus in a true world, whatever Nietzsche might say. Of course there are poets who only relate words to words, not to their models in things, but their artistic defeat indicates that they are breaking some sort of rule of poetry. (57)

Ashbery, if not most poets since modernism, certainly breaks the "rule" Milosz suggests; whether that entails "artistic defeat" is arguable. The new formalists, while not self-described proponents of engagement, have much in common with Milosz's position, since they do not advocate merely a return to meter and rhyme but, like Milosz, a commitment to coherence and to mimesis. From their perspective, Ashbery's work is so eclectic, promiscuous, and ironic as to destroy value of any kind. Frederick Pollack writes, in the new formalist anthology of criticism *Poetry after Modernism*, that Ashbery's work "destroys the past by sentimentalizing it until memory itself becomes first questionable, then laughable. Finally, when there is no value, anything can be equated with (sold for) anything. I am describing, among other things, a poetic" (24–25). Ashbery's refusal of real places, his belief only in their names (as in "the England of the sonnets" ["And You Know," *Some Trees*], "Names of cities that sounded as though / they existed, / But never had" [*April Galleons*], and so forth), while not, I think, "sincere," is grounds for dismissal if one demands that the world's material troubles deserve a "faithful" mimetic treatment in poetry.

The language-based critics, dedicated to undermining bourgeois assumptions about the self and the world, deplore the personal in poetry, which is to say the vast majority of contemporary poetry. This group differs sharply on the subject of representation from a poet such as Milosz and from numerous historicist and postcolonial critics of narrative. When Walter Kalaidjan, for example, indicting the direction of American poetry since the New Critics, writes that "the course of contemporary American poetry has actually reproduced, rather than contested, formalism's swerve from social change" (4), he is not complaining that the poets fail to represent material struggles in their work. Rather, in his view, they have not devised a *poetics* that might question underlying bourgeois assumptions. Thus, though the language might match that of a Lucaksian realist—in statements such as "The 'new' poets largely eschewed any overtly political commitments or affiliations in the wider social field" (7) or "[p]oetry's social text was largely silenced throughout the 1960s" (10)—the complaint is different. In Kalaidjan's opinion, almost everyone connected with postwar poetry, *except Charles Olson* (note Rasula on Lowell earlier), is commodified and "academic," including the anthologists, who, like the poets, have emphasized the personal while ignoring the political.

Kalaidjan's description of the plight of poetry is extravagant. He describes, for example, a market whose poets are "bought and sold by the same conglomerates that marginalize their art" (17). Here, the critic—listing CBS, Time, Reader's Digest, and Doubleday—takes a paranoid leap into a world where gigantic media powers care enough about poetry to repress it. He also argues that the critical establishment has "rendered verse writing acceptably apolitical for the university" (20). Surely, anyone associated with a major U.S. university in the past thirty years would be unlikely to report a preference for apolitical texts in humanities departments. In a similar vein, Kalaidjan refers to the university's "conservative swerve from social commitment" during the three decades since the mid-1950s. From what viewpoint might one see a *conservative* drift in literature departments during those thirty years, or the twenty-five since?

Toward the end of an introduction tracing the history of the repression of the social, Kalaidjan reveals what this history has been leading toward: a paragraph on the language poets, whose poetics questions and resists the critical assumptions underlying bourgeois culture. These assumptions include, in Kalaidjan's words, "the unified identity of the expressive lyric subject, poetry's transcendence of historical reference, and the dominance of signified meaning over the play of the signifier" (31). While most who have written on language poets agree on the first of these three "bourgeois" assumptions, the last two stand in a vexed relation. If one deconstructs poetry's transcendence of historical reference, that is, if one restores poetry to history or vice-versa, can one at the same time deconstruct the dominance of signified meaning? To restore historical referentiality to the poem is to restore signified meaning. Indeed, to argue for "free play" is not, usually, to argue for history. Kalaidjan illustrates a contradiction in the perspectives described thus far, between, on the one hand, the agenda of materialist representation in the sense of forging a connection between literature and the social sphere and, on the other, the repudiation of continuities, realist assumptions, and "bourgeois" coherence.

Kalaidjan also argues that Charles Bernstein's project is to deploy language "so as to interrupt and estrange commodified discourse, thereby contesting the normalizing reading habits that reflect and reproduce advanced consumer culture" (31). While Bernstein's own work warns against assuming the self as the chief organizing feature of writing, Kalaidjan's eagerness to make certain this fits a political program leads to an important error. Bernstein, far from interrupting or challenging commodified discourse, savors it and mines it for a variety of purposes. Ashbery's poetry is an equally clear example of composition often made entirely of commodified materials. The found (often used up) languages that surround us in capitalist culture, whether in advertising or academia, song lyrics or sentimental fiction, provide raw material for these poets. Whether the deployment of these commodified languages really critiques capitalism is unclear. Certainly, it need not reinscribe it.

Kalaidjan's complaint, in short, is not against irreferentiality, as Milosz's is—or Pollack's or Simpson's or others'—but against the personal. As such it is a well-rehearsed complaint among critics of contemporary poetry. A general uneasiness exists—among critics such as von Hallberg, Perloff, and many others, and poet-critics such as Bernstein, Hejinian, and Perelman—with inward-looking poetry. At this late date, many readers no longer want to hear about Robert Lowell's "trouble." (Nor did numerous poet-critics—Hall, Rich, Levine, et al.—want to hear about it in Lowell's own time.) And, among academic readers at least, this applies also to poets such as Galway Kinnell, Sharon Olds, Philip Levine, et al., and to their students, Joy Harjo, Li-Young Lee, Marilyn Chin, Lorna Dee Cervantes, Cathy Song, et al. These latter poets, however, as members of ethnic minority groups are unlikely to be disparaged for being personal, since even though they use the same "naïve" modes of the creative writing workshops, their personal is seen as collective.[4]

Kalaidjan's example is indicative of discussions of poetry that do not offer a vocal disapproval of Ashbery but an implicit rejection: in Kalaidjan's discussion of the most important mid- to late-century poets of America, John Ashbery, arguably the most celebrated poet of our time, goes unmentioned. The absence is doubly curious, given early views of Ashbery as a "language" poet and his own frequent repudiation of the personal. But it is curious only until we understand that Kalaidjan reads Ashbery as a *personal* poet! Kalaidjan's complaints are important since they represent some of the misunderstandings that the "language" position—in its more excited manifestations—can lead to (though need not lead to, as Perelman's, Bernstein's, or Hejinian's writings, among others, demonstrate). How, in what regard, might critics see Ashbery's work as an example of that most critically reprehensible—but publicly embraced—genre at this time in American literary history, *personal* poetry?

Ashbery's second book, *The Tennis Court Oath*, deployed a difficult and disjunctive poetics that displeased those who, like Harold Bloom, looked to Ashbery as a Romantic or transcendentalist poet. But however disruptive of the reified terms of discourse and therefore politically subversive that poetry may then have seemed, a subversive marginality is, by and large, no longer the light by which Ashbery's work is read. Ashbery himself does not believe that his disruption of poetic form—if at this late date it is still a disruption—is a mark of political commitment. The terms of "international politics," he remarks, are too important to be clouded by the terms of "poetry politics" ("Frank" 6). Just after Frank O'Hara's death, Ashbery praised his friend's poems for their disregard for politics and world events:

> Frank O'Hara's poetry has no program . . . it does not speak out against the war in Viet Nam or in favor of civil rights . . . it does not attack the establishment. It merely ignores its right to exist, and is thus a source of annoyance to partisans of every stripe. (qtd. in Longenbach, *Modern* 6)

In reaction to these remarks, Louis Simpson accused Ashbery of "sneering at the conscience of other poets" (Longenbach 86), to which Ashbery responded that all poetry is against war and in favor of life, or else it wouldn't be poetry, but that it stops being poetry when it is forced into the mold of a particular political program.

Jerome McGann echoes Simpson's critique, writing that Ashbery, who once seemed to represent "a swerve from the poetries of the fifties and sixties," has failed to develop "his own work's 'oppositional' features" and has turned instead to "suburban and personal interests"(146). In a similar vein, Hank Lazer comments,

[O]nce the cutting edge and the flashpoint for debates about poetry's direction and function, Ashbery's poetry is now seen as an elegant, somewhat wistful, poetically nostalgic but *easily thematized poetry* on the passage of time, on the phenomenology of dailiness, and on the indirectness and instability of self-portraiture. (35)

The charges of elegance, nostalgia, and suburbanism should sound familiar. (As for "elegance," remember that this is the poet of countless phrases such as "sucking dicks" [*FC* 184] and "Popeye chuckled and scratched / his balls" ["Farm Implements," *DDS* 48].) Nevertheless, here is the figure of the comfortable, aesthetic dandy again, as necessary to American criticism now as in the past. Notice some similar key phrases in Jonathan Holden's discussion of what he sees as the ethical choice facing today's poet:

> . . . to trust one's vision and presume to impose upon the world, by sheer force of character, an individual aesthetic and ethical order, or to continue the modernist hegemony of Eliot and Pound, to retreat in an elitist disgust from modern civilization and indulge in the facile despair of the parodist, recapitulating all the bad languages that comprise our environment, holding our own civilization up before us as if the sad facts could only speak for themselves. (Holden 32)

It is obvious which choice Holden favors. It comes as no surprise, either, that expressions such as "elitist disgust" and "the facile despair of the parodist" turn out to refer to John Ashbery. According to Holden, Ashbery has "impersonality" in common with the modernists, but the Eliot-Pound-Ashbery linkage is hardly self-evident. Harold Bloom has long argued for an Emerson-Stevens-Ashbery genealogy instead. And those conversant with French modernism would argue another genealogy, something like Mallarmé-Stein-Reverdy-Roussel-Ashbery—a genealogy that emphasizes the linguistic and programmatic more than do the other lineages.

The worthy poets are, in Holden's account, those who do *not* give in to elitist disgust and facile despair. What they do instead—that is, what their "force of character" consists of—is suggested by a list of the poets Holden discusses with favor: Galway Kinnell, Carolyn Forché, Richard Hugo, William Stafford, Denise Levertov, John Logan, and Philip Levine, among others. Obviously, these preferences are utterly different from those of the more linguistically and more socially oriented critics quoted earlier, both groups also complaining of effete dandies and tenured bards. Those critics include Rasula, Damon, Bernstein, and Kalaidjan, among numerous others who would reject everyone on Holden's list as hopelessly transparent, clichéd, and *personal.*

Did Ashbery somewhere along the line become "personal"? Richard Howard once commented that Ashbery is "the first poet in history in whose work anxiety had no place, our only poet not writing of anxiety, a poet for whom the poem was poem *all through*" (32). Ashbery comments in an interview: "My own autobiography has never interested me very much. Whenever I try to think about it, I seem to draw a complete blank" (Bellamy 10). In another interview, he says,

> I don't write about my life the way the confessional poets do. I don't want to bore people with experiences of mine that are simply versions of what everybody goes through. For me, poetry starts after that point. I write with experiences in mind, but I don't write about them, I write out of them. (Plimpton 399)

According to a few of the critics cited here, this is the whole problem, while according to others—Rasula, Kalaidjan, McGann, and possibly Lazer—the problem is the opposite, that Ashbery hasn't sufficiently lived up to the antisubjective poetics he describes. Perhaps unexpectedly to both groups, the "real" John Ashbery does stand up from time to time, even by the poet's own account, but as no less a construction than all his other constructed personae. Ashbery's book-length *Flow Chart* offers a poetic account of his own ascendancy, even while defining that ascendancy as antipersonal: "The *culte de moi* being a dead thing, a shambles. That's what led to me" (187). The seventh section of *And the Stars Were Shining* opens with the remark, "Rummaging through some old poems / for ideas—surely I must have had some once?" (85). Ashbery mentions this latter passage—as well as "my own shoes have scarred the walk I've taken," echoing Lowell's "My eyes have seen what my hands did"—as an instance where he is "talking of myself rather than through a persona" (Herd 426). The "*culte de moi*" lines, along with numerous others from *Flow Chart*, similarly make fairly clear, if self-mocking, reference to the poet's own life and career: "I am the sawdust of what's around" (29) seems an apt self-description, as does "All along I had known what buttons to press, but don't / you see, I had to experiment" (123).

And though Howard views Ashbery as "our only poet not writing of anxiety," certainly the *language* of anxiety, love, and nostalgia is everywhere in Ashbery's poetry. What happens when we compare his affective language with that of Sexton, Snodgrass, or Byron? In some cases we might see a wide ironic distance between those poets' exclamations and Ashbery's mock sentimentalism, as in "I felt the tears flow with all their might" (*DDS* 94) or "I shall never forget this moment / Because it consists of purest ecstasy" (*RM* 44). In others, however, irony is not opposition. How should we regard "clouds of anxiety, of sad, regretful impatience / with ourselves, our lives" (*HD* 24) or lyrical passages that do not concern the self, as in "golden / Pollen sinking on the afternoon breeze" (8) or "magic, glittering coastal towns" (10), to choose randomly among hundreds of such phrases? While Ashbery may be following Stevens in confessing the "personal" through abstraction, it is not clear that these "poetic" descriptions are parodic.

A number of critics—among them Charles Altieri, Helen Vendler, John Koethe, and Harold Bloom—have long seen Ashbery as a romantic poet, even, in Altieri's case, as a "love" poet. Koethe writes that "the traditional resources [Ashbery] seeks to conserve are the fundamental impulses of romanticism, which I would characterize as subjectivity's contestation of its objective setting in a world which has no place for it" (87). Alfred Corn says that Ashbery's originality comes "as a by-product of sincerity" (235). Ashbery himself comments, "All my stuff is romantic poetry" (Packard 129) and "The pathos and liveliness of ordinary human communication is poetry to me" (Plimpton 409).

As with the personal, so with the political. Admittedly, an engaged, post-colonial, or Marxist approach to Ashbery may not find much to work with. Irony is not a trope of the poetry of witness. Marjorie Perloff's essay "Empiricism Once More" recounts a young scholar's sociological but tone-deaf interpretation of "The Instruction Manual" as a racist, imperialist, and elitist version of Mexico; the writer had managed to ignore the pervasive irony, the obvious cardboard construction of Ashbery's "Mexico," and thus the whole action that constitutes the poem (58–59). When Ashbery writes, in *Flow Chart*, that "the Reagan / administration insists we cannot go to heaven without drinking caustic soda on the floor / of Death Valley" (175–76), it can hardly be seen as taking a position or as "answering Ashbery's harshest critics," as Susan Schultz suggests it does (4). Yet the *discourse* of politics, as interesting and appropriable as any other discourse, is present in the poetry. What interests Ashbery is the texture of such phrases, not only the contours of the words but also the contours of the idiom as it emerges from a time and a place. Ashbery explains,

> I don't think that any subject ought to be excluded a priori from poetry, and politics is one of them. Politics is something we think about and talk about, so it gets into my poetry. But with few exceptions political poetry has the effect of turning me off. Whereas unpolitical poetry, if it is good, makes one want to behave politically and on other levels as well. (Herd 425–26)

The Center Again

The relative centrality in their respective times of Robert Lowell and John Ashbery should be clear. The critical responses surveyed here form only a small facet of something more deeply pervasive in U.S. culture: that is, the almost Republican antipathy to centers. Perhaps it does not matter who occupies such centers, but it is significant that the center today should be occupied by a poet whose poetics is based on the idea that underlying meanings are not as important as language, which, by its own inherent powers, should "carry" the poem.

The critiques of Ashbery cited earlier, in which the poet appears variously as elegant, nostalgic, suburban, modernist, apolitical, formalist, ironic, aestheticist, and parodist, have in common a particular objection to Ashbery's work: the slipping of moral ties in favor of escape, defamiliarization, and release. The objections are to *play*, whether in the sense of linguistic sampling or collage from films or advertising; in the tonal sense of incorporating daffy, childish platitudes and personae; or in the thematic sense of using tropes of maps, territories, travel, and trains that go nowhere.

To many readers, including some of those most critical of this poet, Ashbery's work *does* depict the verbal, visual, and moral textures of the contemporary United States and, increasingly, of the world, but this is not a mimesis for everyone. Having never been tempted toward a truth-telling of "real" life, his own or anyone else's, Ashbery constructs journeys and scenes that allow us to sense—not because of their realism but because of their constructedness—their indistinguishability from "reality." A history of American poetry of witness eventually will have to account for this, to explore the trajectory between Whitman's "I am the man, I suffered, I was there" and Ashbery's "I have seen it all, and I write, and I have seen nothing" (*FC* 214).

Our journey

flows past us like ice chunks, maybe it is we that

are stationary

JOHN ASHBERY, *Flow Chart*

The Great Escape
John Ashbery's Travel Agency

I see I am as ever
a terminus of sorts, that is, lots of people
        arrive in me and switch directions but no one
moves on any farther.
John Ashbery, *Flow Chart*

                                                you do not pass
From point A to point B but merely speculate
On how it would be, and in that instant
Do appear to be traveling, though we all

Stay home, don't we.
John Ashbery, "Cups with Broken Handles," *A Wave*

                        there was nothing to do except wait
for another train, yet this one still stayed at the platform.
John Ashbery, "Film Noir," *Hotel Lautréamont*

We know that we are en route in a certain sense, and also that there has
been a hitch somewhere: we have as it were boarded the train but for some
unexplained reason it has not yet started. (John Ashbery, "The System," *Three
Poems*)

It was time to be off, in another
Direction, toward marshlands and cold, scrolled
Names of cities that sounded as though they existed,
But never had.
John Ashbery, "April Galleons," *April Galleons*

And I shall be traveling on
a little farther to a favorite spot of mine, O you'd like it but no one can go there.
John Ashbery, *Flow Chart*

                        Why,
it almost seems as if we are arriving

in a port of Cyprus, the damaged
storm in ruins, past the mole
and the breakwater to the incredible piles
of volcanic tuff no one esteems, if indeed

we're here.
John Ashbery, "Fascicle," *Can You Hear, Bird?*

Soon all was drift. They had a feeling
they had better go inside, yet none could make a move
in that direction.
John Ashbery, "Yes, Dr. Grenzmer. How May I Be of Assistance to You? What!
    You Say the Patient Has Escaped?" *Can You Hear, Bird?*

Ashbery: "I don't know what my life is, what I want to be escaping *from*. I want to move to some other *space*, I guess, when I write, which perhaps was where I had been but without being fully conscious of it. I want to move in and out of it, while I'm writing."

Gangel: "Take a journey?"

Ashbery: "Yeah, but also realize, more, where I am." (Sue Gangel, Interview)

His journey is false, his unreal excitement really an illness
On a false island where the heart cannot act and will not suffer.
W. H. Auden, "A Voyage," *Collected Shorter Poems*

Now, from all these travels I never took anything for my books. It seems to me that this is worth mentioning, since it clearly shows just how much imagination accounts for everything in my work. (Raymond Roussel, *How I Wrote Certain of My Books*)

All of these quotations—most from books of poems by John Ashbery, and the last two from his most immediate poetic fathers—suggest something representative in Ashbery: a version of travel in which movement is paralyzed, stopped at its origin, or in which the voyage is, at least, subjectively constructed. The Crusoe of "The Skaters" (*Rivers and Mountains*) does not travel to an island but imagines the journey from the comfort of his apartment; the technical writer of "The Instruction Manual" (*Some Trees*) daydreams his trip to Guadalajara from the tedium of his Manhattan office; the filmgoer of "The System" (*Three Poems*) finally admits that he's really been watching a mirror, "with all the characters including that of the old aunt played by me in different disguises" (105). Some of Ashbery's book titles reflect this dynamic stasis or static movement—*The Mooring of Starting Out*, for example, or *Houseboat Days*. Ashbery's way of showing that mastery is over—whether as history or as fiction—is not through a trope of vulnerability, as in Lowell, but through a parody of the mythology of access to being, which is often, as these examples suggest, a parody of travel's penetration to interiors.

Childish Geographies

A trope for the apparent disengagement discussed in the prior chapter, as well as for Ashbery's famous irreferentiality, can be found in tourism, which, in Ashbery, is imagined travel, clichéd, eroticized, commodified, and always within quotation marks. A traveler visits, or imagines he visits, places whose inhabitants have no, or completely other, expectations of him and whose constraints, since he cannot understand them, do not constrain him. This is travel as release from duty, from the law of the father, the *patria*—travel, in other words, as infantile and oedipal, tied to the pleasure principle. These are Allen Ginsberg's "ports of childish geography." Consider the fantasies of oral (and aural) gratification in Ashbery's "Hop o' My Thumb":

> There are still other made-up countries
> Where we can hide forever,
> Wasted with eternal desire and sadness,
> Sucking the sherbets, crooning the
> tunes, naming the names.
> (*Self-Portrait* 33)

Ashbery's narrators are often either children or childish. Their travel is play-travel; the countries where they "can hide" are "made-up." In the early "And You Know," the students say to their teacher,

> Goodbye, old teacher, we must travel on, not to a better land, perhaps,
> But to the England of the sonnets, Paris, Colombia, and Switzerland
> And all the places with names, that we wish to visit—
> . . . .
> It is too late to go to the places with the names (what were they, anyway? just
>   names).
> (*ST* 57–58)

In "The Skaters," the traveler fondly imagines: "No more dullness, only movies and love and laughter, sex and fun" (*RM* 44). To suck on sweets (or "dicks," also associated with travel, in *Flow Chart*), to sing, to watch movies, to be caressed, to fantasize romantic loves, and not to have to work or obey or, in the case of "The Instruction Manual," *write*—these are some of the releases that the voyage promises.[1]

Richard Howard, writing of Ashbery, borrows the term *blazon en abime* from heraldry to indicate how one finds, in an artwork, its self-referring text (18).[2] The inner blazon I trace in Ashbery's poems is the trope of travel. It functions in perhaps the most obvious sense at the level of signification. Ashbery's deferral of meaning is legend and indeed obvious to most readers. Since poststructuralist theory presents the signifying act as one of continual displacement, signification itself can be regarded as an exercise in travel. Travel becomes the gesture toward a meaning which, because the displacement continues, is always deferred. We may contrast this with the mythic circularity and unity popular in discussions of the journey (and parodied in "The Instruction Manual," considered below). One thinks particularly of Joseph Campbell's—and, earlier, Hume's—idea of the tripartite journey, consisting of departure, initiation, and return.

In this way, the journey is also a key to the formal procedures of the poetry. How, after all, are we meant to read Ashbery's poems? Not, certainly, to probe for meanings—whose existence the poet, in numerous interviews, has disclaimed—but to enjoy a lazy, luxurious way of writing and reading (a "lazy way of moving forward" [*TP* 19], Ashbery writes of writing). Ashbery, critics seem to agree, presents us with the activity of consciousness (or "imitations of consciousness" [Corn 236]), not its power to fix or communicate its content (Kalstone, *Five Temperaments* 201). Thus, methodology coincides with subject, if we take "subject" in its current usage, not as topic but as the experiencing, speaking consciousness.

Finally, and most traditionally, travel serves as a figure of spiritual understanding, "the way" described in the contemplative and devotional *Three Poems*: a way with all roads and options remaining open and with no "road not taken." *Three Poems*, read as a vade mecum, offers a conflation of Whitmanesque, Buddhist, and post-Symbolist ideas of how to live and travel in the world.

While Ashbery's poetry has continued to develop during half a century of continual writing, in a sense, after *Hotel Lautréamont* and *Flow Chart*, it becomes thinner, lighter, and more ludic. I deal in this chapter with the poems I take as the most significant, a few poems from the first three or four decades with occasional mention of later volumes.

Some similarities exist between Ashbery's "innocent, ravished, astonished" narrators, as Richard Howard calls them (34), and Elizabeth Bishop's naïve tourists, but clearly no traumatized or vulnerable traveler can be identified with the historical John Ashbery, as one might identify, say, Robert Lowell's speakers closely with Lowell. Thus, though Ashbery spent ten years living in France (1955–1965), roughly parallel to Bishop's principal years in Brazil

(1951–1967), the topic of geographic travel is less germane to him than to other poets, since travel serves in his work not as account but as trope. Nevertheless, because Ashbery's poetry owes much to French literature and particularly to Raymond Roussel, some account of his years in France and his attraction to Roussel is necessary.

In 1955, to escape a dead-end editing job with McGraw-Hill in New York City, Ashbery applied for and received a Fulbright to Montpellier for the purpose of translating modern French poets. He renewed the fellowship in 1956, the same year his first book, *Some Trees*, was published in the Yale Series of Younger Poets. When the second Fulbright ran out, he returned to New York, where he enrolled in the PhD program at New York University. Having decided to write his dissertation on Raymond Roussel, he persuaded his parents to support him in France while he did the research. In the fall of 1958, he moved to Paris to stay. He never finished the dissertation, in part because he could not face an academic life, especially if it meant returning to America. He stayed in Paris till 1966, surviving by writing art reviews and articles for *Art News* and for the *International Herald Tribune*, as well as, for a year or so, a regular "Paris Letter" for *Art International*. He then returned to New York to accept a position as executive editor for *Art News*.[3]

Ashbery's investigation of Roussel was crucial to his poetic career. Without Roussel's example, it is unlikely that Ashbery would have written as he has. While collage and the use of found phrases date from the surrealist era, the completely programmatic methods of Roussel do not. In studying Roussel, Ashbery saw the possibility of a writing generated by the mechanisms of language, in which the world no longer precedes language but originates in it. He found at the center of Roussel's linguistic labyrinth what Michel Foucault also found: "the inexorable absence of being" (*Death* 19), the loss of all presence.[4]

When Roussel began to travel in the early 1920s, he did so in a specially constructed *roulotte*, a luxurious proto-Winnebago. In India, Australia, the South Pacific, China, or Japan, among other places, he stayed either in his roulotte, his cabin, or his hotel room, seldom sightseeing and almost always working. Michel Leiris comments:

> Roussel never really traveled. It seems likely that the outside world never broke through into the universe he carried within him, and in all the countries

he visited, he saw only what he had put there in advance, elements which corresponded absolutely with that universe that was peculiar to him. Placing the imaginary above all else, he seems to have experienced a much stronger attraction for everything that was theatrical, trompe-l'oeil, illusion, than for reality. (qtd. in Ashbery, introd., in Roussel xi)

When in France, Roussel enjoyed taking long chauffered drives while reading a book (or the pages he'd torn out for the purpose), never looking up to see the landscape. This is an image to keep in mind when reading Ashbery's many train poems—for example, "Pyrography" and "Melodic Trains"—in which the passenger has the luxury of looking out or of turning away toward the interior of the car, as he pleases.[5]

As eccentric as Roussel was, he followed the French tradition of the Symbolist hero who spurns geographic travel as inferior to that of the imagination, such as the character Des Esseintes in J. K. Huysmans's *A Rebours* or Axel of Villiers de L'Isle Adam's play of that title. To this tradition also belongs Gerard de Nerval, who once said to Théophile Gautier that "for one who has not seen the Orient, a lotus is still a lotus; for me it is only a kind of onion" (qtd. in Said, *Orientalism* 101).[6]

Ashbery began taking Roussel as his model as early as 1955, while working for McGraw-Hill. Turning away for a few minutes from his editing job, he wrote the poem "The Instruction Manual," a late addition to *Some Trees*. The pre-text for "The Instruction Manual" was Roussel's prose poem *La Vue*, as Ashbery recounted much later:

[J]ust glancing at the poem *La Vue* I could figure out what he was doing in the poem and I did in fact get the idea of writing the poem from Roussel. It was one of the last poems in the book, a rather paint-by-numbers poem written in '55 just before I submitted the manuscript. (Herd 425)

The poem has less parodic antecedents in twentieth-century Anglo-American pastoral poetry, where the dreamed-of place is conceived from the perspective of the urban blight one wants to escape. In Wallace Stevens's "An Ordinary Evening in New Haven," the speaker inhabits an ugly (and "ordinary") place and dreams of lemon trees, toucans, and brilliant colors. Yeats's "Lake Isle of Innisfree" is a wish driven by the tedium of "pavements grey." Merely mentioning the pavements or the job—in this case the midtown Manhattan office of McGraw-Hill, across from the Port

Authority—suggests a narrative, which "The Instruction Manual" plays out, with a beginning and end: the dream, the call, and the return.[7]

In "The Instruction Manual," the earliest instance in which Ashbery introduces the idea of an unrecoverable presence (the "real" Guadalajara), we see, through a hackneyed touristic narrative, that the staged and the unstaged are indistinguishable. Here, too, prefiguring the poetry to come, the fantasy of travel is seen as a flight from duty. The importance of the poem within Ashbery's work is twofold: it establishes the parodic treatment of bourgeois travel discourse that the poet will use in many books to follow, and it locates the desire for travel and dream travel in the discourse of present disenchantment, a condition constitutive of most if not all of Ashbery's poetry. Home is the present stasis; travel is the future mobility. Travel in space, real or imaginary, transpires in, and is a figure for, time. Of several Freudian concepts at work here—transference, the conflict between the reality and pleasure principles, and the "uncanny" familiarity of the unfamiliar—the Oedipal relation between traveler and home is the most central.[8] The traveler leaves the patria out of dissatisfaction and the desire to understand it from a new, foreign perspective.

As the poem begins, the narrator, bored with his job as writer of an "instruction manual on the use of a new metal," looks out his office window and begins to daydream of Guadalajara: "City of rose-colored flowers! / City I most wanted to see, and most did not see, in Mexico!" Then, "under the press of having to write the instruction manual," he imagines he *does* see the city—with its plaza, its bandstand, fruit sellers, and boys and girls falling in love. Parodying "off-the-beaten-track" touristic pitches, he invites us to "tiptoe into one of the side streets," where an elderly woman on a sunny patio offers a cool drink and shows us a photo of her son in Mexico City. This visit is followed by a climb to the vantage point of the church tower for a panoramic view of the city, with its rich and poor quarters, market, library, and finally the square where we began.[9] The poem concludes,

> How limited, but how complete withal, has been our experience of
>   Guadalajara!
> We have seen young love, married love, and the love of an aged mother
>   for her son.
> We have heard the music, tasted the drinks, and looked at colored houses.

What more is there to do, except stay? And that we cannot do.
And as the last breeze freshens the top of the weathered old tower, I turn
    my gaze
Back to the instruction manual which has made me dream of Guadalajara.
(*ST* 29–30)

The drudgery of writing the instruction manual has led the writer's gaze first out the window onto the street, with its enviable pedestrians, "each walking with an inner peace," and then beyond them into a calendar version of "old Mexico," where everyone is colorful—the bandsmen, the polite old caretaker, the dutiful daughter scrubbing the steps. These two-dimensional figures indicate the limitations of the homebound writer, whose talent extends only to such utilitarian projects as manual writing. The "travel" that might have served as a *critique* of home/work/stasis instead identifies the subject with—and locates him in—that same realm.

The other point—that is, the parodic treatment of travel discourse—is crucial to an understanding not only of the place of travel but also, more broadly, of the relation between irony and nostalgia in Ashbery's poems. Ashbery reminds us in this early instance that the voyage is a topos of the most banal kind, its discourse correspondingly hackneyed. The banality of travel in "The Instruction Manual" lies in part in its circularity, the movement from reality to dream to reality again—that is, the pattern traced by the traveler's departure, accumulation of touristic "markers," and safe return, laden with memories, however artificial.

But is the falsehood of travel rhetoric due to the inauthenticity of the touristic experience or to the banal language embodying it? The representation is only false if we have a true travel experience or true travel language for comparison. Because the experience transpires through a narrow and familiar set of conventions, it is "limited," the narrator admits, and yet "complete." The irony of parody, therefore, is itself ironized: no language available is devoid of banality.

The "city of Guadalajara" is the "City I most wanted to see, and most did not see," not because the narrator stayed in his office but because, even had he left, the "authentic" Guadalajara is not recoverable. Touristic failure to achieve presence is a sign of linguistic failure and vice-versa. The mythology of discovery is that of penetration, of the self's phenomenological access to being. But insofar as this mythology is informed by a rhetoric of loss and a modernist nostalgia for the "authentic," for the thing behind the sign, Ashbery's work repudiates it. Again, the irony does not consist of a clear binarism of the ironic and the sincere.

Further, the pseudo-events that the armchair traveler witnesses do not result from touristic poor taste but from tourism's social relations, which represent the proliferation of versions of reality, of simulations and reality effects, in consumer culture. The manual-writer's journey, for example, includes the off-the-beaten-track episode—the digression from the main square to the side street with its private encounter with the elderly mother—a detour essential to the beaten track of tourism.[10] "Real" lives are thought to be always backstage; hence the tourist gaze must be intrusive. Locals and entrepreneurs contrive backstages to protect themselves from the tourist and to take advantage of obvious opportunities. Pseudo-events, then, do not proceed from the tourist's immersion in the inauthentic but from the social relations of tourism itself. Modern society, as Dean MacCannell writes, recognizes and accommodates the rights of outsiders to look into its workings. Thus, "Institutions are fitted with arenas, platforms, and chambers set aside for the exclusive use of tourists" (*Tourist* 49).

But if the encounter with the elderly Mexican mother is immediately recognizable as staged authenticity, this staging for the tourist's sake is no different from what happens "in Mexico" anyway. In like manner, Ashbery's "phony" rhetoric—which he has made a career of mining and exploiting from every imaginable source—is no less real than the "real" John Ashbery speaking, a notion whose barrenness this poet has worked to reveal at every turn.[11]

"The Instruction Manual" does, after all, leave us with instruction: daydream all you like, but you can't live in your dreams; you must come back home. So says Dorothy at the end of *The Wizard of Oz*: "Oh, Auntie Em, there's no place like home." One's sympathy, however, must go to George Bailey in *It's a Wonderful Life*, who never enjoyed Dorothy's hallucinatory option to find out one way or the other. George has travel longings, but, though he does find love, he is beaten into submission and must finally, in the face of family, job, and mortgage, give up forever, as does the poor writer of the instruction manual, the dreams embodied in the travel posters decorating his office.

Ashbery's parody of presence, of travel's access to interiors, is also, then, a parody of the morality of travel accounts, which, from *The Odyssey* to *The Wizard of Oz*, instruct us to stay home. One may read this parody as directed at the kinds of readers discussed in the previous chapter, readers who demand fidelity to place. Just as Ashbery parodies the "stay home" moral at the end of "The Instruction Manual," so does he at the end of "The Painter" (*ST*) and in "Variations, Calypso, and Fugue on a Theme of Ella Wheeler Wilcox," where the speaker exults, echoing Dorothy, "But of all the sights that were seen by me / In the East or West, on land or sea / The best was the place that is spelled H-O-M-E" (*DDS* 15).[12]

Ashbery's much longer and more digressive "The Skaters," from *Rivers and Mountains*, incorporates touristic parody to illustrate how the experience of travel rests on the idea of home. Based on a book titled *300 Things a Bright Boy Can Do*, "The Skaters" explicitly raises the question of the place of irony in the postmodern poem. Irony ordinarily presumes a position beyond the immediately apparent one of the speaker, from which one can subvert the latter's language, but the binary system of a "real" meaning opposite a surface meaning is not sustainable in "The Skaters," just as it is not in the later *Three Poems*.

Section II of "The Skaters" introduces the topos of the ironic voyage suddenly, along with the equation of the future with travel, and the past with home, as in "The Instruction Manual":

We are nearing the Moorish coast, I think, in a *bateau*.
I wonder if I will have any friends there
Whether the future will be kinder to me than the past, for example,
And am all set to be put out, finding it to be not.
(*RM* 43)

The parodic Symbolist dream travel carries the real fear that, despite the traveler's hopes, the future may merely be a replay. The visited place promised by the cruise may be just another version of home, of "the past, that attic" (43). Nevertheless, the extravagant rhetoric continues and compensates:

Its sailboats are perhaps more beautiful than these, these I am leaning against,
Spangled with diamonds and orange and purple stains,
Bearing me once again in quest of the unknown. These sails are life itself to me.

I heard a girl say this once, and cried, and brought her fresh fruit and fishes,
Olives and golden baked loaves. She dried her tears and thanked me.

Now we are both setting sail into the purplish evening.
I love it! This cruise can never last long enough for me.
(44)

In these lines, the adolescent extremity of both emotion and scene—a "purple" passage—indicates the gratification dreams offer up. In contrast, after the two lovers, transported by their own words, sail off "into the purplish evening," "home" intrudes, with all the familiar weight of its workaday *furniture*. It is instantly, and childishly, refused: "But once more, office desks, radiators—No! That is behind me. / No more dullness, only movies and love and laughter, sex and fun" (44).

The workaday voices then step up their demands, and the energy expended on repression becomes more taxing. After a climax of "purest ecstasy" (44), the narrator and girl from the "purplish evening" sail away, or try to, from home's demands:

And, as into a tunnel the voyage starts
Only, as I said, to be continued. The eyes of those left on the dock are wet
But ours are dry. Into the secretive, vaporous night with all of us!
Into the unknown, the unknown that loves us, the great unknown!
(46)

This ecstatic chant echoes not only Baudelaire's "Le Voyage" but also the urgently infantile travel anxiety of another of Baudelaire's poems, "Anywhere, Out of the World!" The *l'inconnu* (the unknown) and the *n'importe óu* (no matter where) come from those two poems, respectively. Such metaphorized and fantasized travel is not, however, left to pursue its ends unqualified by the burdens and threats of home, which now obtrude in the form not merely of dullness and duty but of the guilt of desertion. "The [wet] eyes of those left on the dock" haunt the dry-eyed voyager still more in "Melodic Trains," where, at a less id-driven level of awareness, he speaks of the "sadness of the faces of children on the platform" and of others on the platform who "are my brothers" (*HD* 24).

In section III, with the help of a now much more localized and identifiable speaking subject, the transgressive and escapist aspects of travel become clearer. In this section, we learn for the first time that the speaker of "The Skaters" is a latter-day Crusoe, whose daily duties on his island home include food-and-water gathering, drudgery that he contrasts with the liberating "distraction" of climbing to the top of a cliff to scan the horizon: "Not for a ship, of course—this island is far from all the trade routes— / But in hopes of an unusual sight, such as a school of dolphins at play" (*RM* 55).

He then tries to remember the name of a nineteenth-century English painter, perhaps Turner, judging from the description of the "pale gray and orange distances," where a waterspout is becoming visible, "delicate, transparent," but his memory is poor:

> I am beginning to forget everything on this island. If only I had been allowed to
> > bring my ten favorite books with me—
> But a weathered child's alphabet is my only reading material.
> (55)

The "ten favorite books" question is a staple of interviews with authors, but the narrator is as limited (or regressed) in resources as he is in memory. Elizabeth Bishop's Crusoe, in her poem "Crusoe in England," remembers trying to remember:

> > —well, I tried
> reciting to my iris beds,
> "They flash upon that inward eye,
> which is the bliss . . ." The bliss of what?
> (*Complete* 164)

Both Crusoes, in the absence of texts to remind them, forget cultural icons and revert childishly to the visual. The books Bishop's Crusoe had previously read are now, in memory, "full of blanks" while Ashbery's Crusoe retains only "a weathered child's alphabet." Bishop's Crusoe plays his tuneless flute as he whoops and dances among the goats. Ashbery's, fluteless and bookless, stands on the cliff, marveling at the violence and beauty of the coming storm. But adult responsibilities continue to pester:

> I had better be getting back to the tent
> To make sure everything is shipshape, weigh down
> > the canvas with extra stones,
> Bank the fire.
> (*RM* 56)

Flip-flopping between desire and duty, he becomes lost in contemplation

of the "luminous" landscape. Then, "I really had better be getting back
down, I suppose." Then, again:

Still it is rather fun to linger on in the wet,
Letting your clothes get soaked. What difference does
    it make? No one will scold me for it,
Or look askance.
(56)

The duty-desire oscillation parallels another opposition, between survival
(securing the shelter, banking the fire) and the death drive (the "freedom"
not to care, to make oneself sick), but the oppositions are themselves nested
within a larger slippage of duty: we soon learn, following the previous lines,
that the whole scene of the castaway has been a child's dream of "sleeping
out," a fantasy of the wilderness. The adult narrator admits that what he
has described as an island is really an apartment:

In reality of course the middle-class apartment I live in is nothing like a desert
    island.
Cozy and warm it is, with a good library and record collection.
Yet I feel cut off from life in the streets.
Automobiles and trucks plow by, spattering me with filthy slush.
The man in the street turns his face away. Another island-dweller, no doubt.
(56)

Now that his condition is revealed as urban and mundane, he invokes
not islands but John Donne's metaphor of islands: indeed, the narrator's
isolation and distance are familiar from the situation of the instruction-
manual writer, who also looked down at the urban passersby, envying them,
cut off from them. The narrator in "The Skaters" reads the daily news but

None of this makes any difference to professional
    exiles like me, and that includes everybody in
    the place.
We go on sipping our coffee, thinking dark or transparent thoughts.
(RM 57)

The island castaway's story now has become the story of the sensitive soul's
alienation in modern society, the "professional exiles" among the masses,
who "continue to tread the water / Of backward opinion" (57).

"The Skaters" is, as David Shapiro wrote in an early introduction to Ashbery's work, "a flurry of parodies" (105). Added to the parody of presence that characterizes all of Ashbery's work is the parody of the modernist philosophical poem of Stevens or Eliot; the parody, in Section I, of the postmodern self-referential text; the parody of the exotic, sublime, Baudelairean voyage with its dream of finding the new in the unknown; and perhaps a parody, in Section IV, of ancient Asian poetry in translation, particularly Pound's Chinese translations:

> This is my fourteenth year as governor of C province.
> I was little more than a lad when I first came here.
> Now I am old but scarcely any wiser.
> So little are white hair and a wrinkled forehead a sign of wisdom!
> (60)

Ashbery's wizened sage pens haiku-like reflections: "Today I wrote, 'The Spring is late this year / In the early mornings there is hoarfrost on the water meadows. / And on the highway the frozen ruts are papered over with ice'" (60). At one point, using "Chinese" (actually Chinese restaurant) words, the poem becomes a burlesque of Pound's "The River-Merchant's Wife":

> Seventeen years in the capital of Foo-Yung province!
> Surely woman was born for something
> Besides continual fornication, retarded only by menstrual cramps.
>
> I had thought of announcing my engagement to you
> On the day of the first full moon of X month.
>
> The wind has stopped, but the magnolia blossoms still
> Fall with a plop onto the dry, spongy earth.
> The evening is pestiferous with midges.
> (62)

In "The Skaters," then, travel functions not only as a trope but also as a means of questioning an ironizing subjectivity. As in the lines just cited, the subject's viewpoint, far from indicating a lack of value in what it parodies, suggests its importance. In thinking of Ashbery's irony, we may be helped by Charles Bernstein, who, regarding his own work, comments,

So that the stuff that seems the most to be made mock of, when I hear it, is interesting to me because my negative reaction suggests that in my relation to it there's something beyond just that I believe it to be false. (*A Poetics* 460)

"Whatever I include [in a poem]," Bernstein continues, "I *like*, am fascinated or engaged by, in some way that doesn't reduce simply to irony" (461). He wants "humor that opens out into a multivolitional field destabilizing to any fixed meaning" (462). He cites Octavio Paz's idea of a meta-irony that "destroys its negation and, hence, returns in the affirmative." But, Bernstein qualifies,

I don't want to stop at that flip back to the affirmative but to go beyond yes and no. Humor as destabilizing not only the negation to mean affirmation but the affirmation also—the idea of a perpetual motion machine that never stops pinging and ponging off the walls, ceilings, floors. So returns to . . . let's say "the absolute," maybe the ineffable—everywhere said, nowhere stated. (462)

Certainly the ping-pong effect is observable in Ashbery, both, taking the case of "The Skaters," in Crusoe's movement back and forth between pleasure and reality and in the combined poignancy and banality of that narrator's meditations. In a general and perhaps obvious sense, Ashbery's irony—in which a borrowed rhetoric reinscribes a sentiment as it undermines it—returns us to the idea of deferral, where meaning and value are indefinitely postponed. In none of these journeys does a traveler arrive.

Maps as Territories

Travel in Ashbery represents two kinds of escape: unconstrained childishness and unconstrained textuality. Though they are often inextricable, here I try to treat these separately: first, the "childish geography" discussed in the form of escape, orality, and ekstasis; and, second, what may be called the map-territory problem. Both "The Instruction Manual" and "The Skaters" trace the routes of childish escape, the fantasies of elsewhere arising out of the sense of separation from others as well as out of boredom with duty. Through these poems and many others, we see the pleasure-seeking, commitment-fleeing man-child or tourist. But these and other Ashbery poems also give us the sense of travel as reading, of geography as text, and, with this, a sense of the subject's losing himself somewhere between map and territory. The loss sometimes takes the form of pleasurable release, sometimes of helplessness. This textual dimension of travel, then, part of Ashbery's debt to Roussel, is the principal feature of the poems I examine next.

A major source of confusion in Ashbery's traveler (as in his reader) lies in his inability to distinguish between the mediated and the unmediated, between representation and "reality." For some, the traveler's inability to "map" will evoke Frederic Jameson's discussion of "cognitive mapping" in his *Postmodernism, or the Cultural Logic of Late Capitalism*. In Jameson, the complexity of the current world system defies our attempts to grasp and represent it, so that no map is adequate. But Jameson implies that material systems *can* be—even *ought* to be—mapped, an assumption that Ashbery's travelers would be unlikely to endorse.

"Rivers and Mountains," a shorter and more widely anthologized poem than "The Skaters," offers a relatively early example of a poem that explores and dismantles the opposition of the "true" versus the constructed travel site. The poem begins and ends with references to a group of plotting assassins. Though much of the body of the poem ignores that plot, the fact that a subversive group and the state opposing it are involved with navigation, strategies, and maps confers coherence, since notions of territory preoccupy the poem more than particular plots, whether hatched or aborted.[13] In fact, the poem's actions transpire *on* the map. "Rivers and Mountains" begins,

> On the secret map the assassins
> Cloistered, the Moon River was marked
> Near the eighteen peaks and the city
> Of humiliation and defeat—
> (*RM* 10)[14]

The "Moon River" theme (from the film "Breakfast at Tiffany's") places us in the early 1960s, as do references to what could be the topography of Vietnam, to U.S. military strategy during the Vietnam War, and to the assassination of a leader (perhaps Ngo Dinh Diem). But we are denied the satisfaction of historical grounding when we see, in the next few lines, that the trail of the assassins ends among

dry, papery leaves
Gray-brown quills like thoughts
In the melodious but vast mass of today's
Writing through fields and swamps
Marked, on the map, with little bunches of weeds.
(10)

While references to state apparatuses—"The rioters turned out of sleep in the peace of prisons" or "public / Places for electric light / And the major tax assessment area"—appear intermittently, the poem, from this point onward, pays more attention to the troubled relations of texts to "reality." The second verse paragraph begins

So going around cities
To get to other places you found
It all on paper but the land
Was made of paper processed
To look like ferns, mud or other
Whose sea unrolled its magic
Distances and then rolled them up
(10)

The actors in this drama—not the assassins now but "you," their trackers—tramp out of jungle and into text. This simulated and dissimulating world of papier-mâché and maps, unrolled and then rolled up again, offers experience only through simile. "Moonless nights [are] spent *as on a raft.*" A melody is heard "*As though through trees*" (10–11; emphasis added). (In "The Skaters," "*as into a tunnel,* the voyage starts" [46; emphasis added]). Compensation for the evanescence of moonless nights seems at first to lie in the less evanescent "homes," "seminaries," "fisheries," or "places" (11), but these end up equally indeterminate and fleeting (or rhetorical, like the hackneyed "H-O-M-E" in Ashbery's "Variations," *DDS* 15). Even "Moon River" proves moonless.

The third section of "Rivers and Mountains" identifies "your" military strategy, presenting the map-territory problem as a mundane opposition of theory and practice, in the sense that an infantryman would say to a tactician, an Iago to a Cassio, "The map is not the territory":

Your plan was to separate the enemy into two groups
With the razor-edged mountains between.
It worked well on paper
But their camp had grown
To be the mountains.
(11)

If the map will not work, one must revert to the "real" camp and the "real" mountains. But the enemy has surpassed us: its world, no longer confined to maps and plans, has grown into Nature itself. And what follows removes any possibility of recourse to that Nature:

                    and the map
Carefully peeled away and not torn
Was the light, a tender but tough bark
On everything.
(11)

Jorge Luis Borges's fragment "On Rigor in Science" had not yet been translated into English when Ashbery composed "Rivers and Mountains," but the parallel is too striking to pass over. Borges's piece, purportedly an excerpt from a seventeenth-century Spanish travel text, describes a group of cartographers in an unnamed empire who, obsessed with accuracy, kept enlarging their maps until the map of the empire was the size of the empire itself and "coincided with it point by point" (90). Succeeding generations saw little use for this map and abandoned it to the elements, but, every so often, in forgotten corners of the empire, Borges "quotes," pieces of the map surface, "inhabited by Animals and Beggars" (90). (Later Ashbery poems also—for example, the following line from "Flow Chart"—suggest this Borgesian idea: "Scratching around one is sure to uncover bits of the ancient way" [191].) In "Rivers and Mountains," two problems arise with "your plan . . . to separate the enemy." One is, as we have seen, that the enemy's camp has become indistinguishable from nature; the other, which Borges's fable helps us see, is that the map we have been using to trace, contain, and define the assassins is now seen to be the light that, like bark— in a double substitution or metalepsis—covers all of nature, so that it, too, is indistinguishable from perceived reality, forming a "tender but tough bark / On everything." The map has become so much a part of our way of seeing that we do not see without it; it is the light by which we see, not only mediating but covering, even obscuring by its interposition. In the Borges story, too, the map superimposes an extra layer over everything, so complete it matches every detail of the earth.

In *Simulations*, Jean Baudrillard takes Borges's idea still further:

> The territory no longer precedes the map, nor survives it. Henceforth, it is the map that precedes the territory . . . if we were to revive the [Borges] fable today, it would be the territory whose shreds are slowly rotting across the map. . . . But it is no longer a question of either maps or territory. Something has disappeared: the sovereign difference between them that was the abstraction's charm. (2)

Though Baudrillard emphasizes the precedence of the map over the territory, his crucial (and contradictory) point is the indistinguishability of map and territory. No longer does one thing represent or mirror another, nor can one be measured in terms of another. Ashbery later writes, in "The New Spirit," "Today is cooler or warmer than yesterday, and it all works itself out into a map, projects, placed over the other real like a sheet of tracing paper, and these two simultaneously become what is going on" (*TP* 18).[15]

No single event concludes the political drama of "Rivers and Mountains," yet a remarkable ending subsumes all events ("all this") in text. After we are told "the war was solved / In another way by isolating the two sections / Of the enemy's navy," subject-verb and pronoun-antecedent agreement fairly disintegrates (12). "Light" in the following, final passage may be the grammatical subject of several verbs and participles, but even making such connections does not produce an event:

Light bounced off the ends
Of the small gray waves to tell
Them in the observatory
About the great drama that was being won
To turn off the machinery
And quietly move among the rustic landscape
Scooping snow off the mountains rinsing
The coarser ones that love had
Slowly risen in the night to overflow

Wetting pillow and petal
Determined to place the letter
On the unassassinated president's desk
So that a stamp could reproduce all this
In detail, down to the last autumn leaf
And the affliction of June ride
Slowly out into the sun-blackened landscape.
(11–12)

If we take "scooping" and "rinsing" to be actions of "light," what are the "ones" being rinsed? And can we include "wetting" among those participles, or is its agent not "love" instead? And is it "light" or "love" or neither that is "Determined to place the letter / On the unassassinated president's desk"? This syntactical slippage is not unusual in Ashbery's work; often the poet accomplishes his leaps within and by means of it —in this case, leaps from what seem to be events transpiring in a "real" world to maps, plans, stamps, paper simulacra.

The last of these leaps brings us to Borges once again. One of his most famous stories, "The Lottery in Babylon," tells of the unknowable "company" that runs the lottery and whose existence gives rise to a conspiracy theory of such proportions that the paranoid and the mystical become one. In Ashbery's poem, all of "this"—the light falling, bouncing, rinsing; love rising and overflowing in the night; and the letter finally placed on the unassassinated president's desk—has occurred so that a stamp might reproduce it, "down to the last autumn leaf." In Borges's story, the narrator contemplates the possibility that one's dreams, the hues of leaves, "a bird's call," "the shadings of rust and of dust" are all manifestations of the company and finally that "it is indifferent to affirm or deny the reality of the shadowy corporation" (*Labyrinths* 35). Whether the company exists or not has no significance. This erasure of difference—between "reality" and representation, but also between state control and individual autonomy—brings us to the hyperreal, the universe of maps, theories, and mediations, which offer no recourse to anterior realities.

Two later poems, "Melodic Trains" and "Pyrography," both from *Houseboat Days* and both about train travel, make explicit the shape-shifting of the travel subject in motion across textually confounded terrains, a topos that is streamlined in the cyclical "The Instruction Manual" and submerged in the thick paranoiac texture of "Rivers and Mountains."

Trains seem to be Ashbery's favorite means of transport, in both senses of the word *transport*.[16] "Melodic Trains" plays out the travel-as-escape theme but develops the traveler's moral relation to others beyond the scant treatment of that relation in "The Instruction Manual" and "The Skaters." The adolescent fantasy of a life of sweets, sex, and movies is overcast now by the shadows of those who share the speaker's limited world. Delight and release are thus mixed, as the poem proceeds, with the pain and loss associated with departures.

The traveler in "Melodic Trains" seems to be a child playing at adulthood, riding the train and wearing adult clothes for "fun." The clothes he wears also constitute the landscape he passes:

And it is fun to wear other
Odd things, like this briar pipe and tweed coat

Like date-colored sierras with the lines of seams
Sketched in and plunging now and then into unfathomable
Valleys that can't be deduced by the shape of the person
Sitting inside it—me, and just as our way is flat across
Dales and gulches, as though our train were a pencil

Guided by a ruler held against a photomural of the Alps
We both come to see distance as something unofficial
And impersonal yet not without its curious justification.
(*HD* 24)

As the traveler examines his coat, he sees that its herringbone pattern resembles the peaks of mountain ranges and that the seams of the sleeves resemble valleys, features that cannot be related to his own shape. (We may recall Roussel's discovery of landscapes in small objects, such as the advertisement on the side of a pen in "La Vue.") The coat's seam, running straight through the herringbone, parallels the train trajectory, so that, as in "Rivers and Mountains," the geography conflates with a constructed text. The journey is uneasy:

Only the wait in stations is vague and
Dimensionless, like oneself. How do they decide how much

Time to spend in each? One begins to suspect there's no
Rule or that it's applied haphazardly.
(24)

Just as "unofficial" and "impersonal" in the previous passage suggest a longing for travel that is *official* and *personal,* so here "dimensionless" reveals a desire not only for rules in the systemic world of trains but in "oneself" as well. The dissatisfaction is compounded by the subject's lack of agency. Other people decide—those who build trains, lay tracks, and write schedules—and one cannot know their motivations. One can only ride the train and look out the window. The traveler is concerned about this impersonal distance as an empathetic gap between himself and others. Looking out the window, he sees the "sadness" of the children who are *not* traveling and whose welfare is still uncertain. He cannot feel carefree because

> any stop before the final one creates
> Clouds of anxiety, of sad, regretful impatience
> With ourselves, our lives, the way we have been dealing
> With other people up until now. Why couldn't
> We have been more considerate? These figures leaving
>
> The platform or waiting to board the train are my brothers
> In a way that really wants to tell me why there is so little
> Panic and disorder in the world, and so much unhappiness.
> If I were to get down now to stretch, take a few steps
>
> In the wearying and world-weary clouds of steam like great
> White apples, might I just through proximity and aping
> of postures and attitudes communicate this concern of mine
> To them? That their jagged attitudes correspond to mine,
>
> That their beefing strikes answering silver bells within
> My own chest, and that I know, as they do, how the last
> Stop is the most anxious one of all, though it means
> Getting home at last, to the pleasures and dissatisfactions of home?
> (24–25)

In "The Skaters" the dry-eyed traveler sails off, leaving the wet eyed behind on the dock, but in "Melodic Trains" such a carefree departure is no longer possible. An important knowledge is ascribed to the homebodies. "They"—on the platform—know something of the "last stop," the trouble of arrival, the deathlike stasis of endings. The child traveler aspires to that knowledge and that maturity, sensing in himself some as yet unplumbed depth of pain and experience. Thus, the passage begins by saying that all stops *except* the last one are fraught with anxiety and ends, under the influence of those others' perspective, by saying "the last / Stop is the most anxious one of all." At every stop the traveler is reminded of his brotherhood with those would-be passengers outside; the "[c]louds of anxiety" settle over him as he reflects with dissatisfaction on "the way we have been dealing / With other people up until now."

The traveler's remorse, at privilege, luxury, and mobility, sets in as soon as the travel reflections begin—that is, from the second stanza onward. Any "fun" remaining is heavily qualified and comes toward the end, at the celebration of arrival. As also in "Pyrography," the poem's last principal image is that of the train hurtling through the landscape:

It's as though a visible chorus called up the different
Stages of the journey, singing about them and being them:
Not the people in the station, not the child opposite me
With currant fingernails, but the windows, seen through,

Reflecting imperfectly, ruthlessly splitting open the bluish
Vague landscape like a zipper. Each voice has its own
Descending scale to put one in one's place at every stage;
One need never not know where one is

Unless one give up listening, sleeping, approaching a small
Western town that is nothing but a windmill. Then
The great fury of the end can drop as the solo
Voices tell about it, wreathing it somehow with an aura

Of good fortune and colossal welcomes from the mayor and
Citizen's committees tossing their hats into the air.
To hear them singing you'd think it had already happened
And we had focused back on the furniture of the air.
(25–26)

The windows, "[r]eflecting imperfectly," split open the landscape "like a zipper." Logically, that split would be not the windows' reflection but the train's movement along the track; if one imagines the track as a zipper, the train's movement opens what had been a seam or a suture. The zipper-track is the *via rupta*, the rupture of nature by culture, articulated tie by tie (or tine by tine if the track is a zipper; a strong visual and operational similarity functions here, as also with the stitch or suture). According to Derrida, this primordial rupture is nothing less than writing itself, the violent inscription of difference ("Violence" 107–8). Yet the zipper image in "Melodic Trains" suggests not so much a reunifying as a closing off of possibilities. It both "ruthlessly" splits and closes.

All the stops together are the stages of the journey, each called up by "a visible chorus," which both sings *about* these stages and sings them into existence.[17] The would-be travelers on the platforms may seem to constitute this chorus, but the poet withholds this interpretation: "Not the people in the station, not the child opposite me / With currant fingernails, but the windows, seen through // Reflecting imperfectly." The windows are the agents that both sing the journey into existence *and* split the landscape. Most crucially, they "put one in one's place at every stage." They are the medium through which the subject perceives and judges and the means by which he locates his own subjectivity.[18] "One need never not know where one is," unless one stops traveling. Location in place is not important, but location in movement is. (In a later poem, Ashbery writes, echoing Emerson, "Our strength lies / In the potential for motion, not in accomplishments" ["Cups with Broken Handles," *A Wave* 51].) To stop traveling produces the need to know where one is, to give up continual self-construction through discovery and adventure or to "give up listening, sleeping, approaching a small / Western town that is nothing but a windmill."

Giving up this travel would mean becoming the armchair traveler of "The Instruction Manual" and "The Skaters," merely telling a story "[o]f good fortune and colossal welcomes." The traveler of "Melodic Trains" indeed hears that story but comments, "To hear them singing you'd think it had already happened / And we had focused back on the furniture of the air." For the traveler the trip is *not* over, not until (most likely, not even after) the final stop. Only with stasis does one need to focus back on "the furniture of the air," which one might read as furniture *made* of air, the devalued, empty equipment associated with home and work (the "office desks, radiators" of "The Skaters").

But the traveler of "Melodic Trains" is troubled by his effect on those left behind in the rejected patria, as well as in the new territories where he trespasses. While he repudiates such anxieties at the poem's opening, reveling instead in motion and costume, the anxieties insistently become the burden of the poem. The more mature traveler at the poem's end has to accept them even while knowing that the movement of travel is the only "place" he can inhabit. The alternative, to be bound in a static past, however guilt free, is unacceptable.

The other train poem from *Houseboat Days,* "Pyrography," also a poem of goodbyes and receding landscapes, has a pointedly American dimension. "Pyrography" is a "State" poem, like few poems of the twentieth century, commissioned by the U.S. Department of the Interior for its Bicentennial Exhibition, America 1976, and appearing in the exhibition catalogue published by the Hereword Lester Cook Foundation.[19] The poem's first stanza echoes the American romance of hobo travel, of the lone, sensual ego, from Whitman through Crane to Kerouac, free of the demands of town:

This is America calling:
The mirroring of state to state,
Of voice to voice on the wires,
The force of colloquial greetings like golden
Pollen sinking on the afternoon breeze.
(8)

Like "Melodic Trains," the poem suggests both the disillusion of home and the disappointment of travel:

If this is the way it is let's leave,
They agree, and soon the slow boxcar journey begins,
Gradually accelerating until the gyrating fans of suburbs
Enfolding the darkness of cities are remembered
Only as a recurring tic. And midway
We meet the disappointed, returning ones, without its
Being able to stop us in the headlong night
Toward the nothing of the coast.
. . . .
Why be hanging on here?
. . . .

The land wasn't immediately appealing; we built it
Partly over with fake ruins, in the image of ourselves
. . . .
                              The land
Is pulling away from the magic, glittering coastal towns
To an aforementioned rendezvous with August and December.
The hunch is it will always be this way,
The look, the way things first scared you
In the night light, and later turned out to be,
Yet still capable, all the same, of a narrow fidelity
To what you and they wanted to become:
No sighs like Russian music, only a vast unravelling
Out toward the junctions and to the darkness beyond
To these bare fields, built at today's expense.
(8–10)

"The land is pulling away," one would think, from the train; that is how it looks to us as we depart a place. But here the land pulls away from the coastal towns, toward a future season. We may recognize, first, the disjunction between "land" and "town" as the familiar map-territory problem, a discrepancy between geography and cognitive grids. Remember that Elizabeth Bishop's peevish tourist, on sailing into Santos, Brazil, expresses surprise at the flag and the presence of coins and paper money, and apprehends the difference between a "country" and a "nation," the latter inscribed in ways the former is not. In Ashbery's poem, as we head toward "the nothing of the coast," the site of commerce and internationalism, the (relatively) unconstructed land pulls away.

But if the disappointment of town is its flags and coins, its contamination or constructedness, the disappointment of land is its failure—"our" failure—to achieve the sublime; we must colonize it to give it meaning. Because the land disappoints us, "we built it / Partly over with fake ruins, in the image of ourselves." Only by this construction are these "things" capable of meeting our expectations and their own, faithful "[t]o what you and they wanted to become." And what did they and you want them to become? Not, apparently, the sadness of departure and of failed presence, but the huge sweeping vista of the poem's ending, a sense, strongly American, of the "vast unravelling" space, the prairies and the "darkness beyond" them. This is almost the sublime, the pathos of an ending that swells out of the landscape, beyond the dimensions of its characters and action. But Ashbery does not allow it; instead, the moment's constructedness has the last word: "built at today's expense." The "vast unravelling" is created out of the moment of perception, the subject's movement across the landscape (and, not least, the moment of Ashbery's writing it out "today"). A sense of wonder arises at this "unravelling" that is less troubled by the dissonance and guilt of the traveler in "Melodic Trains." Nostalgia, loss, and disappointment are, here, part of the experience of pulling in and out of "magic . . . towns" and hurtling on through a dark, starry landscape into the unknown.

The Tao of Ashbery

Three Poems differs from the rest of Ashbery's poetry in that it consists almost entirely of prose and in that its rhetorics, rather than drawn from multiple worlds of discourse, are of a particular stamp: the devotional and metaphysical. But, as elsewhere in Ashbery, what seems parodic or satirical is really a means of tapping a discourse, and whatever the degree of irony in *Three Poems*, the book also can be read "straight," its strange, moving, and plausible philosophy constituting a spiritual guide.

References to the "way" run especially through "The New Spirit," making it, variously, a text of spiritual progress or awakening, a parody of that text, and a deployment of the trope of travel:

> our shared apprehending of the course as plotted turns it into a way, something like an old country road. (24)

> The way is narrow but it is not hard, it seems almost to propel or push one along. One gets the narrowness into one's seeing, which also seems an inducement to moving forward into what one has already caught a glimpse of and which quickly becomes vision in the visionary sense . . . a limited but infinitely free space has established itself. (27)

> But it is hard, this not knowing which direction to take, only knowing that you are moving in one, not because no rest was decreed for you but because the force that shot you here remains through inertia, and . . . you have begun to evolve in that other direction not included by the archer. (30)

There is probably more than one way of proceeding but of course you want only the one way that is denied you. (31)

While some such passages have biblical antecedents ("strait is the gate and narrow is the path," for example), most echo either Taoist or Zen teachings concerning the path toward spiritual awakening, "where the false way and the true way are confounded, where there is no way or rather where everything is a way, none more suitable nor more accurate than the last" (17). Such a "teaching," like many in *Three Poems*, is coherent with the Buddhist antiessentialist idea that no true way exists just as no true Buddha exists. As an old Zen koan says, when you meet the Buddha, you must kill him. Or as another koan goes, "Not two": it is not that the universe is all one; it is that one should resist dualistic thinking. What we see is always construction, there being, to use a title by Gary Snyder, *No Nature*. Thus, amid Ashbery's mystical clichés ("The end is still shrouded in mystery" [70]) are plausible Buddhist ideas, such as that "we have only to step forward to be in the right path, we are all walking in it and we always have been, only we never knew it" (78).

The metaphysics that postmodernism purportedly abolished seems always about to be restored in *Three Poems*. "The New Spirit," in particular, interlarded with references to astrology, Tarot cards, mysticism, and the rhetoric of radiance, stars, and "diamond light," evokes the generational foundation-seeking of the late 1960s, when this poem was written. The figures of spring and the dawn supplant that of travel to explore a personal (I do not mean Ashbery's) as well as a generational burgeoning: "The light continues to grow. . . . All this happened in April. . . . Something *is* happening. . . . It was a new time of being born" (43–45). In the following passage, the trope of travel combines with this radiance of the "new time":

At this point an event of such glamour and such radiance occurred that you forgot the name all over again. It could be compared to arriving in an unknown city at night, intoxicated by the strange lighting and the ambiguities of the streets. The person sitting next to you turned to you, her voice broke and a kind of golden exuberance flooded over you just as you were lifting your arm to the luggage rack. At once the weight of the other years and above all the weight of distinguishing among them slipped away. You found yourself not wanting to care. Everything was guaranteed, it always had been, there would be no future, no end, no development except this steady wavering like a breeze that gently lifted the tired curtains day had let fall. And all the possibilities of civilization, such as travel, study, gastronomy, sexual fulfillment—these no longer lay around on the cankered earth like reproaches, hideous in their reminder of what never could be, but were possibilities that had always existed. (37)

"Glamour," "radiance," "exuberance," "intoxication"—this diction permeates "The New Spirit" at the same time that it characterizes earlier poems such as "The Skaters" and even "The Instruction Manual," where Guadalajara is full of light, love, and gaiety. A concordance for Ashbery would show hundreds of uses of the word "stars," for example. The presence the quoted passage seems to offer becomes specific when the narrator lists the paths one might still take, the "possibilities," which, if not acted on, turn into "reproaches," failures of imagination or resolve.

The passage also, as in "Pyrography" and "Melodic Trains," depicts a train scene, in this case one reminiscent of a 1940s Hollywood film, reminding us of the romantic and religious capital invested in travel, where the fantasized male journey—at night, into the unknown, with an unknown woman—entails a lifting of the bans of time and responsibility. "Everything was guaranteed, it always had been." Among these releases—from care, from the future, from "the weight of the other years," and from "the weight of distinguishing among them"—stands the oxymoron of "steady wavering," like the poet's idea of houseboats as "on the move and . . . stationary," a dialectic central to Ashbery's poetics.[20]

But if presence is always at the brink of restoration in *Three Poems*, it is also always thwarted. All the mostly sensual "possibilities" remain possibilities because "the way" remains primarily linguistic. Writing itself is depicted as a journey—exploring, discovering, getting lost, suffering crises of pain and ecstasy, pausing to take notes, fighting through densities, coming out into clearings, resting, and returning. Many of the moral and spiritual "lessons" of *Three Poems* apply equally to travel and to composition:

But there is no help for it and it must be remembered that the halfhearted, seemingly lazy way of moving forward is both the impetus and the nature of the work. (19)

These ample digressions of yours have carried you ahead to a distant and seemingly remote place. (105)

The "seemingly lazy way of moving forward" is how composition as travel is to be carried out, the digressive way of life spurring an equivalent composition. The effect of this on the question of "presence" reveals a peculiar aspect of Ashbery's poetics that merits attention and indeed yields its own blazon en abime in *Three Poems*. I refer to the stylistic and grammatical quirk of irreferentiality, specifically the fact that pronouns often have no or unclear antecedents. This habit, well known in Ashbery (see, especially, Kinzie), assumes more importance in *Three Poems* than in other Ashbery texts in that *Three Poems* gestures continually toward grand secrets and revelations. A passage from "The System" at once exemplifies and examines this unrecoverability of referents:

> Suddenly you realize that you have been talking for a long time without listening to yourself; you must have said *it* a long way back without knowing it. . . . And the word that everything hinged on is buried back there; by mutual consent neither of you examined it when it was pronounced and rushed to its final resting place. . . . [I]t is best then that the buried word remain buried for we were intended to appreciate only its fruits and not the secret principle activating them—to know this would be to know too much. Meanwhile it is possible to know just enough, and this is all we were supposed to know, toward which we have been straining all our lives. (95)

Reference is withheld precisely when everything in life urgently depends on it. What "we were supposed to know," what we have been straining toward all our lives is "this," which will not be told. At one point, "it" and "this" settle on "the word" as a referent. But "the word" has no referent beyond itself. Or, more accurate, according to the passage, it had a referent, now buried somewhere in the preceding prose, but it would do us no good even if we could find it. Ashbery here makes simultaneously a grammatical (why we cannot/should not find the pronoun's antecedent) and a theological point (why God's name should not be spoken; why ultimate foundations should remain unexamined; and why first principles are unknowable). In one of a handful of verse lapses in "The New Spirit," he writes,

> So this meaning came to arise
> Towering above the rest
> . . . .
> Simultaneously it was penetrable

And was being saturated by the direction of the journey
   we must take
Since it is before us helplessly waiting:
It must exist once the idea of it exists.
(34)

Here, "it," untypically, has a grammatical antecedent, but that antecedent—"meaning"—is as unspecified as "it" is. Once having its pronoun uttered, something that is "it" exists, but the signifying chain, backward or forward, promises no referent, even, or especially, when matters are most weighty. Insofar as this irreferentiality may be seen as a movement toward irreducibility, where "The truth was obstinately itself," as Ashbery writes early in "The System" (55), it may also, paradoxically, constitute a movement toward, rather than away from, presence. Given the inscrutability of God or Nature, the matters to which *it* or *this* refer are irreducible. The most that could be offered would be another name, which would lead only to the infinite regression familiar to readers of Derrida. Thus, the parodic travel movement, with its deferred arrivals and withheld interiors, plays out at the level of grammar.

Like "The New Spirit," "The System" appears to address big questions of mind and universe in the context of the American counterculture crises of the late 1960s and early 1970s, when there was "exaltation on many fronts" and "a sense of holiness growing up" (57). Its emphasis is on the theme of unity, the "full circle" of the journey—not merely the arc tracing beginning to end, as in Joseph Campbell's analyses of mythical travel, but the collapse of beginning and end into one. Indeed, "The System" brings us back to the trope of motionless travel, where movement is revealed as apparent, where "even the dullest of us knows enough to realize that he is ignorant of everything, including the basic issue of whether we are really moving at all" (74); where "the pendulum that throughout eternity has swung successively toward joy and grief had been stilled by a magic hand" (60). The young people of "The System" have come to realize that "the progress toward infinity had crystallized in them, that they in fact were the other they had been awaiting, and that any look outward . . . was as gazing into a mirror" (61). They see that "the twin urges, to act and to remain at peace with yourself," are the same (83), and, especially, that happiness is "both fixed and mobile at the same time" (83).

The realization of this unity, however, comes at the cost of a spiritual surrender, wherein

> all traces of doubt will have been pulverized by the influx of light slowly mounting to bury those crass seamarks of egocentricity and warped self-esteem you were able to navigate by but which you no longer need now that the rudder has been swept out of your hands, and this whole surface of daylight has become one with that other remembered picture of light, when you were setting out. (80)

The loss of mastery described here is often seen, in Buddhist as well as in Romantic and Symbolist thought, as requisite to awakening. Rimbaud's "Le Bateau Ivre" depicts a similarly liberating but deadly sea voyage: "The typhoon spun my silly needle round. . . . / Rudderless, I was driven like a plank / on night seas stuck with stars and dribbling milk" (Lowell's translation, *Imitations* 81–82; ellipsis added). The helplessness is exchanged for the transcendence that follows: "then heaven opened for the voyager. / I stared at archipelagoes of stars. / Was it on those dead watches that I died— / a million golden birds, Oh future Vigor!" (83).

In the discourse of mysticism, one is forced to give up the ego when the voyage's intensity sweeps worldly instruments and assumptions out of one's hands. At this point, the light engulfing the traveler becomes one with the memory of the light of first setting out—that is, in Freudian and Wordsworthian imagery, the still-remembered light of infantile oceanic consciousness, always there, waiting to emerge once the ego is cast aside and linearity is revealed as illusion. This identity of light is the "full circle" so often invoked in "The System": "[I]t is certain now that these two ways are the same . . . the risk and the security . . . an amalgam of both, the faithful reflection of the idealistic concept that got us started along this path" (81). The collapsing of distinctions, whether of risk and security, action and inaction, or beginning and end, leads eventually to Ashbery's rewriting of Robert Frost:

> You discovered that there was a fork in the road, so first you followed what seemed to be the less promising, or at any rate the more obvious, of the two branches until you felt you had a good idea of where it led. Then you returned to investigate the more tangled way, and for a time its intricacies seemed to promise a more complex and therefore a more practical goal for you. . . . And in so doing you began to realize that the two branches were

joined together again, farther ahead; that this place of joining was indeed the end, and that it was the very place you set out from, whose intolerable mixture of reality and fantasy had started you on the road which has now come full circle. (90)

In this version of travel, there is no road not taken. The terminals of birth and death, as of home and abroad, meet and are one. In Frost's poem, "knowing how way leads on to way" is knowing that no return is possible; in Ashbery's, "you returned to investigate the more tangled way" (though even Frost concedes, the ways were not much different—"the passing there / Had worn them really about the same" [105]) and found it more to your liking.

Eventually, the speaker views this sameness from an even wider perspective: one need never have chosen a path; indeed, one need never have left the house. Not only were the choices themselves illusory, but also no difference exists between traveler and nontraveler—both are in motion in the passage of time:

One must move very fast in order to stay in the same place, as the Red Queen said. . . . [Y]ou must still learn to cope with the onrushing tide of time and all the confusing phenomena it bears in its wake, some of which perfectly resemble the unfinished but seemingly salvageable states of reality at cross-purposes with itself that first caused you to grow restless. (90–91)

No one escapes "travel," then: one is in motion relative to the rush of time, and those unsatisfactory "states of reality" that first prompted the travel impulse—Ashbery at his most supremely general—cannot be purged from the "System."

In the final pages of "The System," the full-circle theme returns ("Today your wanderings have come full circle" [101]), together with a history of "your" way of living—your early rejection of unity in favor of multiple lives and your subsequent realization that diversity is only apparent, that all the "individualistic ways" actually merge with each other. This final emphasis on unity culminates, at the end of "The System" (and on through "The Recital"), in a reversion that may seem surprising in a poet such as John Ashbery. Throughout *Three Poems*, we had been repeatedly warned against nostalgia, particularly for those Ur-sites on which travelers pin religious hopes. "There must be nothing resembling nostalgia for a past which in any case never existed," the narrator warns (19). Moreover, once one is infused with the "new spirit," "one can then go about one's business unencumbered by nostalgia" (28). But the speaker now claims to repudiate the indeterminate, diverse, and inclusive realities we associate with the postmodern. Now he embraces nostalgia.

Specifically, he embraces movies, with their "windows on the past" that tempt the narrator back toward presence, unity, and coherence, arguing against the indeterminacy and moral poverty of contemporary thinking. The artifice of movies now stands for what is knowable about ourselves. Movies enable us to "stay on an even keel in the razor's-edge present which is really a no-time," but in which "Unfortunately we have to live" (102–3). As appalling as the present is, the movies can save us from it and restore us to life:

> But only focus on the past through the clear movie-dark and you are a changed person, and can begin to live again. . . . [W]e can live as though we had caught up with time and avoid the sickness of the present, a shapeless blur as meaningless as a carelessly exposed roll of film. There is hardness and density now, and our story takes on the clear compact shape of the plot of a novel. (103)

The present is "sickness," its narrative blurred and meaningless. Only a hard, dense, and clear story can offer us meaning. The speaker complains that the present story has too many "adventures," "pleasures," and "experiences that somehow don't fit in but which loom larger and more interesting as they begin to retreat into the past" (103):

> There were so many things held back, kept back, because they didn't fit into the plot or because their tone wasn't in keeping with the whole. . . . One sometimes forgets that to be all one way may be preferable to eclectic diversity in the interests of verisimilitude. (104)

Again, the passage refers both to a mode of composition and a way of life. Congruent with the emphasis throughout "The System" on the "full circle" and on unity, the narrator rejects postmodern eclecticism, preferring the sameness of "all one way" as the mode of greatest power. Indeed, he argues that "the most powerful preachers" teach lessons that are

> deeply moving just because of this rigidity, having none of the tepidness of the meandering stream of our narration with its well-chosen and typical

episodes, which now seems to be burying itself in the landscape. The rejected chapters have taken over. For a long time it was as though only the most patient scholar or the recording angel himself would ever interest himself in them. Now it seems as though that angel had begun to dominate the whole story: he who was supposed only to copy it all down has joined forces with the misshapen, misfit pieces that were never meant to go into it but at best to stay on the sidelines so as to point up how everything else belonged together, and the resulting mountain of data threatens us; one can almost hear the beginning of the lyric crash in which everything will be lost and pulverized, changed back into atoms ready to resume new combinations and shapes again, new wilder tendencies, as foreign to what we have carefully put in and kept out as a new chart of elements or another planet—unimaginable, in a word. (104)

But something curious happens in this passage, which begins by preferring the powerful (because rigid and homogeneous) lesson of the preacher and ends by arguing for the return of the repressed "foreign" content. Indeed, the first contrast the passage sets out is not a contrast at all: that between the preacher's "all one way" discourse, on the one hand, and "our narration with its well-chosen and typical episodes," on the other. These seem equally formed and equally guilty of leaving out the dynamic but not well-formed elements that now gather into a "lyric crash." What finally has power, what finally *takes over*, are the "rejected chapters," the "misshapen, misfit pieces."

Of many such self-referential passages in Ashbery's work, of many blazons en abime, this one directly engages the point of the poet's lifted rhetorics and establishes the rhetor's position regarding them. What is the alternative to these rhetorics, any one of which wields power but none of which the speaker can identify himself with completely or for long? A tepid, "meandering stream," even more hackneyed than "the rejected chapters" which interested no one but the "recording angel himself"? That angel is, in fact, now the dominant force behind "the whole story," and the "rejected chapters" gather themselves into a mountain of data about to fall on our heads.

And would you believe that this word could possibly be our salvation? For we are rescued by what we cannot imagine: it is what finally takes us up and shuts our story, replacing it among the millions of similar volumes. . . . At last we have that rightness that is rightfully ours. But we do not know what brought it about. (104–5)

The poet's ambivalence about nostalgia is just this, that those past spurious subjectivities, which made claims for truth and agency and which Ashbery rejects implicitly through most of his work, still lie there in the rigid "false" rhetorics abandoned by contemporary thinking, to be recuperated, if only momentarily, by the poet. In those rhetorics, as in the movies, inheres at least *something*—"that rightness that is rightfully ours." In fact, the poet has been drawn into rhetorics that he dreamed he was merely collecting, parodying, and trying on for size in the absence of any language of his own; he "who was supposed only to copy it all down has joined forces" with it. The "lyric crash" that threatens us marks the end of any distinction between what one has left out and what one has included. Remember how *Three Poems* begins: "I thought that if I could put it all down, that would be one way. And next the thought came to me that to leave it all out would be another, and truer, way" (3). If this inclusion/exclusion choice constitutes another collapsing set, it is perhaps the master set of the poem's making. The "mountain of data" building up around the sidelines of a planned construction, "foreign to what we have carefully put in and kept out," has already collapsed; the "unimaginable" has already happened. No distinction is maintainable between what is and what is made.

"The Recital," the last, shorter prose poem of *Three Poems*, completes the discussion of the construction's indistinguishability from the raw materials left out of it. The illusion of a separate, created, "real" thing keeps surfacing, only to be submerged again.

> No, but this time something real did seem to be left over. . . . At first it seemed to be made merely of bits and pieces of the old, haggard situations. . . . Then it became apparent that certain new elements had been incorporated, though perhaps not enough of them to change matters very much. (117)

The speaker tacks back and forth during this final section of the book, but the collapse of the alternatives leads him finally to the unity developed in "The System." This time the unity is not of the journey's beginning and end, nor of apparent forking paths, but of the included and excluded rhetorics of the poem's composition:

> But already it was hard to distinguish the new elements from the old, so calculated and easygoing was the fusion, the partnership that was the only element now, and which was even now fading rapidly from memory. (118)

Revisiting the Frostian dilemma of forking paths and its compositional correlative of what material to include, "The Recital" argues that a narrative requires choices, just as thinking requires, in Borges's words, "forgetting a difference." We must return to the Argentine fabulist a last time. The protagonist of Borges's story "Funes, the Memorious" is an idiot-savant who sees and remembers everything. Unable to reduce any observation to a category—unable to think, in other words—he lives in a world overwhelmed with data, which his memory is capacious enough to name and which he sets out to catalogue in an endless dictionary of irreducible specificities (for example, a dog seen in full profile at 3 P.M. requires a different name than the same dog seen in three-quarter profile at 3:01 P.M.). "The Recital" is a response to that hopeless task and that hopeless perceptual mode: choosing a path and following it, however much regretting the "road not taken," is the price of coherence, a price the speaker here, as often throughout *Three Poems*, suggests we pay. After all, our *shaping* of data, not the mountain or chaos of data itself, produces meaning. We must exclude a great deal to make the plots of our stories cohere. Indeed, the speaker advises us to forget about verisimilitude, arguing that "to be all one way" is better. But oneness is in peril because the repressed material hovers and threatens, demanding inclusion in (and as) the real. Such an inundation of data will destroy everything we have carefully put in and left out. Yet, the speaker suggests, it will save us, not by eliminating narratives but by substituting new and needed, if always provisional, ones.

That the voyage has been imaginary, that the speaker has been seeing all this in a film does not diminish it. To the contrary, the data had to be shaped: a story, a voyage, or a movie does that work of shaping. Exiting the theater at the end of "The System," he wonders how to go on living "except by plunging into the middle of some other [movie] you have doubtless seen before" (106).

Three Poems deals with collapsing oppositions. Certainly home and travel collapse, but so do maps and territories, parody and parodied, staged and nonstaged, and irony and "sincerity." With its extravagant spirituality—highly conventionalized and yet rhetorically subverted by ruptures and non sequiturs—*Three Poems* is perhaps the strongest example of the ways in which the trope of travel can illuminate the function of irony, the pathos of the erased hope of presence, and the primacy of artifice in Ashbery's poetry. In addition, these prose poems illustrate how the figure of an ecstatic movement away from the patria can begin by seeming childish and solipsistic and end in a liberating transcendence; how the topos and rhetorics of travel are both infantilized and spiritualized (sequentially, if we move from Ashbery's 1950s poems to those of the 1970s). The liberation that banishes time and care is the recapitulation of infantile irresponsibility at a new level. But even in Ashbery at his most ironic, questions of travel—travel as figure for time's passage, as the map's failure before the territory or the territory's before the map, and as the unstable subject in transit across borders—are all concerns at the heart of the poetry, not vitiated by parody.

So I dream nightly of an embarkation,

. . . .

And a long journey unaccomplished

   yet, on antique seas

rolling in gray barren dunes under

   the world's waste of light

toward ports of childish geography

GINSBERG, "Siesta in Xbalba," *Collected Poems*

Shooting the Gulf

Three Beat Questions of Travel

In *American Poetry and Culture, 1945–1980,* Robert von Hallberg catalogues American poets who traveled or lived abroad in the 1950s, including Charles Olson, who spent a year in the Yucatan; W. S. Merwin, who lived in England, Spain, and France (later in southern Mexico and Hawaii); Robert Lowell, who spent two years in Europe; Elizabeth Bishop, who had been traveling since the mid-1930s and who settled in Petropolis, near Rio de Janeiro, in 1951; James Merrill, who lived in Rome and later in Greece; James Wright, who had a Fulbright to Vienna; Richard Howard, who was studying at the Sorbonne; Adrienne Rich, who had a Guggenheim year in Europe; Robert Creeley, who moved to Mallorca in 1952; Richard Wilbur, who won the Prix de Rome fellowship in 1954; and John Ashbery, who left to Paris on a Fulbright and stayed for ten years.

This list can be supplemented by cataloguing American poets of a different stamp and by extending the time frame slightly. George Oppen, Muriel Rukeyser, and Denise Levertov, like Olson, all lived in Mexico; Paul Blackburn, Allen Ginsberg, William Bronk, and many others wrote there. Ginsberg, Bronk, Nathaniel Tarn, and Clayton Eshleman also traveled to Peru. Olson's letters to Creeley from the Yucatan celebrated the Mayan hieroglyphs, in which Olson found, as Pound had in Chinese, the model of a language for poetry. Indeed, the U.S. poets whose interests leaned toward Latin America are too numerous to list, as are the poets who translated, whether from Cuban, Chilean, Peruvian, or Mexican poetry and whether from Spanish or from indigenous languages. Many writers on the West Coast tended to look west, that is, to the "Far East." Both Gary Snyder and Kenneth Rexroth spent years in Japan, where Cid Corman edited and published the poetry magazine *Origen* out of Kyoto.

Ginsberg traveled and lived in the Yucatan, Spain, Morocco, Italy, and Germany in the 1950s. In the 1960s, he traveled in Greece, Israel, India, Vietnam, Japan, Cuba, Poland, Czechoslovakia, Russia, and again France and Morocco. Later, like Rexroth, Rukeyser, and Snyder, he lived in India, eventually becoming a Tibetan Buddhist. Ginsberg would write many travel poems, but *Howl* is already a travel poem, as the poet writes of Kerouac, Burroughs, Snyder, and Neal Cassady:

> who retired to Mexico to cultivate a habit, or Rocky Mount to tender
> Buddha or Tangier to boys or South Pacific to the black locomotive
> or Harvard to Narcissus to Woodlawn to the daisychain or grave.
> (18)

In the 1960s, Donald Allen referred to the "international school of poetry," thinking of the negritude poets; of Kenneth Rexroth, who translated from the Chinese and Japanese; and of "deep image" poets such as Robert Bly, James Wright, Clayton Eshleman, and Jerome Rothenberg, who translated from Lorca, Vallejo, Neruda, Transtromer, Apollinaire, and others. By the 1970s, Howard Moss, then poetry editor of the *New Yorker*, had begun to deplore what he called the "international style": too many American poets were influenced, he thought, by poetry in translation, by Chilean surrealism, or by the Russian or Swedish tone, and not by the materiality and muscularity of English. Poets had stopped trying to write like Yeats, Auden, or even Lowell, whose "translationese" carried over from his versions of

Montale, Ungaretti, and Rimbaud into his own later poems. If Lowell's translation style was not travel per se, it was certainly border crossing—not purifying but problematizing, even, for some, betraying, the "language of the tribe."

To understand the travel impulses of the beats and related poets of the period and to distinguish them from those of the Pound-Eliot era, as well as from established poets of the 1950s and 1960s such as Lowell, we would need to remember the travel of the French Symbolists, the travels and travel fantasies of Nerval and Rimbaud, the travel poems of Baudelaire, and, several decades later, the poetry and travel of Antonin Artaud, who took peyote with the Tarahumara Indians, hoping to enrich or supplant his European mind-set with a magical, collective consciousness. Artaud may have been a primitivist, but travel, for him as for some English and American writers, was an antidote to modernity, an escape from dehumanizing capitalist labor and from spiritual moribundity.

In this chapter, I examine three separate but interrelated questions of travel: Allen Ginsberg's travel seen as a critique of home, in the senses I have just mentioned; Gary Snyder's scroll-like poem *Mountains and Rivers without End*, whose form raises the issue of the constructedness of travel in a rather different way than Ashbery's poetry does; and Robert Creeley's reintroduction of a central topos of the present book, that is, the anxiety and remorse attached to travel and their effect on both the sensibility and the poetics of the traveler.

Economy, Ecstasy, and Critical Travel (Ginsberg)

Midcentury travel abroad by Americans, although advertised as "getting away from it all," was not ordinarily anti-American. Those modestly affluent Americans who toured France and Italy with *Europe on Five Dollars a Day* in hand experienced travel as scenic, cultural, historical, gastronomic, and erotic, without entertaining any notions of something wrong at home. This situation changed in the 1960s, when for a younger generation of travelers, with many writers among them, travel took the form of a critique of the West, its systems of economy and labor, its desacralized society, and its exploitative geopolitics. Usually this travel-as-critique is toward or in non-Western or developing countries. As in John Ashbery's poetry, the idea of travel as critique owes something to Freud. Travel, Freud notes, is always *from* a place as much as it is *to* a place, and thus it implies a rejection of the place one leaves, explicit or not. While Freud never developed an actual "travel theory," many of his best-known ideas—scopophilia, the uncanny, the return of the repressed, the Oedipus complex, the struggle between the pleasure and reality principles, and particularly transference—are rich sources for understanding both the motivations behind travel and the experiences of the traveling subject.[1]

For the travelers in question here, the objects of critique are first the ugly systematism of America, its jobs, mortgages, installment plans, and instruction manuals, and second, concomitantly, its soulless secularism, its shortage of ecstasy, religious or sexual. The escape is from "Moloch," as Ginsberg's *Howl* names it. The religious hopes attached to travel are a measure not only of the intensity of the longing for the other place but also of the repudiation of what is found on United States soil and in U.S. depredations abroad. "There is a god / dying in America," Ginsberg writes in Mexico in the 1950s, contrasting this dying god with, a few lines later,

> an inner
anterior image
of divinity
beckoning me out
to pilgrimage.
(*CP* 105–6)

In an early poem, Gary Snyder—who traveled most often on the U.S. West Coast and not by plane or train but on foot or by hitchhiking—sets out with unusual clarity the oppositions of work and play, profane and spiritual, and mundane and transcendent, but without recourse to travel abroad or to indictments against Moloch.[2] In the Pacific Northwest in the 1960s, he writes,

> Hitched north all of Washington
Crossing and re-crossing the passes
Blown like dust, no place to work.

> Climbing the steep ridge below Shuksan
  clumps of pine
  float out of the fog

No place to think or work
   drifting.

. . . .

I must turn and go back:
   caught on a snowpeak
   between heaven and earth
And stand in lines in Seattle
Looking for work.
(*Rip Rap* 2–3)

Snyder's title, "The Late Snow & Lumber Strike of the Summer of Fifty-Four," like Ashbery's "The Instruction Manual," suggests an economic circumstance, but the poem is imbued with the Japanese haiku's pathos and serenity. The image of "clumps of pine / [that] float out of the fog" evokes the scrolls of Sesshu and Snyder's later *Mountains and Rivers without End*, in which the mist—actually empty space on the scroll—veils the connectedness of peaks and treetops to earth so that they seem to float in space. In the context of this serenity of picture and tone (even the distress of being "[b]lown like dust" evokes Basho's *Back Roads to Far Towns*), it almost escapes notice that every other line concerns, as does the title, the need for work, shelter, and survival.

Unlike a British pastoral poem, whose poet may stand on a crowded London street dreaming of the solitude of a wooded island, here the narrator must make the opposite trek, to leave behind the unpeopled landscape and return to the city, where he will "stand in lines," resuming his role in industrial capitalism. Snyder's turn back from the heights of nature toward the city and work does not critique value as unequivocally as Ginsberg's excoriations of the West, but it nevertheless implies the predicament of being "caught . . . between heaven and earth"; the journey ahead, for the time being, is clearly toward earth.

In Ginsberg, travel as critique has more typically meant the movement away from the patria's demands of work and responsibility, toward an alternate world of spirituality and gratification. (Spiritual aspirations are seldom ascetic in Ginsberg.) "What childishness is it that while there's a breath of life / in our bodies we are determined to rush / to see the sun the other way around?" asks Elizabeth Bishop in "Questions of Travel" (*Complete* 93). If Bishop's view of childishness is at all pejorative, Ginsberg's is not. His phrase "childish geography" acknowledges the traveler's naïve projections onto the other place, projections that set up an overt struggle between play and transgression, on the one hand, and duty and guilt, on the other. Ginsberg was arguably the most candidly adolescent of American poets when celebrating the ecstasy lying on the other side of economy: "Haha! what do I want? Change of solitude, spectre of drunkenness in para- / noiac taxicabs, fear and gaiety of unknown lovers"(*CP* 159).

The "innocent, astonished, ravished" voice that Richard Howard attributed to John Ashbery's poetic personae (34) is practically a generic convention in the poetry of Ginsberg, Gregory Corso, Lawrence Ferlinghetti, and indeed poets not associated with the beats, notably Kenneth Koch and Frank O'Hara. The latter poet, traveling in Spain, writes:

I think of you
and the continents brilliant and arid
and the slender heart you are sharing my share of with the American air.
("Now that I Am in Madrid and Can Think" 356)

The grand scope and the unabashed adolescent but surreal romanticism— less so the deft dactyls and near rhymes of "brilliant and arid" and "sharing my share of"—could as easily be Ginsberg's, as could, in many other poems by O'Hara, the homosexual desire and scatology. Travel in O'Hara—as in Ashbery and Ginsberg—promises oral, sexual, and economic gratification. The release from constraints is sometimes, as in "A Little Travel Diary," put in the most primal sense possible:

there for the first time
since arriving in Barcelona I can freely shit
and the surf is so high and the sun is so hot
and it was all built yesterday as everything should be
what a splendid country it is.
(357–58)

In Ashbery, O'Hara, and Ginsberg, orality and sexual gratification are the chief objects of travel as escape. We can see this as much in Ashbery's book-length *Flow Chart* as we can in Ginsberg's rhapsodies about Mexico and the unabashedly exploitative sexual economics of a favorable exchange rate:

To Mexico! To Mexico! . . .
genitals and thighs and buttocks under skin and leather.

Music! Taxis! Marijuana in the slums! Ancient sexy parks! . . . And here's a
hard brown cock for a quarter!

(*CP* 159)

In Mexico in the mid-1950s, writing of a Europe, Morocco, and India
he has not yet visited, Ginsberg, in "Siesta in Xbalba," fabricates a childish
fantasy of those places, with an excitement built entirely of anticipation.
He imagines Europe as a "continent in rain, / black streets, old night, a
/ fading monument" and himself in North Africa as "penniless among
the Arab / mysteries of dirty towns around / the casbahs of the docks"
(105). He romanticizes being "penniless," seeing (or projecting) the poverty
and squalor of the other place as attractive alternatives to the glut and
sanitization of home. The last section of "Siesta in Xbalba" takes the form
of a series of rhetorical questions—"Toward what city / will I travel? What
wild houses / do I go to occupy?" (105)—pointing up, in Symbolist fashion,
the gap between the present of imagination and the future of the unknown.
But Ginsberg is adolescent, naïve, and kitsch at the same time that he is
Symbolist and transcendental:

I alone know the great crystal door
    to the House of Night,
a legend of centuries
    —I and a few Indians.

And had I mules and money I could find
    the Cave of Amber
and the Cave of Gold
    rumored of the cliffs of Tumbala.

(103)

One might find these images in *The Raiders of the Lost Ark* or its predecessors,
H. Rider Haggard's *She* and W. H. Hudson's *Green Mansions*. While writing
in a personal and expressivist mode, Ginsberg nonetheless draws on exotic
adventure lore, ironized but not necessarily distanced from the poet's own
romantic projections and concerns.

The traveler's turn away from the West's instrumental reason, science, and
organization, though it provides a critical perspective, may be as disturbing
as it is liberating. Travel is more often an unraveling than a consolidation,
more a loss, however productive, than a gain. Of the poets discussed here,

this loss, particularly in the form of disintegrating identity, is most obvious in Ginsberg and illustrates a register much less comic and self-gratifying than the previous examples from his poetry. In "Patna-Benares Express" (1963), for example, he writes:

> no money in the bank of dust
> no nation but inexpressible gray clouds before sunrise
> lost his identity cards in his wallet
> in the bald rickshaw by the Maidan in dry Patna
> Later stared hopeless waking from drunken sleep
> dry mouthed in the RR station.
> (300)

In "Galilee Shore," he writes, "I have no name I wander in a nameless countryside" (289). In Warsaw, admiring the beautiful youth, the poet sees himself as a "wild haired madman who sits weeping among you a stranger" (351). In "The Moments Return," he recalls his "vow to record" (352) but, approached by a stranger, realizes he is helpless to do the one thing vital to a poet: "Alas, all I can say is 'No Panamay'—I can't speak" (352).

But loneliness and loss of orientation and language are just the beginning. Ginsberg writes third-world dystopia as if he were V. S. Naipaul on a bad acid trip. Take his 1962 vision of Calcutta:

> Forty feet long sixty feet high hotel
> Covered with old gray fur buzzing flies
> Eye like mango flowing orange pus
> Ears Durga people vomiting in their sleep
> Got huge legs a dozen buses move inside Calcutta
> Swallowing mouthfuls of dead rats
> Mangy dogs bark out of a thousand breasts
> Garbage pouring from its ass behind alleys
> Always pissing yellow Hooghly water.
> ("Heat" 294)

These catalogues, and others from Ginsberg's international travel poems, are grislier even than those of *Howl*. The hallucinatory misery suggests subjective horror, a shift from description as a log of events transpiring in the world to a log of internal psychic and physical miseries. The eighteen-page "Angkor Watt" (1963) is traumatic from its opening stanzas: "shivering / and throat choking / with upsurge / of stroke fear / cancer Bubonic /

heart failure / bitter stomach juices / a wart growing on my rib"(306). The physical fears and threats proliferate through these lines, from the external cold to nausea and vomiting to the imagined cancer, plague, and heart failure and finally to the minor symptoms of a wart and "bitter stomach juices." None of these real travel possibilities bears particular relation to the geographic and historical Angkor Watt, the Cambodian temple to Vishnu built in the thirteenth century. Ginsberg's hypochondriac poetics allows the catalogue of internal ills to spread out and finally to substitute for the exterior landscape. Travel to the *interior*, to use the term from nineteenth-century exploration texts (and from Bishop's poem "Arrival at Santos"), inevitably involves one's own interior. Travels back into time, whether in the more parodic and dreamlike "Siesta in Xbalba," where the land that time forgot is imagined in pulp-novelistic terms, or in literal travel to developing, non-Western, preindustrial societies, are also travels downward into the self and the body.

In "The Change: *Kyoto-Tokyo Express*" (1963), written a month after the previous poem, the dystopia is all interior: "vomit thru / tears, snot ganglia buzzing" (325), horrific images of masochistic physical and sexual anguish, "shitting the meat out of / my ears on my cancer deathbed," and "crying dysentery boneface on / the urinal street of the Self" (326). Most of the poem is a sequel to the earlier paranoia in India, occasionally with Indian allusions ("Kali mother hung with / nightmare skulls" [327]) and, despite the title, no reference to Japan.

The "I" of Ginsberg's travel poems, while sometimes Yahweh-like ("I am that I am" [327]), agonizes in a swamp of obsessional neuroses, paranoia, and horror of the repressed, which, in the manner of Whitman, the poet tries to embrace: "Yes I am that worm soul"; "I am / a mass of sores and worms / and baldness and belly and smell" (327). Bemoaning his separation from his own image, however, the poet moves in "The Change" toward a prayer of reconciliation, addressed to God and Self: "Come, sweet lonely Spirit, back / to your bodies, come great God / back to your only image, come / to your many eyes & breasts" (328). The reconciliation is both personal and spiritual. To Ginsberg, one's interior, if it exists, lies back in time and down in the body. If these are constructed axes of the imagination, they are no less real for that: praying, beseeching, and invoking *up*ward has been the pattern in most societies. Similarly, one grows *up*, presumably into a higher consciousness, as one dies *down*, back into the earth. But the myth of the return characteristic of traditional cultures, as Mircea Eliade explains it, entails a downward journey. The invitation, the call offered in "The Change," is for the spirit to descend into the morass of desire, illness, "sores and worms" that the flesh is heir to. Once the traveler's gaze shifts, as it does in these poems, from the outer to the inner landscape, the vertical rather than the horizontal travel axis predominates.

Ginsberg's long "Wichita Vortex Sutra," written back on American soil, searches the nation's heartland for the source of its homegrown evil and its depredations in Southeast Asia and Latin America. Some sections of the poem place the speaker in Vietnam, China, and Guatemala, suggesting that the flight from America toward more "authentic" or spiritual sites— imbued, of course, with the Western traveler's projections—is complicated by the signs or residua of "home" abroad: "The first thing we see as we travel round the world is our own filth, thrown into the faces of mankind," complains Lévi-Strauss in *Tristes Tropiques* (38). What Ginsberg's traveler sees on the streets of Vietnam is United States based, but, as in the travel poems of Lowell, the traveler's psychology overwhelms the specificities of place. The "flight" from the Mekong Delta is the flight from the United States within oneself as much as without.

> I fled the Mekong delta, fled the 12,000
>   Military speaking hot dog guts on the
>   downtown aircooled streets,
> fled the Catinat Hotel, flushed my shit
>   down the bathroom—
>
> jumped in the cab suddenly, afraid
> after left Xaloi temple like a
>   Negro disintegrated in New Orleans,
> afraid to publish that or they bomb
>   my typesetter's woodsy Balcony
>   in Louisiana—
>
> Everywhere it's the fear I got in my own
>   intestines—
> (*CP* 318)

While "elsewhere" (India, Vietnam, Mexico, or Japan) easily underwrites critiques of home, Ginsberg's Whitmanesque, panoramic, freewheeling road poems jotted down in buses, cars, and planes across the United States also offer pointed critiques, as one of his book titles suggests: *The Fall of America*, a continuation of the "poem of these states" begun with "Wichita Vortex Sutra" (from *Planet News*). In the "After Words" to *The Fall of America*, Ginsberg explains, borrowing from Whitman, that this "long poem of these States" continues the

> chronicle taperecorded scribed by hand or sung condensed, the flux of car bus airplane dream consciousness Person during Automated Electronic War years . . . headlights flashing on road through these States of Consciousness. (189)

In the book, the poet begins in the Northwest, travels down through California, across the Midwest to the East Coast, returns to the West, and then makes a leap across the Pacific, ending with a lament for the Vietnam War. A good part of the long travel sequences "Thru the Vortex West Coast to East 1965–1966" and "Zigzag Back thru These States 1966–1967," together covering seventy-three pages, consists of radio news of the war, advertisements, religious services, talk shows, and, most of all, music, along with the poet's commentary on these, rather than description of what passes by the car or bus window. Sometimes the news, opinions, and music are collaged so as to be almost indistinguishable: "Shanghai water power cut off by Mao's enemies / I am a Rock, I am an Island—radio souls cry" (*Fall* 66). In the first pages of the sequence, each place visited begins a line—"At Nespelem," "At Grand Coulee," "On plains toward Pasco" (1)—but each place is also a heard melody, not emanating from that place but from more centrally commodified sources; thus: "Walking Boogie teenager's tender throats, 'I wish they all could be California girls,'" "Bob Dylan's voice on airways, mass machine-made folksong of one soul," and "Radio the soul of the nation. The Eve of Destruction and The Universal Soldier" (1).

The critique is of the music as an emanation of the very things some of the songs purport to attack—remembering that one of those popular folk-rock songs, "The Eve of Destruction," was a commercialization of protest music. Similarly, in "Kansas City to Saint Louis," Ginsberg writes,

> artificial rock & roll, Beach Boys
> & Sinatra's daughter overdubbed microphone

antennae'd car dashboard vibrating
False emotions broadcast thru the Land
Natural voices made synthetic,
                phlegm obliterated
Smart ones work with electronics—
(56)

Far from inspirational, the radio emanations are sinister. The music and messages do not complement the geography or the inner world. Instead,

Hypnosis of airwaves
In the house you can't break it
        unless you turn off yr set
In the car it can drive yr eyes inward
        from the snowy hill,
        withdraw yr mind from the birch forest
                make you forget the blue car in the ice,
Drive your mind down Supermarket aisles
        looking for cans of Save-Your-Money Polishing-Glue
made of human bones manufactured in N. Vietnam
        during a mustard gas hallucination:
        The Super-Hit sound of All American Radio.
(56)

The poem itself, reflecting the inescapability and fascination of the radio, testifies to the hypnotic potential of that medium. Advertising mantras numb the traveler to the natural world around him, while they exhort him to buy products whose manufacture entails exploitation of foreign resources and peoples. Ginsberg wrote these lines well before the advent of postcolonial theory, but "culture" and "imperialism," to borrow key words from an Edward Said title, are very much in league in the broadcasts saturating this listener. The synthetic voices and false emotions, the popular songs Ginsberg cites—*"Home I'm Comin Home I am a Soldier—" / "The girl I left behind . . . / I did the best job I could / Helping to keep our land free / I am a soldier,"* and many more, not all directly associated with the Vietnam War—"lull" us "into War" at the same time that they train us to buy (56; ellipsis added). The poem's collage style demonstrates that the "Super-Hit" song, the "Save-Your-Money" product, and the human loss on Asian battlefields are not separate phenomena but part of the one "Moloch," the critical object of most of Ginsberg's life's work. The demonic emanations, as Ginsberg depicts them, infiltrate every part of the nation: "Isolate farmhouses with radios / hearing the Horror Syndicate / take over the Universe!" (24).

The American individualist dream of driving down the highway in one's own car is compromised by the fact that the car is equipped with the very instruments and voices one wished to escape by buying the car, illustrating the forms of modern hegemony, not centralized but dispersed, even "implanted" in each person. At the time Ginsberg wrote, before cell phones, pagers, and palm pilots, this implantation applied only to each individual car and home, not yet each individual body. But the radio is nevertheless "shoving voices into myriad innocent ears" (23), voices that take the form of love and "protest" songs, as well as spiritual, martial, and patriotic songs "pulsing through radio stations. . . . What Patriot wrote that shit? Something to drive out the Indian / Vibrato of Buffie St. Marie? / Doom call of McGuire? / The heavenly echo of Dylan's despair" (24; ellipsis added). These latter are the voices to which Ginsberg imputes authenticity and an alternative set of values, but they are drowned out by "Come to Jesus / where the money is! / Texas voice / singing Vietnam Blues / Twanging / 'I don't like to die / I'm a man I ain't about t'crawl' " (23–24).

In these U.S. travel poems, Ginsberg's critique is consistent with that he mounts from abroad, in that the music, like its source, is "false," "artificial," or "synthetic," obliterating its grounding in the body ("phlegm") and alienating the listener from nature and the present moment. Of course, this critique has been established and hallowed by two centuries of poetry—romantic, Georgian, and modernist—deploring the dehumanizing effects of technology and the alienation from nature. Ginsberg's expressivist poetics are thus traditional, particularly in that the speaking subject, whether anguished or elated, is always recognizable, often ailing and conflicted but seldom deconstructed. What differs are the terms of the critique, the specific American and global reference points, the first-thought-best-thought poetics, and the funny, prophetic, and hallucinatory sensibility.

The principal difference between Ginsberg's U.S.-based critique and his critique from abroad is that the "god / dying in America" is not offset, in the U.S. poems, by the promise of an alternative, "inner / anterior image / of divinity / beckoning me out / to pilgrimage" (CP 105–6). The Kerouac-like energy and excitement of the road still operates, but not the magical-religious hopes and aspirations the poet attaches to journeys abroad. I return to these lines about the "image / of divinity" also to emphasize an earlier idea: that the "divinity" lies in both an "inner" and an "anterior" image, reminding us that, at least as the Western subject usually perceives it, the journey backward in time ("Back out of all this now too much for us," as Frost wrote in "Directive," in a pastoral mode but running nevertheless from "Moloch") is also the journey to the interior.

Scrolling the Journey (Snyder)

I have discussed at length, particularly in my chapter on John Ashbery, the idea of travel as construction, as *not* biogeographic. Elizabeth Bishop prized imagination over "reality" but felt trapped by her "George Washington handicap." Robert Lowell, in *Day by Day* and notably in the poem "Epilogue," dwelt on this problem, asking "Why not say what happened?" yet never suggesting that one should or *could* say what happened. In Derek Walcott's endlessly textualized landscapes, too, "nature" is seen in mediated or textual terms.

Gary Snyder provides another variety of the world-as-imagined or world-as-text trope in his *Mountains and Rivers without End*, the long sequence he worked on intermittently during most of his writing life. The book's endpapers and frontispiece feature scenes from an early-twelfth-century Chinese scroll painting, "Streams and Mountains without End," and the first poem, "Endless Streams and Mountains," meditates on that painting. The painterly model is explicit: we are invited to read the "endless" landscape as we would a Chinese scroll (as perhaps Snyder wanted it printed), unrolling it on the left and rolling it up on the right. It unfolds to us scene after scene, where, as Snyder says in an earlier poem, "clumps of pine / float out of the fog" (*Rip-Rap* 2–3) or inland valleys open up to view, then close as a new mountain range rises from the plain or an inlet reveals fishermen or villagers dwarfed by the landscape. The Chinese scrolls belong to a genre of painting in which mountains, pines, valleys, and tiny boats float in and out of deep mists. Mist acts as a connective tissue such that the logic of one image need not cohere with that of another. The mist, like our own perceptive lapses while viewing or reading, obviates that need for coherence.

Snyder's epigraphs to the collection consist of a remark attributed to Buddha and several short glosses on that remark by Dogen, the thirteenth-century monk who introduced Soto Zen to Japan. One might think Buddha's remark—"A painted rice cake does not satisfy hunger"—self-revealing to a Zen student. It seems to invite us not to confuse a map with a territory, not to let representations and simulacra interfere with a material reality such as the body and its need for solid food. Why, as a Zen master once asked, look at the moon's reflection when you can look at the moon itself?

But Dogen's glosses suggest something different: that *only* the painted rice cake can satisfy, since all the phenomenal world is painting: "If you say that the painting is not real, then the material phenomenal world is not real, the Dharma is not real." And, finally, "Without painted hunger you never become a true person" (*MR* ix).

This latter remark, particularly, seems to offer a license to write, surprising perhaps from a Buddhist sage. Snyder prepared this ground in *No Nature*, a book that also presents nature as construction. The insight is crucial: nothing exists, not even "Nature," as a foundational referent for our interpretation. Plato's indictment of poets for merely representing (and that unfaithfully) fails to acknowledge that the object of the representation, real or ideal, is equally constructed. To turn that indictment around, a painter may say, as Jackson Pollock once did, "I *am* nature." Dogen's insight comes out of Buddhist philosophy rather than French or Californian postmodernism, but it leads to the same place: the collapse of the distinction between the real and the represented.

The structure of "Endless Streams and Mountains" mimes that of the painting as viewed by the poet as he stands in a Cleveland Museum, "[c]learing the mind and sliding in / to that created space" (5). Several verse paragraphs of description follow this preparation of the mind, leading us along the scroll's paths, trails, mountains, and streams. Well into the poem, and into the painting/scroll, we look inland: "gentle valley reaching inland / The watching boat has floated off the page" (6). While humans still occupy the landscape—travelers, plowers, homesteaders—the "watching boat" floating off seems to remove the last vestige of subject-object.

The poem's next stage is a transition from the painting to the glosses supplied by a series of owners and commentators. These are part of the artwork, not separate in the way art is conventionally separated from commentary in the West. "At the end of the painting, the scroll continues on with seals and poems. It tells a further tale" (7). The most interesting gloss is the first, written in 1205:

"The Fashioner of Things
    has no original intention
Mountains and Rivers
    are spirits condensed"
(7)

The others are unremarkable: "I love the company of streams and boulders," "truly a painting worth careful keeping," and, the final gloss written in the mid-seventeenth century, "My brother brought over this painting to show me" (7–8).

After reading all the commentaries, the viewer looks again at the landscape and instructs rather than quotes: "Step back and gaze again at the land" (8). The "Old ghost ranges"

                tell their tale,
    walk the path, sit the rains,
    grind the ink, wet the brush, unroll the
        broad white space:

    lead out and tip
    the moist black line.

    Walking on walking,
            under foot   earth turns.

    Streams and mountains never stay the same.
    (9)

This first poem frames the book in two concrete ways. First, the "moist black line" begins and ends a book about the art of evoking and the poignancy of having to end somewhere: "The space goes on," Snyder writes on the last page, but "the tip drawn to a point, / lifts away" (152).

Second, the lines "*Walking on walking / under foot   earth turns. / Streams and mountains never stay the same*" turn out not only to frame but also to permeate the book, appearing five more times in "The Mountain Spirit," where that spirit asks to hear the lines recited, and once at the end of the book's last poem, "Finding the Space in the Heart."

These lines seem to recapitulate Dogen's glosses in Snyder's epigraphs. Just as we understand Buddha's admonition that a painted rice cake is not a rice cake but fail to see that the "real" rice cake is also a construction; or, to move to a pre-Socratic model, just as we understand Heraclitus when he says you do not step into the same river twice but forget that the foot is just as ephemeral as the water, reconstituting its molecules by the moment; so we are likely to remember our mobility over the landscape but forget the landscape's mobility, at a different rate, underfoot. This is the first sense of the phrase "*Walking on walking*": that we walk over something—the turning earth—that is itself walking, a moving spirit, according to the poem "The Mountain Spirit" and to the first commentator on the painting. Everything lives and travels, not only the living traveler. The corollary sense is that representation is always layered, that a gloss or painting always precedes our own, that our representing, like our perceiving, is always mediated.

We often think of Asian poetry, especially the haiku forms that provide Snyder's models, as pictographic, but this is a misunderstanding, according to Rey Chow ("How" 72), on the part of Pound, Fenollosa, and, for that matter, Derrida. In fact haiku almost always emphasizes, as here, a moving moment, an unpinnable transience.

"Finding the Space in the Heart," the final poem of *Mountains and Rivers without End*, represents a quest undertaken to perceive and appreciate the past of the American land. It concerns a series of visits, from the 1960s to the 1990s, to the edge of the great continental basin, once an enormous sea, that lies to the east of the Cascade Mountains. The poem also tells the story of the poet's own vicissitudes, the circumstances that brought him, and the different mates and children who accompanied him over the decades, to this site.

This is a poem of travel in the most elementary sense, a description of covering ground: "Driving a Volkswagen camper . . . we came down from Canada" (ellipsis added) or

We followed the rim of the playa
to a bar where the roads end

and over a pass into Pyramid Lake
from the Smoke Creek side,
by the ranches of wizards
who follow the tipi path.
The next day we reached San Francisco
in a time when it seemed
the world might head a new way.
(*MR* 149)

The entire poem reads as a concrete travel account, but it also constitutes an homage to the object of the trip, the place where "it all drops away," where one sees the past, the vanished ocean:

the faint shorelines seen high on these slopes
long gone Lake Lahontan,
cutthroat trout spirit in silt—
Columbian Mammoth bones
four hundred feet up on the wave-etched
   beach ledge.
(150)

Beyond this shoreline stretches the vast, flat, and dusty plain, "mile after mile, trackless and featureless" (150). The language here belongs to the genre of "gaunt wastes" described in Paul Fussell's *Abroad*, though here it takes lyric rather than narrative form. The description of the vast, empty basin leads to a reflection at the heart of Snyder's book: the Buddhist realization of nothingness once binary oppositions are broken down, not only those of self and not-self but also of high and low, past and future:

all equal, far reaches, no bounds.
Sound swallowed away,
no waters, no mountains, no
bush no grass and
   because no grass
no shade but your shadow.
No flatness because no not-flatness.
No loss, no gain. So—
nothing in the way!

—the ground is the sky
the sky is the ground,
no place between.
(151)

The lines describe a condition of entropy and diffusion, but the genius of the place, as travel writers used to say, produces an understanding impossible in a forest or a city. Not only is "nothing in the way" to obstruct your movement in any direction but also the place offers no obstacle to the Buddhist realization of emptiness within all things: "all equal, far reaches, no bounds."

The poem's third movement describes the third trip, when, "now in the nineties desert night" (151), the poet returns to the site, finding the moment less mystical if more communal and down-to-earth: "old friends, old trucks, drawn around; / great arcs of kids on bikes out there in the darkness," eating "grasshoppers roasted in a pan," the "foolish loving spaces // full of heart" (151–52). Then, Snyder adds the now familiar: *"Walking on walking / under foot   earth turns. / Streams and mountains never stay the same"* (152).

"Walking on walking" might have closed this poem, the repetitions having built up rhetorical and thematic power throughout the sequence, were this not the final poem of a scroll-book. The book begins with the epigraph of a "painted" universe, and its first poem concerns a painting of mountains and rivers, which themselves paint out their existence, unrolling the space and "lead[ing] out and tip[ping] / the moist black line." That metaphor, then—the "art" metaphor—closes both poem and book:

The space goes on.
But the wet black brush
tip drawn to a point,
    lifts away.
(152)

The lines may signal not only the end of a piece of writing but also of a life of writing, if we note the place-dates at the end of the book: *"Marin-an 1956–Kitkitdizze 1996."* The metaphor is that of life as a writing and death as the moment when the brush tip, instrument of our inscription, rises, leaving the space to go on without us. Omar Khayam offers a different version, seeing a "Moving Finger" as writing our lives, as does Keats in his epitaph, where water is the page where life is written. Perhaps these precedents reinforce the metaphor. But the image of the Chinese ink brush and the delicacy of a "tip drawn to a point" that then "lifts away" make it the apt figure for the Zen traveler who realizes that, all along, the *space* lives and moves, not the subject who writes and lives on and through it.

Of twentieth-century American "nature" poets, Robert Frost, Robinson Jeffers, Theodore Roethke, and A. R. Ammons are perhaps those one thinks of most readily. Of these four, Ammons most resembles Snyder, particularly in his melding of the anthropological, ecological, and transcendent, though Ammons looks more to Emerson than to Asian or Amerindian lore. Neither Ammons nor Snyder is a poet of romantic or sublime exclamation, as Roethke or Jeffers often were. Neither constructs, as Frost did, a countrified persona spinning homilies (though late Ammons comes closest). And neither Ammons nor Snyder is as fond of poetic closure as Frost and Roethke were. Ammons and Snyder also share a penchant for description that is at once poetic and scientific. Snyder's volumes of poetry *Turtle Island*, *Regarding Wave*, and *No Nature* are often interlarded with ecological or scientific prose passages. (The phrase and the concept "no nature" appear also in Ammons: "there is no nature, / no nature of stones and brooks, stumps, and ditches" ["Tombstones," *Sumerian Vistas* 22].) Snyder's lines in "Endless Streams and Mountains"—"these spits of low ground, rocky uplifts / layered pinnacles aslant, / flurries of brushy cliff receding" (*MR* 5)—would be at home in any of a number of Ammons poems ("bending sandpit lakes, crescent / round groves of dwarf pines" ["Gravelly Run," *Selected* 11]; "mesquite roots / crazed the stone / and rains / moved glinting dust / down the crevices" ["I Came upon a Plateau," *Selected* 6]). In Snyder's "The Mountain Spirit," he writes, "Buttresses fractured, looming," "abraded gritty mudwash glide," and "barren flanks of magma-swollen uplands" (*MR* 144), again in the poetic-scientific vein of Ammons.

But it is not only the affinities of sensibility, style, and vocabulary that suggest the relevance of A. R. Ammons to what may appear a peculiarly Zen or West Coast sequence; a larger conceptual parallel exists as well. Ammons developed a scroll metaphor and project like *Mountains and Rivers without End* in several early typescripts, notably *Tape for the Turn of the Year*, first composed in 1963 with the title "Today" on a roll of adding machine tape.[3] The second day's entry of that sequence explains:

```
          the story, tho
                    contained,
          unwinds on this roll
          with time and event: grows
          like a tapeworm, segment
          by
          segments: turns
                    stream-corners: issues
          in low
          silence
                    like a snake
                    from its burrow: but
          unwinding and unwound it
          coils again on
          the floor
          into the unity of its
                    conflicts
          (12/7/63)
```

This sequence, typed between the narrow margins of the tape-scroll, explores its own continuous writing as Snyder's does. As we have seen, Snyder writes of the process:

> grind the ink, wet the brush, unroll the
>   broad white space:

> lead out and tip
> the moist black line.

As the space unrolls, the story unwinds. Ammons's *Tape* foregrounds the story's growing (like a tapeworm) and turning, issuing (like a snake from its burrow), unwinding, and coiling. The similes are not entirely fanciful, since the poet describes the form the tape takes as it accumulates on the floor or, later, coils in a wastebasket. Snyder's scroll-poem, while also self-referential, traces the story itself—not only its contours, that is, but also its content, the journeys not only of pen over paper but also of human over creek bed, *playa* (shore), and city. Ammons depicts the poem itself as a journey, with the same tug-of-war between duty and desire we have seen in other poets of travel. He writes, for example,

journey, journey, what is
   the way home?
home? who wants to go home?
what's wrong with these
   excitements, shows,
excursions?
. . . .
my poem is now twenty feet
long:
of course, it's a little
thin. . . .

   maybe this poem
will be all about getting
home
and figuring out some
excuse for leaving again:
that wd be good bth cmng &
gng:
(12/10/63; ellipsis added)[4]

The last two lines, shorthanded from Frost's "Birches," remind us of that idea most central to Ammons's poetics: the dynamism and restlessness of natural processes. "Corsons Inlet" is his most famous statement of this Heraclitean flux, *Garbage* a very late one, but the idea infuses all the poems, and the colon remains Ammons's most characteristic punctuation mark. The poem, "now twenty feet / long," he reflects, may be "all about getting / home," but home is not a place to go, only a place to turn from again in a different direction.

What gives *Tape*'s self-referential axis coherence are the geological, archeological, and anthropological reference points that Snyder and Ammons share. Both poets interrogate life and history to seek broad commonalities. In *Tape*, after meditating for several feet (not pages, in this case) on life since the Miocene and on the lateness of human arrival, Ammons arrives at the ultimate reduction of human activity: "get food: / get water: / get sex:" (12/9/63). Modern concerns and pursuits immediately muddy the formula's simplicity, however:

gets dense: play golf,
church clothes:
  lawn sod: boss:
social security:
    get food:
    get water:
    get sex:
(12/9/63)

The last three lines, a motif in *Tape*, appear as often as the "walking on walk-ing" of Snyder's book. Each time they appear, the accreted complication of contemporary Western life threatens them anew:

    get food:
    get water:
    get sex:
bank account, nice car,
good address, retirement
plan, investment portfolio,
country-club membership,
monogrammed shirts, summer
home, cabin cruiser, big
living room
(12/11/63)

The poem thus deals with the same moral and practical problem that oc-cupies Snyder's poetry: the need to live in a "primitive"—preindustrial and elemental—world, despite the obstacles. That dreamed-of world, however, presupposes a consciousness different from the one that contemplates it. What constitutes the "I" that seeks that world? For Snyder, as we saw, there are "no bounds . . . no waters, no mountains . . . [n]o flatness because no not-flatness . . . nothing in the way" (151), while for Ammons,

we are, as bodies,
"localizations"
supported by barriers,
  holding in &
  shutting out:

We are systems of
exclusion, permitting
certain inlets,
refusing others:
(12/10/63)

Of these two inquiries into the nature of "Nature," Snyder's lines remind us that we understand and distinguish bodies in the world by contrasts, and that if we break down those distinctions, we will not see beings (including ourselves) as separate. Ammons's lines qualify Snyder's to say that, for life to exist, barriers between entities must be maintained; human bodies hold themselves together by allowing certain constituent chemicals in and keeping others out. Entropy for both poets is thus attached to a system of value. Ammons, from "Corsons Inlet" onward, claimed to witness and record entropy and not to place forms and structures in its way, a claim perhaps impossible to sustain for anyone, least of all a writer. But scientific (geological, biological, anthropological) observation, for both poets, keeps the vision of a paleolithic consciousness from ever becoming romantic. For Ammons, the dialogue between oneness and multiplicity, as between stasis and dynamism, is worked out in the histories of natural forms:

that is all I have ever
said: that
        the circular lichen
        spotting the tree
trunk
is
like a moral order: there
is a center
where with threads it
knitted in, the
    "holding-on" point
    that gathers stability
    from bark: and there
    is
the outward multiplication
of forms (cells and patterns)

to an unprescribed
periphery
    that marks the moment-to-
    moment
    edge of growth.
(12/27/63)

Throughout such reflections, the commonality of reference points is striking. Ammons writes, as does Snyder, of the plains Indians, who "centered /
their lives / on the chase . . . stabilized / in instability" (12/28/63; ellipsis
added), and of a "climax forest" under water "since the Miocene / when it
was an / island" (12/30/63).

Of two differences from Snyder, at least in this phase of Ammons's work,
the first is the greater level of self-reference in writing the poem: Ammons,
in discussing the body, simultaneously discusses the poem, which is likewise
one of the "systems of / exclusion," posing the same question of what to
let in and what to shut out. The second difference is Ammons's humor,
including frequent asides about the length of the tape and the labor of
writing, as in "you may think this / is pretty awful: / but I doubt seriously
/ you could do any better" (1/5/63).

Toward the end of Ammons's poem, the controlling metaphor of writing
as journey returns:

    in voyages, there
    are wide reaches
    of water
    with no islands:
I have given you the
interstices: the
    space between
    electrons:
    I have given you
    the dull days
of the voyage
when turning and turning
reveals nothing.
(1/11/63)

This is in part a comment on composition, on leaving things in rather than taking things out, on the concept of including space, not just event, in the text, whether that space is between islands or between electrons. (Transposing the poem from adding-machine tape to book represents a visual aspect of this principle.) Space may be the vast, sublime expanses between stars (or electrons), but it also may be, for the traveler eager to arrive, monotony. Consider C. P. Cavafy's poem "Ithaca"—appropriate here, since A. R. Ammons spent the better part of his life living and teaching in that island's New World namesake. Cavafy reminds travelers that they should not be too eager to arrive at a final destination. Ithaca is nothing in itself: "what Ithaca has given you is the beautiful journey" (36). Thus, days must pass, in writing as in traveling, when Ammons's "turning and turning" (echoing Yeats) "reveals nothing." This is the nature of the journey, as it is the nature of the scroll. In Snyder's *Mountains and Rivers without End*, the painterly device of the scroll is the use of space—the mist—as a rest area and transition between scenes, like Ammons's "interstices," offering "nothing" in itself.

At the end of Snyder's scroll, the pen lifts from the paper, though the space goes on, offering a figure for ultimate nonclosure. In *Tape*, the paper's physical finitude is a given all along, since the only space has been the space of the poem.

> Well, the roll has
> lifted from the
> floor
> & our journey is done:
> thank you
> for coming:
> thank you for coming
> along:
> (1/11/63)

Robert Creeley and the Remorse of Travel

> If, then, the problem is the road
> and the passion we call traveler and one
> who has remained; *if it is to blame one*

for coming or going, remaining or staying the same
or, perhaps, for not explaining or, better,
for not complaining; is there a name
for it? What is there, after all, to explain?
That passion is wild, the road runs, the traveler
has come back and sits and talks and goes again?
(Creeley, "Poem for Beginners," *Collected* 10; emphasis added)

In this section of a poem written in the late 1940s, Robert Creeley raises a question of travel posed in Elizabeth Bishop's "Questions of Travel" and developed further in the poetry of Derek Walcott, whose anxiety of travel derives from conflicts about home. Despite its title, "Poem for Beginners" appears to be a traveler's defense in response to "one who has remained," one who has blamed the traveler ("to blame one for coming or going"). To the traveler's question, "What is there, after all, to explain?" the answer is, quite a lot: the wild passion, the running road, and the traveler who comes, talks, and then "goes again." From home's perspective, this behavior is distressing and requires explanation. Creeley returns to these preoccupations in the late 1970s with a travel diary called *Hello: A Journal, February 29–May 3, 1976* (later published in a larger collection, *So There: Poems 1976–83*, which I use here as the source) and again in the much later retrospective book *Life and Death* (1998).

In these two later books, Creeley writes brief, fleeting poems that are perhaps more typically "travel poems"—in their casual, notational style—than those, say, of Walcott or Bishop. Indeed, the poems are at times so notational as to be apparently trivial. For example, in "Wellington, New Zealand," the first poem of *Hello: A Journal*, the traveler notes, "It's the scale / that's attractive, / and the water / that's around it" (*So There* 8), and "I wish I / could see the stars" (9). The poem's last two lines seem to offer a cliché universalism: "Same clock ticks / in these different places" (9). But Creeley, in developing his idiosyncratic pulse and prosody, has always courted minimalism; the whole of the poem's action is more than the sum of its often deliberately throwaway lines. If the sentiments are cliché—as in "South, north, east, west, / man—home's best" (12)—how does cliché operate here? Creeley in his late work begins to use obvious rhymes and meters, for example, combined with sentiments that have just enough quirk to make them *not* Hallmark cards:

What is Williams' (Raymond's) tome . . .
Where have all the flowers gone?

I put them right here on the table . . .
No one's been here but for Mabel.
(37; ellipses added)

In *Life and Death*, the courting of absurdity and, more to the point, sentimentality points to a sense of connectedness the writer sees as missing in
his life and work, a lack he attributes to travel. "Histoire de Florida," the
longest sequence of the book, includes verses such as these:

You thought
you were writing
about
what you felt

You've left it out
Your love
your life
your home

your wife
You've
left her
out

No one is one
No one's alone
No world's that small
No life

You left it out
(17)

"Histoire de Florida" is a Donne-like moral exhortation to the "individual" footloose and irresponsible traveler, the answer to travel as self-
gratification. The extreme simplicity, like the sentimentalism, is linked to
an exacerbated pathos in late Creeley. That is, he connects homesickness
and remorse about travel to the urge to transcribe with the least opacity
possible:

Simple things
one wants to say
like, what's the day
like, out there—
who am I
and where.
("Speech," *So There* 99)

A great many U.S. poets have tried to be "simple"; Creeley's genealogy
from Williams might, to some, imply that effort, and his work always has
been famously spare—but not with this motivation. The idea that one
must be faithful to reality, that "simple things" are sayable, and that one
must witness and give account are deeply problematized in the poems of
Lowell, Bishop, and Walcott, to use the most obvious examples of what
happens to representation in the course of travel. As I suggest at the outset
of this study, representation of a group or constituency is tied to mimetic
representation. Freedom from one may mean freedom from the other, but
at considerable cost.

In "The Dogs of Auckland" (*Life and Death*), a backward glance over
traveled roads, the poet accounts for the pass at which he has arrived:

Almost twenty years ago I fled my apparent life, went off
into the vast Pacific, though it was only miles and miles

in a plane, came down in Auckland Airport.
(47)

He demystifies travel by describing the "vast Pacific" as really "only miles
and miles // in a plane" and a few lines later asks, "How to stay real in such
echoes? How be, finally, anywhere the body's got to?" (47). The "stay" of
"to stay real" is as important as the "real," in that it suggests a status quo
encroached on by influences that threaten to destabilize it. To travel is to
become something else, to be false to what is known and given at home.
On a return, does one return to what one was? "Curious, coming again
here, / where I hadn't known where I was ever" (46).

These late books both have titles of finality: *Life and Death* and *So There*.
Life and Death is a book of deep indefiniteness, a frail, funny, and vulnerable
book that mocks the grandeur of its own title. In *So There*, *there* always ends
up being *here*, but the remorse running through the book suggests that,

finally, from a perspective of age, *here* has more value than *there*: "home's best." All that freewheeling individualism is fine while you are young or rich or secure, Creeley has said in conversation, but when trouble comes, one needs a home and loved ones.

The anxiety of travel, Freud thought, is a facet of the guilt of enjoying what not all are given to enjoy, whether through lack of imagination or lack of means ("A Disturbance"). The return home is in a sense the bodhisattva's denial, the refusal of an *ek-stasis* that not all can share, the hunkering down instead for the long wait. The wait may be very long indeed, as Creeley suggests in "Desultory Days," yet another version of Elizabeth Bishop's question of travel and a last position on the traveler's accountability:

Were it then wrong
to avoid, as might be said,
the heaped-up canyons of the dead—
L.A.'s drear smut, and N.Y.C.'s

crunched millions? I don't know.
It seems to me
what can salvation be

for less than 1%
of so-called population
is somehow latent fascism

of the soul. What leaves behind
those other people,
like they say,

reneges on Walter Whitman's
19th century Mr. Goodheart's
Lazy Days and Ways In Which

we might still *save the world*.
I loved it but
I never could believe it—
(*So There* 162)

Is it, finally, wrong to travel? As I noted in the first chapter, Emerson thought so, and poets as different from one another as Bishop, Walcott, and

Creeley raise the question for surprisingly similar reasons. Freud's anxiety about travel in "A Disturbance of Memory on the Acropolis" was so acute that he doubted the existence of that canonical site even as it lay before his gaze. Freud viewed his own depression and subsequent disbelief at finally seeing the Acropolis as deriving from his having achieved the forbidden: the surpassing of his father. If other loved ones cannot enjoy this experience, how, with what right, can I? In the previous lines, Creeley extends this anxiety from the context of immediate family to that of the patria, where the fidelity to "home" entails a *collective* obligation. Such travel anxiety figures in more poems by more poets than can be mentioned here, but consider one of the poetic sources of Walcott's anxiety: Anna Akhmatova, witness first to the Russian Revolution and then to the Stalinist era, who refused to leave Russia. In "I Heard a Voice," she describes her resistance to the call to leave: "Leave Russia, leave your sinful, / Godforsaken land, forever" invites the voice, to which the poet responds "I covered my ears with my hands, / Lest my sorrowing spirit be / Defiled by such sentiments" (173). Five years later, in "I Am Not One of Those," she claims, "I am not one of those who left the land," adding that "I pity the exile's lot / Like a felon, like a man half-dead, / dark is your path, wanderer." She ends that poem with a vision of the last reckoning, when those who left and those who stayed behind will stand up for moral comparison: "We are the people without tears, / straighter than you . . . more proud" (173–74). She returned to the theme at the end of her career in this "Requiem" of the years 1935–1940:

No foreign sky protected me,
no stranger's wing shielded my face.
I stand as a witness to the common lot,
survivor of that time, that place.

(180)

Does an American or an American poet have an obligation of this kind, a duty to witness the "drear smut" of Los Angeles and the "crunched millions" of New York City? Can a parallel be drawn between the poets of witness of Eastern Europe or Latin America—so charismatic from the U.S. perspective—and American poets who, while they might hunger for it, suffer no repression from a largely indifferent government and public and who come and go as they please? (One can always argue for a Foucauldian, interiorized repression, but poets in the United States do not face prison, torture, or even censorship to speak of.) The "drear smut" and "crunched millions" compare to the gulags only to those with little idea what gulags were.

But what is freedom or travel or even enlightenment worth, asks Creeley, if only 1 percent can have it? Should this be the poet's and traveler's question? Or should the traveler respond by asking, What are the "crunched millions" to me? Are they not just clouds of the sky when the horizon fades? And insofar as they are present and material, could I and would I do anything about them if I *did* stay home?

Creeley's misgivings are not those of a frustrated traveler—of George Bailey in *It's a Wonderful Life*, who never realized his dreams of travel—but those of a traveler at the end of the road, one who has exhausted desire and imagination and who longs to rest and enjoy community. In other words, his comments are an "adult" response to Ginsberg's "childish geography," a response to travel as escape or gratification. Salvation for the mere self, he says (before undercutting this with his last doubt—"I never could believe it"), means reneging on Whitman's promise. Whitman promised the open road and the open form. Does Creeley expect too much of Whitman's promise? Can the open road or form "save the world"? Creeley's tribute to Allen Ginsberg, which introduces Ginsberg's posthumous book *Death and Fame*, closes as follows:

> Yet the heroic voices, the insistent intimacies of their tenacious humanity, hold us in a profound and securing bond. Where else would we think to live? Our friend gave his whole life to keep faith with Whitman's heartfelt insistence, "Who touches this book touches a man." So Allen Ginsberg will not leave us even now. "To see Void vast infinite look out the window into the blue sky." (xvi)

Unlike Snyder, whose largely West Coast travels were never far from roots, and whose commitment to the local seemed to come naturally, Ginsberg held onto his childishness, recanting neither it nor travel and never doubting that, despite the claims of home, government, and occupational and social norms, room exists—or, rather, with courage and irreverence enough, one *makes* room—for the free agent traveling through space and time.

In the same essay where Emerson deplores both travel ("Travel is a fool's paradise" [134]) and, for similar reasons, prayer ("Prayer looks abroad"

[132]), he sets out as clearly as anyone has the ethos of the traveler that Ginsberg—and Creeley, for all his late remorse—followed:

> Power ceases in the instant of repose; it resides in the moment of transition from a past to a new state, in the shooting of the gulf, in the darting to an aim. This one fact the world hates; that the soul *becomes*. (129)

There was no treachery if he turned his back

on the sun that plunges fissures in the fronds

of the feathery immortelles.

DEREK WALCOTT, *Tiepolo's Hound*

And yet so many fled, so many lost

to the magnetic spires of cities, not the cedars,

as if a black pup turned into the ghost

of the white hound, but a search that will lead us

where we began: to islands.

DEREK WALCOTT, *Tiepolo's Hound*

The Problem of Witness
The Travels of Derek Walcott

"Subject position," by now a cliché in the politics of identity, has been for Derek Walcott the motive of a figurative abundance unparalleled in late-twentieth-century poetry. From "A Far Cry from Africa" and "The Divided Child" onward, Walcott has crafted hundreds of metaphors for conflicted identity, for the Subject poisoned by, gifted by, caught between, or shuttling between two worlds. The awards and distinctions conferred on him reflect this emphasis. Homages on the occasion of the Nobel Prize, awarded to Walcott on the five hundredth anniversary of Columbus's first landfall in the New World, celebrated the poet's exile status, his homecomings, and his commutes between Boston, St. Lucia, and Trinidad. Apparently unconscious of racist overtones, Swedish Academy member Kjell Espmark characterized Walcott's poetry as "a meeting place of the virtuosity of Europe and the sensuality of a Caribbean Adam" (Grunquist 153).[1] "[A]n ambiguity without a crisis" is how Walcott himself has termed his being both American and West Indian ("Caribbean" 3), but the questions of his earliest poetry continue to be asked in his latest: How can I, and for whom do I, speak?

Walcott has rejected descriptions of himself as exile or emigré, but he has, in many poems, described himself as a traveler. He has set his poems not only in St. Lucia but also in Manhattan, Miami, St. Petersburg, Cracow, Rome, San Juan, and London; he has written not only of island fishermen but also of John Clare, Balzac, Pisarro, Antonio Machado, Ovid, and Kurtz. But if to translate is to betray (*traduttore, traditore*), it is also to travel (*trasladar*, to translate; to move, to remove), so travel, home voices say, is a kind of treachery. Emerson thought we were *responsible* to places: they depend on us and become venerable by our "sticking fast" to them, as he writes in "Self-Reliance" (133). Walcott often seems to agree with that indictment of travel: "Traveling widens this breach," he writes at the end of his 1970 essay "What the Twilight Says" (35). And, graver still, in his Nobel acceptance speech: "The Traveler cannot love, since love is stasis and travel is motion" ("Antilles" 77).

Critics who find Walcott's work too distanced from the material realities of the Caribbean usually voice one of at least three related complaints: Citing the poet's immersion in European traditions, they ask whether Walcott is re- or decolonizing the Afro-Caribbean by stealing literary types from former slavers. Second, they note, as Paul Breslin has of *Another Life*, the poet's tendency toward the sublime and the allegorical, his movement from the historically concrete to the universally symbolic. (Specifically, Breslin is uneasy with "claims to Adamic transcendence of history . . . claims of elemental kinship to the earth that circumvent cultural mediation" [177].) Finally, critics question the poet's biogeography. While Walcott repeatedly emphasizes his ties to St. Lucia and to the Caribbean in general, he has taught in the United States for the past twenty years and now spends half the year in Boston. He was commissioned by the Royal Shakespeare Company to stage the *Odyssey* in London, helped Paul Simon pen the short-lived Broadway musical *The Capeman*, and staged Robert Pinsky's translation of the *Inferno*.[2] These are sore points with critics such as Dionne Brand, who insists Walcott sees the Caribbean "with the eye of the imperial stranger" (Gingell 44).

Beyond this, fame has a double edge in the Caribbean. While Walcott's many awards represent long overdue acknowledgement of Caribbean literary value, they also confirm his work's appeal to, and coherence within, old centers of power in Europe and America. As Paula Burnett observes, giving an award to a Caribbean artist can be seen as a sign of the North's "growing enlightenment, in that the honour is going to a hitherto unacknowledged quarter," or "as yet another manifestation of neo-colonialism, in that once again the North acts as global arbiter of quality and manipulator of power. The ambivalence is acute" ("Hegemony" 1–2). Even Walcott's winning the Nobel prize—certainly a source of pride for many islanders and an event celebrated in at least one calypso song—has confirmed, for others, his distance from Caribbean material concerns.[3]

Can the Caribbean poet-traveler speak for home, "wherever that may be?" To some Caribbean writers, the idea of home has long been problematic and the need to leave the Caribbean self-evident. Kamau Brathwaite, Aimé Césaire, Jamaica Kincaid, Maryse Condé, and V. S. Naipaul are among the most famous of a large group of such writers. Condé was virtually unknown in her native Guadeloupe until her books were published in France. Césaire began the *Notebook of a Return to My Native Land* while vacationing in Yugoslavia and completed it in Paris.[4] Brathwaite has taught for years at New York University, and Naipaul's home base has long been the English countryside. Writing in the St. Lucian *Star* on the occasion of the Nobel award, John Robert Lee admonished his compatriots: "If Derek Walcott lived here he would not be popular. . . . Derek had to go outside. Do not foolishly blame him for that. Our generation has to stay home and make it here. A hard ground. But he has made the path clear for us" (qtd. in Burnett, "Hegemony" 10).

That this defense needs to be made at all suggests that if travel raises questions for writers in general, the questions are graver for Caribbean writers. Read as an ethnic Caribbean poet, or as hybrid of Europe and Africa, Walcott is subject to a burden of representation, and therefore to a kind of criticism, to which many poets are not. No one demanded of Robert Lowell or Elizabeth Bishop that they speak for their people; no one now demands of John Ashbery that he be faithful to local, ethnic, or national constituencies. Readers in search of such fidelities simply turn elsewhere.

But this conversation between an accusatory home and a transgressive, cosmopolitan artist is carried on at an even more compelling level in Walcott's poems, which are frequently haunted by the fear that the poet's border-crossing—geographic and linguistic/metaphorical—distances him from his origins. Of these kinds of movement, the last is most conspicuous and necessary in a discussion of poetry, for at least two reasons: first, the movement of figuration itself constitutes a betrayal of presence (or of the dream of presence), and, second, the fields of postcolonial studies and new historicism have for at least twenty years studied the narrative almost exclusively. If poetry dispenses with plot, with character, and with continuities of time and place, how can the poet speak for home? Can he or she be both exile and neighbor?

In what follows, I pursue these two dimensions of travel: first, the geographic voyages where the poet scrutinizes the subject position of the privileged, often airborne traveler; and, second, linguistic and metaphorical travel, where the act of substitution offers a corollary to geographic travel as betrayal. These two dimensions are in fact inseparable in the poems, which locate the anxiety of the estranged traveler within an unusually thick metaphorical and linguistic texture and which develop their own commentary on figuration, often more demanding than that of the poet's critics.

Witness and Flight

While Walcott has said he belongs in and to St. Lucia, he also has noted the luxury of catching a plane out, a privilege not all St. Lucians share. "I'll continue to come back to see if what I write is not beyond the true experience of the person next to me on the bus," he has remarked (Hirsch 223). These comments on departures and homecomings, and even on modes of transport, are more than casual, given the centrality of these as topoi in Walcott's poetry. Apart from the ships of *Omeros* and "The Schooner *Flight*," and, in at least one crucial case ("The Light of the World"), a bus, travel in Walcott's poems is by plane. In "The Schooner *Flight*" (*The Star Apple Kingdom*), the poet-sailor Shabine looks up from his skiff at a jet plane and decries industrial "progress" (4). At the conclusion of "Tales of the Islands" (*In a Green Night*), the poet looks out the airplane window at the receding landscape, a scene repeated in *Another Life* ("I watched the island narrowing" [115]), as well as in "The Gulf" (*The Gulf*), where the receding vista is that of the United States. In the opening poem of *Midsummer*, the jet "bores like a silverfish through volumes of cloud" (I), while in "The Fortunate Traveler" (*The Fortunate Traveler*), one of Walcott's most extended critiques of mobility, the jet provides a metaphor for power, privilege, and invisibility.[5]

In "The Fortunate Traveler," the poet contrasts the cosmopolitan traveler's comfort with the misery of millions in the developing world, trapped as in the hold of a slave ship: "In the hold of this earth / 10,000,000 shoreless souls are drifting. / Somalia: 765,000, their skeletons will go under the tidal sand" (89). The detachment of the traveler, a former academic and now a negotiator of economic interests in developing countries, both invites and anticipates our criticism, since the poem continually glosses the situation described.[6] "One flies first class, one is so fortunate," the traveler says dryly, while he yearns for the earthbound gaze and mourns his own narrowing of vision, his moment-by-moment recession from the individual sorrows below (88). For this lofty perspective, as for the profession enabling it, he has only contempt:

> We are roaches,
> riddling the state cabinets, entering the dark holes
> of power. . . .
>
>   . . . and when
> the cabinets crack, we are the first
> to scuttle, radiating separately
> back to Geneva, Bonn, Washington, London.
> (90, ellipses added)

The poem crawls with insects—cockroaches, lice, locusts, and weevils, particularly these latter, since they attack crops, and this is finally a poem of famine and apocalypse.[7] Indeed, the poem begins with an epigraph from Revelation 6:6 ("A measure of wheat for a penny, and three measures of barley for a penny"), and its ending is the most prophetic of any in Walcott's oeuvre. As the beetle-black taxis and the topcoated diplomats evoke cockroaches, so the jet plane evokes the more harmful insect: "No one will look up now to see the jet / fade like a weevil through a cloud of flour" (89).

The poem's bureaucratic traveler, armed with graphs and World Bank forms, conducts his tractor sales for "Iscariot's salary" and rhetorically asks, "[W]ho cares how many millions starve?" In a plot that lies somewhere between Graham Greene and Ian Fleming, he takes his profits and sails to the islands, where Albert Schweitzer "moves to the harmonium / of morning" and where, "to the pluming chimneys, / the groundswell lifts *Lebensraum, Lebensraum*" (93). Here, far from Europe's centers, Schweitzer's humanitarian high culture conflates with Nazi Germany's expansionism and genocidal technology. (The idea that these are two sides of the same coin may have come, Paula Burnett argues, from Walcott's reading of Chinua Achebe's well-known article on *Heart of Darkness* [*Derek* 177].) In the next verse paragraph, the displacement is explicit—from Kurtz's jungle back to Europe:

> The heart of darkness is not Africa.
> The heart of darkness is the core of fire
> in the white center of the holocaust.
> (93)

Curiously, though, in the tropical context, "the heart of darkness" has also a positive ring, as the last place where a religious life is possible. Walcott has employed "God is dead" themes in other poems than this ("Crusoe's Island" [*Castaway* 54] provides an early example and much of *The Bounty* a more recent one), but here the consequences of that knowledge are especially disturbing. The urbane and secular narrator envies the unenlightened, "backward tribes [that] keep vigil of his Body" (95) even while he compares them to vermin:[8]

> Keep the news from their blissful ignorance.
> Like lice, like lice, the hungry of this earth
> swarm to the tree of life.
> (95)

Must religious belief imply ignorance and even subhumanity? The problem again is that of subject position. We credit this corrupted diplomat with the capacity for regret and self-examination, as well as with nostalgia for a more spiritually connected life. Are we then to share his contempt—albeit mixed with sadness—toward the benighted multitudes who still believe? (Walcott does not as a rule create unreliable narrators; Spoiler, Shabine, and the many unnamed tourist-travelers of Walcott's poems are invariably trustworthy if complex personae.) Still more depressing, though the "backward" natives swarm *to* the tree, the divine union is thwarted: "fires / drench them like vermin, quotas / prevent them" (95–96). From the traveler's viewpoint, they are merely "compassionate fodder for the travel book, / its paragraphs like windows from a train" (96). This traveler's "fortune" is the freedom to turn away from a world that has become mere text or, alternatively, to turn that world *into* text to quiet its demands: "everywhere that earth shows its rib cage / and the moon goggles with the eyes of children, / we turn away to read" (96).[9] The speaker credits Rimbaud with knowing we prefer texts to reality. Rimbaud, in Walcott's telling, "knew that we cared less for one human face / than for the scrolls in Alexandria's ashes" (96).

The simplest of biblical motifs, a reworking of I Corinthians 13, introduced almost unnoticeably in the first section of "The Fortunate Traveler" but gathering force as the poem advances, provides the unity of the poem: "*and have not charity.*" The line occurs three times in the last movement, where the poem takes on its powerful prophetic tone:

> In loaves of cloud, *and have not charity*,
> the weevil will make a sahara of Kansas,
> the ant shall eat Russia.
> Their soft teeth shall make, *and have not charity*,
> the harvest's desolation,
> and the brown globe crack like a begging bowl,
> and though you fire oceans of surplus grain,
> *and have not charity*,
>
> still, through thin stalks,
> the smoking stubble, stalks
> grasshopper: third horseman,
> the leather-helmed locust.
> (97)

Within these biblically cadenced sentences, the phrase from Corinthians erupts, apparently randomly, like a return of the repressed, until in the last last sentence of the poem, it is fully integrated, logically and grammatically following "though you fire oceans of surplus grain," just as it follows "though I speak with the tongues of men and angels" and "though I have the gift of prophecy" in the Bible.

In this poem, unlike any other of Walcott's poems on mobility, privilege, and deracination, anxiety about travel as a sign of the failure to love becomes global prophecy, a credible vision of the world's end, even while the poet plays on words to the last moment—"stalks" as descriptive noun for the wasteland of famine instantly becoming "stalks" as verb, signaling the approach of the Apocalypse. The insects, which may well inherit the earth and which appear only as metaphor earlier in the poem, now make their literal entrance, harbingers of the end of humanity.

The traveler's voice in Walcott's many travel poems typically sounds like Walcott's, or at least "Walcott's," the voice of the St. Lucian poet, playwright, and painter who has made art of his arrivals and departures. The conscience-stricken traitor-prophet of "The Fortunate Traveler" is a special case, as are the Creole narrators, most memorably that of the early "Tales of the Islands" and, in two of Walcott's most compelling longer poems, the 1950s calypso satirist of "The Spoiler's Return," who returns from the dead to satirize local island corruption, and Shabine, the poet-sailor of "The Schooner *Flight*," who answers the call of the sea at considerable cost. These narrators inhabit social strata unlike that of the erudite, globe-trotting narrator of the other poems, but all the narrators have in common their flight from or toward another place.[10] The Spoiler's is a homecoming, Shabine's a departure.

"*Adios, Carenage*," the first section of "The Schooner *Flight*," is a farewell to home and family, which, by the poem's end, becomes a farewell to travel itself: "My first friend was the sea. Now, is my last" (*SAK* 20). The reasons for leaving are those Freud emphasized: not the attraction to the other place so much as the repulsion toward home:

> But they had started to poison my soul
> with their big house, big car, big-time bohbohl,
> coolie, nigger, Syrian, and French Creole,
> so I leave it for them and their carnival—
> (*SAK* 4)

Home, in this case, means island society at large, its unsavory capitalism, corruption, and political games. Shabine subscribes to Shelleyan ideas of the unacknowledged power of the poet over investors and ministers ("All you fate in my hand," he threatens [16]), but, for all this rejection, he also suffers from homesickness. He testifies,

I swear to you all, by my mother's milk,
. . . .
that I loved them, my children, my wife, my home;
I loved them as poets love the poetry
that kills them, as drowned sailors the sea.
(5)

Later, in a moment he thinks is his last, he says, "I have not loved those that I loved enough" (17). In this reflection he resembles Walcott, as he does also in the literary tastes he discusses, his passion for poetry and the sea, and indeed his physical appearance. At the journey's outset, he looks in the taxi's rearview mirror and sees "a man / exactly like me, and the man was weeping" (4). Shabine is "a rusty head sailor with sea-green eyes," who says of himself:

I'm just a red nigger who loves the sea,
I had a sound colonial education,
I have Dutch, nigger, and English in me,
and either I'm nobody or I'm a nation.
(4)

The choice Shabine describes here is more desperate than that between the collective and the individual; it is the choice between the collective and nothing. Only by having left behind collective identity does Shabine see its importance. The phrase, and the choice, suggests that no identity suffices that does not reflect all the history Shabine embodies. Yet Shabine rejects his "nation," as it rejects him. "The Schooner *Flight*" gives us the Creole version of the in-between theme Walcott has pursued from his earliest poetry. In "A Far Cry from Africa," he writes, "I who am poisoned with the blood of both, / Where shall I turn, divided to the vein?" (*GN* 18); here Shabine declares:

After the white man, the niggers didn't want me
when the power swing to their side.
The first chain my hands and apologize, "History";
the next said I wasn't black enough for their pride.
(*SAK* 8)

Shabine's earlier declaration of love, like all of his avowals, is predicated on his having *left* his nation. His poetry of home is possible only from abroad.

He can speak only for a people from whose claims travel has released him. When toward the end of the poem—in the remarkable sequence that begins "Open the map"—he writes,

> from this bowsprit, I bless every town,
> the blue smell of smoke in hills behind them,
> and the one small road winding down them like twine
> to the roofs below
>
> (19)

the condition of this blessing is mobility. He blesses "from this bowsprit," not from the hearth. If "the traveler cannot love," as Walcott later says, he can bless, which may be easier. Indeed his mobility affords both the energy and the clarity to articulate this blessing.

Walcott's narrators—in *Omeros*, "Return to D'Ennery," "Light of the World," and the present poem—want to speak for a nation, in the root sense of the term, a birthplace, a people ("I am satisfied / if my hand gave voice to one people's grief" [SAK 19]), but, at the moment of speaking, they feel the onus of representation, in both senses, as native islander and as writer, and their response is to slip off the burden. At this stage, Walcott's poems often veer toward the "nothing" that the Victorian explorer James Anthony Froude announced and that Césaire and Naipaul, as much as Walcott himself, have taken as theme.[11] The rhetorical corollary to the absence Froude saw ("no people there in the true sense of the word") occurs in the poem's turning self-consciously into a "blank page": the refusal of nostalgia for a prelapsarian state of presence and, instead, the embrace of metaphor. Perhaps the virtue of "The Schooner *Flight*" lies in the fact that it does not execute this move too quickly. Even though the sails of *Flight* are pages, textual transcendence is inhibited, and the material and spiritual predicament of the poet-sailor and his world are not lost to us.[12]

Rei Terada suggests reading "The Light of the World" as Walcott's *ars poetica*. "The Schooner *Flight*" might be nominated more readily for that honor, if only because it contains the following declaration:

> I have only one theme:
>
> The bowsprit, the arrow, the longing, the lunging heart—
> The flight to a target whose aim we'll never know,
> vain search for one island that heals with its harbor

and a guiltless horizon, where the almond's shadow
doesn't injure the sand. There are so many islands!
19)

This, and the lines that follow it, could stand as the most central passage
in Walcott's poetry, as an announcement of the poet's concern and purpose.
Romantic, excessive, and sentimentalized, it is also Georgian without the
compactness and thetic unity of a Masefield poem. But it does more than
announce a terrain (islands, boats, horizons) and a theme (the impulse to
move). It also announces a way of writing. The piling on of metaphors typical
of Walcott, who nearly always prefers four or five to one, emphasizes the
theme's projectile motion. The first two terms ("bowsprit," "arrow") are
concrete, masculine emblems of adventure and battle; the subsequent four
("longing," "lunging heart," "flight," "search") are abstract and diffuse,
losing vigor as they lose concreteness. This passage, like Whitman's open
road or Baudelaire's tribute "to those who leave for leaving's sake," addresses travel as an end in itself. But the chain of substitutions ends with
a telos, since the poet's search, however doomed, is toward "*one* island"
that "heals" and whose horizon is "guiltless." These comforting elements
suggest "home," but such singularity of place dissolves in the context of
islands that spill out like "peas on a tin plate" (19). Just as we had a chain of
signifiers for travel, each displacing the last in an effort to signify adequately,
and thus acting out the movement of travel itself, so now the poem moves
toward its conclusion with an archipelago of names for islands, substituting, for the homely "peas," grander versions of seeing and knowing, and
illustrating Walcott's poetics of excess in the sense, this time, not only of
quantity but also of rhetoric: "As many islands as the stars at night / on that
branched tree from which meteors are shaken / like falling fruit around
the schooner *Flight*" (19–20).

In the heightened pathos of the poem's end, the islands become stars
in the sky, which in turn are visualized as bright fruit on a vast tree, then
as meteors shaken loose like fallen "fruit around the schooner." These
images of chaos, abundance, and endlessness tuck into each other—from
islands, to falling stars, to fruit on a cosmic branch—each thing one in a
myriad, "just as this earth is one / island in archipelagoes of stars" (21).
The repletion answers to the poem's own energy, to the expectations set
up by the sea-yarn genre, by the departure scene at the outset, by the

poem's seventeen-page length, but also by the scale and promise of the announcement: "I have only one theme."

The poem ends with a forlorn Shabine watching the moon on the water make a "road in white moonlight taking me home" (20). Homecoming as an ending, however, is no more happy than homecoming as the topos of an entire poem. Shabine, after all his adventures, has to try to "forget what happiness was." Going home is giving up: the end of a life at sea or simply the end of a life. At best it is a peaceful absence rather than the fullness of completion (and acceptance of rest) such as that offered in a Georgian poem such as "Sea Fever."

The stars falling like fruit in "The Schooner *Flight*" echo the volume's title poem, "The Star-Apple Kingdom," a Caribbean *Gone with the Wind* whose theme, like that of "The Schooner *Flight*," is the contest between pleasure and duty, travel and home, commitment and aesthetics: the conflict, never resolved but endlessly generative, that is Walcott's one true theme. I will turn to this poem at the close of this chapter.

The poem of homecoming is a genre Walcott has mined repeatedly. The tourist persona may be a device from Bishop, but for Walcott it has a special poignancy: other than in the "Tropic Zone" sequence of *Midsummer* and a few poems set abroad, he speaks as a stranger not in a strange land but on the roads and beaches of his native island. In "Homecoming: Anse La Raye," for example, the poet is taken for a tourist by the children, who "swarm like flies / round your heart's sore" (*The Gulf* 84).[13] He remembers his own childhood when, bored by the sea, he hoped he would be these children's poet ("I am your poet, yours") but never contemplated "homecomings without home," returns to a site so estranged that it fails to recognize him, even more than he it. And what has he to offer these begging children? "You give them nothing. / Their curses melt in air" (85). He gives them no money, but he also gives them the "nothing" that he reflects, the nothing of the rotted sea grapes, split coconuts, and beach wrack, of the tropic island as absence. Third, he gives them nothing in the sense that his poetry has never touched them; it is a matter of indifference to them; they do not recognize him as their poet.

An extended treatment of the native as tourist is Walcott's "The Light of the World" (*The Arkansas Testament*), which explores the estrangement of both speaker and poetry from his birthplace. Written nearly twenty years after "Homecoming: Anse La Raye," this poem plays on several senses of "transport" as travel. *Transport* is, first of all, a synonym for *bus* in the English Caribbean. Second, it is the act of carrying or carrying across, even of being, in the Romantic sense, transported or carried away. As in the Greek *metafora*, transport is at once a movement, a substitution (and thus a concealment), and a carrying over. For the poet-traveler, the key facet is that of transport as a substitution of figure for presence, as a metaphorical betrayal of the material and literal, and as an escape from geographic, linguistic, *and* semantic "home."[14]

In the first line of the poem, the poet boards the "transport" to hear Bob Marley's voice "rocking on the transport's stereo" (*AT* 48). He sees a beautiful woman, whom he names "the light of the world," humming to the music. Later, all the passengers will "sing / Marley's songs of a sadness as real as the smell / of rain on dry earth" (51). In this account, Marley's is a poetry evoking "real" emotion and sensation, providing people with the transport the narrator's own work—written, not sung—falls short of. The writer has failed, as he failed in "Homecoming: Anse La Raye," to be his people's poet in the way Marley is—popular, iconic, danceable, hypnotically "transporting," and, incidentally, high (the "kaya" of the poem's epigraph is marijuana). Marley takes his place in the history of visionary artists, who, themselves transported, can transport others and who point the way toward transport: "*Kaya now, got to have Kaya now*" (48).

As the bus begins to fill, an old woman shouts to the driver to wait for her: "Pas quittez moi à terre!" she shouts. The phrase, we find out, is deeply figurative. As the narrator offers his readings of it, further displacements occur—each one a recoding, another remove from the local:

> "Pas quittez moi à terre,"
> which is, in her patois: "Don't leave me stranded,"
> which is, in her history and that of her people:
> "Don't leave me on earth," or, by a shift of stress:
> "Don't leave me the earth," [for an inheritance];
> "*Pas quittez moi à terre*, Heavenly transport,
> Don't leave me on earth, I've had enough of it."
> The bus filled in the dark with heavy shadows
> that would not be left on earth; no, that would be left
> on the earth, and would have to make out.

Abandonment was something they had grown used to.

And I had abandoned them.

(49–50)

The poem provides the glosses for us, but we may wish to gloss them in turn. The poet's first English translation of the Creole "Pas quittez moi à terre," an equivalent of "Wait for me!" makes pedestrian sense (literally) in the situation, but he quickly drops that reading in favor of one that makes the old woman the voice of "her people," as Bob Marley, in the poem, is seen to be of his. Now she is not merely an old woman hailing a bus but also the embodiment of her race. She and "her people" want to be included in the "transport" as an experience that earth cannot offer. But then, "by a shift of stress," the meaning becomes " 'Don't leave me the earth,' for an inheritance." The bus offers a passage out of earth, a train to glory, a boat over Jordan, a "heavenly transport" to a more enlightened (given the poem's title) state. The last reading repeats the second: " 'Don't leave me on earth,' I've had enough of it."

Basking in the warmth and courtesy of the passengers, the returning native wants "the transport / to continue forever, for no one to descend" (51), but he comes to his stop and must himself descend to return to his hotel, "full of transients like myself," his international, not his folk, community.[15] The passengers "went on in their transport, they left me on earth" (51).

The last and shortest verse paragraph contains a poignant epilogue to this apparent abandonment, where the transport stops and a man shouts the poet's name and holds out a pack of cigarettes he had dropped. Walcott turns away in tears. "There was nothing they wanted, nothing I could give them / but this thing I have called 'The Light of the World' " (51). Out of the passengers' respect for the privacy of St. Lucia's most celebrated native son, the poet had been left alone. But now, spoken to, no longer a stranger, he asks himself the question he asked twenty years earlier in "Homecoming: Anse La Raye": what do I have to offer if they want nothing of me? As a reply, in the last line, he offers this poem, refitting the metaphor he had used for the beautiful woman at the poem's beginning. "This thing" sounds offhand, but "The Light of the World" is, like "the star-apple kingdom," grand and immaterial, whether immanent, as in the light the world gives off, or outside and otherworldly. In either case, these title words now describe the poem or, more largely, the world of representation. Rei Terada points out the paradox of gifted poets who use their whole arsenal of powers to claim that these powers are insufficient. However, saying "I have called" the poem "the Light of the World" suggests it may not *be* the light of the world but that Walcott has—extravagantly, perhaps erroneously—seen it as such. *Is* the poem "the light of the world" in the same sense the woman is in the first verse paragraph—that is, in the sense of an overwhelming, charismatic physical presence? If the poem's action is complete, the substitution of text for presence has been acted out, and the light of the world is now the art that must mediate presence for us.

The poignancy of abandonment in "The Light of the World" mixes with erotic desire, since the first of the "transports" occurs while the poet-traveler gazes longingly at the young woman's body, seeing her both as a work of art that he would like to have had a hand in creating ("If this were a portrait . . . I'd have put in an earring / something simple" [48; ellipsis added]) and as an object of sexual desire. The more complex and much more vocal old woman, whose words are the poem's centerpiece, displaces her. But when the realization of abandonment comes up explicitly, the subject's attention reverts to the younger woman—"I was deeply in love with the woman by the window. / I wanted to be going home with her this evening" (50). He fantasizes first a sexual encounter and then a life with her, finally snapping out of it by saying, "But the others too," referring to his other neighbors on the transport. But the pathos of his realization of the distance between himself and his people seems borrowed from the keener regret of not possessing the object of his desire. Even if a reader resists converting the poem into moral allegory, the narrator has already performed much of that conversion, and given the narrative and the interpretations offered, one is compelled to relate these two phenomena: the poet's longing for the young woman on the bus and his anguish at the thought of his irrelevance to his people. The old woman's cry, a collective cry we are told, pleads not to be left behind but to be allowed to be transported (or to be uttered, as seen later in another "Homecoming"). As a response to that cry, however, the poet now offers a poem involved not so much in transporting as in mulling over frustrated desires, at once sexual, professional, and poetic. The popular reggae music drowns out the poet's more self-absorbed agonizing. (This is not a fault, obviously: the poem's topos is exactly this comparison and this alienation.) Despite the heightened affect at the poem's end and the offer of the poem as "light," this is, as at Anse La Raye, a homecoming "without home."

The Charge of Home and the Mourning of Presence

At several points in the readings thus far, a kind of slippage and distancing, other than that of travel, emerges: the betrayal of presence by language. The narrator of "The Light of the World," reminded by the old woman of his duty to represent, offers, somewhat unhappily, the "light" of figurative language instead of the "light" embodied in the young woman who is the poem's impetus. Even while Walcott's metaphors abound and luxuriate, the poems made up of them regularly offer a critical commentary on figuration and its consequences. The reflections of the "fortunate traveler," who is "fortunate" because he can "turn away to read," are symptoms of a malaise regarding the slipping free of material demands by means not only of literal but also of metaphorical travel.

From a poststructuralist standpoint, the poet-traveler's is not a special predicament. Representation can never restore presence. We are all, rather, involved in substituting for the seen world another, unseen, world; Rilke would say not that we are substituting but that we are transforming the seen into the unseen; as he wrote, we are "the bees of the invisible" (133).[16] The transformation may be more tribute and spiritual necessity than escapism, and yet transformation remains substitution. The celebration of, but, more important, the anxiety over, this transformation is acute in Walcott in part because of the stakes mentioned earlier in this chapter and in part because travel has compounded the distance and the difference. The traveler turns away (keeping in mind the sense of the "turn" as trope): the various fortunate travelers of Walcott's poems enjoy both the privilege of airborne mobility and the "gift," as he often calls it, the craft of metafora. Language betrays as travel betrays, precisely by this turning.

Walcott's linguistic turn, while impossible to overlook, is not as often remarked as his postcolonial predicament. Perhaps critics too readily assign linguistic play in poetry to Los Angeles and Buffalo and too little notice it in the poetics of the Caribbean, despite the obvious instances of Walcott, Brathwaite, Chamoiseau, and others. The landscape of contemporary poetry, notable in poetry anthologies published in the United States, often depends on a division between a poetry of subjectivity or confession, on the one hand, and a poetry of linguistic experiment, on the other. Discussions of the former, which has much more currency in classrooms, tend to be content rather than medium centered; this is particularly true of collections representing literatures seen as ethnic.[17] But for Walcott, forms and meters, a penchant for the theatrical, the trompe l'oeil, crafty homophonic slippages, Borgesian conflations of the real and the artificial—aesthetic and intellectual play, in other words—are what fascinate. Indeed, Walcott may offer the most striking example in contemporary poetry of the awkward meeting and mutual misrecognition of the postcolonial and the postmodern.

When, in "The Schooner *Flight*," the poet-sailor Shabine refers to "my pages the sails of the schooner *Flight*" (*SAK* 347), he suggests a textual rather than a geographic adventure. Like Elizabeth Bishop, whose first published poem, "The Map," explores the pleasurable aesthetic confusion between sign systems (colors, lines, and names), material oceans and shores, and national entities, Walcott has written many poems deploying world-as-text figures.[18] He describes islands "like words . . . Erased with the surf's pages" ("Islands," *GN* 77; ellipsis added), "shelves forested with titles, trunks that wait for names" ("A Map of the Continent," *The Gulf* 75), "The monotonous scrawl of the beaches" (*AL* 22), an ocean that "kept turning blank pages // looking for History" ("The Sea Is History," *SAK* 25), and many more such turns in *Omeros* and *Tiepolo's Hound*. By the time of *Midsummer*, the trope hypertrophies: Walcott speaks of "pages in a damp culture," "canefields set in stanzas," and "bright suburbs [that] fade into words" (I), so finally it is impossible to know whether we are traveling through landscape or language. This mutual enfiguring of nature and language constitutes at once an irreferential play, a relentless inquiry into the relation between "reality" and representation, and an assertion of Walcott's sense of the world as mythic (more on this later), existing outside of linear history.

If language itself thwarts the need to recover a paradise of presence, self-conscious artistry—particularly Walcott's genius for the veilings and unveilings of metaphor—exacerbates the problem. Walcott's artistry has long been a subject of Walcott's artistry. One of his chief ironies, often introduced by other voices in the poems, is that craft appears at *odds* with "faithful" representation. The first section of "The Schooner *Flight*" ends with a promise to write well and honestly, and Shabine the poet-sailor pledges,

> Well, when I write
> this poem, each phrase go be soaked in salt;
> I go draw and knot every line as tight
> as ropes in this rigging.
> (*SAK* 5)

Walcott sometimes begins a poem with a prayer: "Let these lines shine like the rain's wires in Santa Cruz / before they leave me, like the mist" ("A Santa Cruz Quartet," *B* 73). In "The Bounty," he refers to "these tinder-dry lines of this poem I hate" (5). But one must write, he says, because "we have no solace but utterance" and because it is "my business and my duty . . . / to write of the light's bounty on familiar things / that stand on the verge of translating themselves into news" (16; ellipsis added).

But duty, in the sense of a commitment to presence, is at odds with pleasure, just as home is at odds with travel. The familiar world, always on the verge of translating itself into "news" (poetry, in the sense Pound had, of "news that stays news"), is consigned to remain on that verge, crossing it only through language, an always incomplete satisfaction. In *Omeros*, the poet's father tells him to come back after his travels and be true to his birthplace, devoting himself to its depiction in poetry. His father shows him a vision of the island women of the past, carrying baskets of coal up ramps into a ship. This, says his father, "is the chance you now have, to give those feet a voice" (76). The poet seems to find in this encounter with history the confirmation of his vocation, a confirmation offered in numerous other poems. But, toward the poem's end, led through hell by Homer, he views the poets as "selfish phantoms" who "saw only surfaces" and who are condemned "to weep at their own pages" (293). Walcott reflects that "that was where I had come from. Pride in my craft" (293). He sees himself sliding toward them, "falling // towards the shit they stewed in," before Omeros pulls him free (293). "Pride in my craft" fills him with remorse. The Dantesque descent is here a figure for the guilt of the poet who cannot represent, not for lack of but *because* of his poetic skill. The writing of the poem is continually imbued with the vanity of writing the poem. The confession of guilt and inadequacy, a poetic device in itself, allows the process it questions: a meditation on representation and the displacement of travel. The watercolorist, the poet who delights in surfaces, whether of his fellow poets' work or of the sea wrack and sea grapes strewn through his poems, cannot stop questioning the relation of his artistry to the social and economic hungers that the world cries out for him, he thinks, to represent.

In "Homecoming," from *The Bounty*—as a final example of this theme—"Nature" itself disapproves of the poet's double betrayal. The oleanders, casuarinas, and breadfruit trees speak in this sequence as critics, acting out the traveler's projection of the rooted "home" from which he has long been a fugitive:

> it was on an ochre road I caught the noise of their lives,
> how their rage was rooted, shaking with every gust:
> their fitful disenchantment with all my turned leaves,
> for all of the years while theirs turned to mulch, then dust.
> "We offered you language early, an absolute choice;
> you preferred the gutturals of low tide sucked by the shoal
> on the grey strand of cities, the way Ireland offered Joyce
> his own unwritten dirt road outside Choiseul."
> "I have tried to serve both," I said, provoking a roar
> from the leaves, shaking their heads, defying translation.
> "And there's your betrayal," they said. I said I was sure
> that all the trees of the world shared a common elation
> of tongues, gommier with linden, bois-campêche with the elm.
> "You lie, your right hand forgot its origin, O Jerusalem,
> but kept its profitable cunning. We remain unuttered, undefined,"
> and since road and sun were English words, both of them
> endowed in their silence the dividing wind.
> (32)

At one level, this is a late installment of the "where shall I turn" topos that Walcott has been writing all his life. At another, this is a commentary on the poet's life work, one developed also in the opening pages of *Omeros*, where the trees are "the old gods" of the island, cut down for man's purposes (5). Here in "Homecoming," the casuarinas rage at the poet's treason, his "turned leaves."[19] We may think first of the tropism of leaves themselves, then of literary tropes as turns, and then of the acts of reading or writing: turning pages (or phrases) is the textual activity that has drawn or withdrawn this poet from island realities. But most of all, given the theme of the return home, we may think of turning back or away, the turning of a turncoat who no longer recognizes nor is recognized by his home.[20] Moreover, when something turns, it turns toward death: when milk sours, it turns, and when leaves turn, they become brown, as does an uprooted plant. While the poet's leaves were turning—northward—the trees' leaves had "turned to mulch, then dust." The first of these transformations ensures other, newer growth, sacrificing one generation of leaves to protect another, but disintegration follows that sacrifice.

The island vegetation hears the poet's reply, "I have tried to serve both," as betrayal. His next assertion that "all the trees of the world shared a common elation / of tongues" is worse than betrayal: it is a false universalism that tries to erase the specificity of island life. The poet has capitalized on his talent—"profitable cunning"—without giving back what he owes to its origin. He has "turned" his gift elsewhere, northward. But the chief accusation of these rooted beings is not that the poet has absconded but that he has failed to represent them to the world, to turn them into text: "We remain unuttered, undefined" (B 32). In *Omeros*, the old trees, the first gods of the island, "endured the desolation / of their tribe without uttering a syllable / of that language they had uttered as one nation" (6). This generation of trees is far less patient. Their charge, while valid in the sense that things must always remain unuttered, unrestored, is scarcely credible in the context of Walcott's work. Walcott rivals both Pablo Neruda and St.-John Perse in his naming of the world, especially its vegetation, detritus, and sea wrack. (See, for example, "Sainte Lucie": "Pomme arac, / otaheite apple, / pomme cythère, / pomme granate, / moubain, / z'ananas," etc. [*SG* 36].)

But "unuttered, undefined" may refer more to nature's insatiable appetite for signs than to the insufficiency of Walcott's gesture of naming (or even the insufficiency of English, since he presents the "English words" as mute, devoid of evocative power). The casuarinas ask too much: since no name can define and contain, the naming process must be continuous and endless. No matter how extensive the naming, "We remain" unuttered because we remain: "we" (the trees) are rooted. In this way, the trees revenge themselves on the mobile poet, demanding he be tethered to themselves; their rootedness confers on them an intimidating authority.[21]

Linguistic nature, in this "Homecoming," takes on a meaning beyond that of the poet's habitual troping. The voices of the trees, raised in reprimand, mourn their own lack; nature speaks yet demands a voice. From the poet's standpoint, Nature's demand for transformation into language is its principal feature. He faces a world of objects that demand signing and meaning, that demand to be something other than themselves.

The Scandal of Universals

To the unforgiving trees of "Homecoming," the poet's remark that "all the trees of the world shared a common elation / of tongues" is as treacherous as the poet's travels. To see universalism as betrayal, as the trees do, is another way of naming language as treasonous. In both cases, the specificity of a moment is betrayed. The trees do not seem to grasp, however, that uniqueness must be sacrificed if one wishes to tell a story, since no unique terms exist; as Saussure observes, a linguistic sign uttered only once is incomprehensible. The charge, then, like the charge that the trees remain "unuttered," is impossible to answer with satisfaction. Nevertheless, in working out this argument between the aberrant, "faithless" traveler and the rooted, demanding "home," "Homecoming" presents us with a key paradox in Walcott—that of the witness in the act of denying the possibility of witnessing—a paradox evident in several other poems of *The Bounty* and of *The Arkansas Testament*.

The Bounty takes up a form, a style, and to a large extent a subject matter set out in *Midsummer*, three books earlier. *The Bounty*'s exuberance, like its form, matches that of this predecessor; indeed the two titles are the most celebratory in Walcott's oeuvre. Universalizing statements run through *Midsummer*:

> Though they have different sounds for "God" or "hunger," the opposing
> alphabets
>   in city squares
> shout with one voice.
> (XXII)

In the controlling metaphor of the book, midsummer is one season spanning all climates: "summer is the same; / . . . summer is the same / everywhere" (VIII; ellipsis added). This sameness, as absence of difference— in seasons and in countries, prefigures *The Bounty*, in whose title poem, addressed to his mother, the poet writes "there is one season, our viridian Eden," and mourns that "[t]here is no change now, no cycles of spring, autumn, winter, . . . / no climate, no calendar except for this bountiful day" (15). Later in *The Bounty*, he makes the connection of that tropical sameness to island life: "but here we have merely a steadiness without seasons, / and no history" (35).[22]

This sameness of the seasons offers an advantage: the freedom to deploy metaphors extravagantly, not to memorialize rootedness but to build a mythic world. In *Midsummer* and *The Bounty*, then, we may see Walcott's universalism as a mission to write *out* of the linear history he deplores in his 1974 essay "The Muse of History." In that essay he offers Whitman, Neruda, Perse, Césaire, and Borges as examples of writers with a New World Adamic vision, poets who reject a version of history defined as linear and culpable. *Midsummer* is explicit about this project:

> my own prayer is to write
> lines as mindless as the ocean's of linear time,
> since time is the first province of Caesar's jurisdiction.
> (XLIII, ii)

Put this way, as a strike against Caesar, the project sounds revolutionary. From a historicist viewpoint, however, it sounds quietistic or "transcendental." Certainly, in many sectors of the academy today, universalism is seen, at best, as naïve and benighted; at worst, as disguising attempts to depreciate if not erase difference. But the charge of betraying historical reference could plausibly be better founded—were the whole argument not already incorporated into the poem—in a sequence such as "Signs" (*The Bounty*), where the war in Bosnia immediately generates its own simulacrum, in the form of a film. After references to "David's star" and "the ethnic cleansing" comes the line, "Arc-lamps come on, and with them, the movie-setting," followed by references to "soot-eyed extras," a "shot" that "elegiacally grieves," and a "sequel" (*B* 22).

Taken as a mourning of presence, rather than an abdication of witness, "Signs" evokes a contemporary problem: that of the televiewer who, in assimilating indiscriminate mixes of reportage, commentary, fiction, and advertising, fails to distinguish, generically and historically, between them. The proliferation of simulacra precludes any sharp distinctions between the events represented. Far from endorsing a nothing-but-text theory, however,

"Signs" explores the competition between material realities and representations. Indeed, "Signs" is key to the paradox in Walcott suggested earlier, in that, while the poem itself generates a surplus of signs, the poem's narrator speaks against signs, not only for the pre-Christian reason that "the ancient tongue / that forbade graven images makes inevitable sense" (*B* 22) but also for the reason behind that injunction: signs limit and define, pretending to contain the uncontainable.

The paradox is that even the conviction that the poet must escape the burden of witness leads Walcott apophatically to witness. Announcing his unwillingness to recover historical tragedy compels him to acknowledge that tragedy. Admittedly, the refusal may sometimes appear as a loss of proportion, as in "Summer Elegies," from *The Arkansas Testament*, much of which reads as if it had been a draft of "Signs":

> There is sometimes more pain in a pop song than all of Cambodia,
> . . . the heart puts love above it
> all, any other pain—Chernobyl, a mass murder—
> the world's slow stain is there; we cannot remove it.
> (96)

But here too, apophasis is at work: the staggering scale of what went wrong in Cambodia or in Chernobyl makes it unrepresentable but unignorable. In "Steam," from the same volume, a Holocaust survivor says, "I believe in 10. In my hands. But more than 1,000,000 / tires them like crabs. All those bald zeros / add up to a lie"(68). In what seems a refusal to represent colossal suffering, the not-to-be-mentioned one million are mentioned, in the same breath as the inadequacy of language, poetry, and the human sensibility to grasp them.

Much of "Elsewhere," also from *The Arkansas Testament*, rewrites Auden's "Musée des Beaux Arts," suggesting that ordinary lives go on despite suffering "elsewhere." But "elsewhere" also suggests that the signified is never *here*, that it is always unrecoverable. Even were the dreadful to happen here—as in the saying "It can happen here" (or in Heidegger's "The dreadful has already happened")—it would still be elsewhere: it would lie beyond representation. Walcott writes,

> elsewhere, in one-third or one-seventh
> of this planet, a summary rifle butt

breaks a skull into the idea of a heaven

where nothing is free.
(66)

The "idea of a heaven," rather than "heaven," marks again a move from the place to the construction. From here to the poem's end, the linguistic takes over, particularly the familiar world-as-text figures:

Through these black bars
hollowed faces stare. Fingers
grip the cross bars of these stanzas
and it is here, because somewhere else

their stares fog into oblivion
thinly.
(67)

The lines suggest that they are the only means of accomplishing witness, as the bars behind which one can see the faces of the inmates. "[I]t is here," because elsewhere the prisoners dissolve, to our view, into an impenetrable fog, just as those vast numbers of the dead in "Steam" dissolve to the understanding. Is the poem, then, a way of apprehending this suffering? Can we see the missing and disappeared by looking through the grid of the lines? The prospect does not seem likely in a poem that questions the whole apparatus of representation. However, the end of "Elsewhere" takes up the question of subjectivity, where work *can* be done:

The world is blameless. The darker crime
is to make a career of conscience,
to feel through our own nerves the silent scream
of winter branches, wonders read as signs.
(67)

The passivity of this, and the denial of its promise to go "somewhere" rather than to relegate all presence to "elsewhere" when so much is at stake, will make it unappealing to readers for whom "to make a career of conscience" is not a bad idea. For Walcott, "it" has to be here in the art, because otherwise it is always elsewhere, which means nowhere, un-locatable, always deferred. The "darker crime" is what history according to "Caesar" conditions us to commit: to see all phenomena as pain, all stories as stories of victimhood. While Walcott's thinking and his poetics have passed through changes over the years, this idea, and this refusal, is consistent, from the early essay "The Muse of History" to the most recent work.

In one of the *Midsummer* poems, Walcott addresses explicitly the problem of locating "it"—the suffering, the tragedy, the crimes—in art. Nostalgic for still-life painting, he stresses the inadequacy of art for anything but surfaces: "the depth of *nature morte* / was that death itself is only another surface / like the canvas, since painting cannot capture thought" (XVIII). But the surfaces change, he records, after the First World War. A new set of images, no less superficial, replaces all those pleasant subjects—bustled skirts and boating parties:

> like dried-up tubes, the coiled soldiers
> piled up on the Somme, and Verdun. And the dead
> less real than a spray burst of chrysanthemums,
> the identical carmine for still life and for the slaughter
> of youth.
> (XVIII)

This may be the baldest admission in Walcott's poetry of the inevitable textuality of art, which must relish and revel in its own medium. It is also a refusal, among many such, of history according to Caesar. As a theory of representation, it is not for everyone. The Adamic mythmaking role Walcott sees for the poet means that play, language's awareness of itself, does not take second place, even in, or especially in, the most historically referential moments. Not a choice or preference, it is, for Walcott, the awareness that it cannot be otherwise.

Walcott's Other Places

I felt history to be the burden of others.
"The Muse of History"

The subject-object relations that have most interested Walcott are those of the estranged traveler in his relation to home, but Walcott's oeuvre also includes travel poetry in the more conventional sense of highly descriptive poems written abroad. A look at these latter poems reveals that, while he celebrates a "sacramental stasis" in his native islands, Walcott concedes and even embraces history in *other* places. Indeed, the kind of history as victimization he deplores in "The Muse of History" is the very kind he seems to envy in his favorite heterotopias: Europe, Latin America, and the Hispanic Caribbean.[23] Particularly, the commitment of poets who have suffered under repressive regimes awes and perhaps intimidates Walcott. In *Sea Grapes* he asks, "Why do I imagine the death of Mandelstam / among the yellowing coconuts . . . ?" ("Preparing for Exile" 17) and quotes Anna Akhmatova, who was not a "fortunate traveler," who did not and *could* not leave home:

> No, not under the vault of another sky,
> not under the shelter of other wings.
> I was with my people then,
> there where my people were doomed to be.
> (23)

The malaise of the privileged traveler, in the face of literary-historical figures such as Akhmatova, has plagued not only Walcott but also many North American poets who have looked with a qualified envy to Eastern Europe, Latin America, or China, regions where totalitarian regimes have sometimes conferred on writers a subversive importance that they lack in the land of instant absorption.[24]

For Walcott, the longing for the fullness and dynamism of the other place's history is too powerful to repress, and his own island's "Nothing," which he has redeemed from Froude and Naipaul, converting it to a positive attribute, again and again seems impoverished and stultifying. In the *other* place history, not just the sea, is "going on."[25] I turn here to Walcott's persona as the tourist abroad, not in his own land—the Anglophone Caribbean poet traveling in the Hispanic Caribbean. This may be Walcott's true "travel" poetry: poems where the geographic and psychological shift entailed by encounters with the poet's Caribbean others brings out a different register of his voice and a different, though sometimes cynical, sensibility.

We find treatments of other Caribbeans in poems such as "Cantina Music" and "The Liberator" from *The Fortunate Traveler* and in "Central America," "Salsa," and "French Colonial. 'Vers de Société'" from the "Elsewhere" section of *Arkansas Testament*. Throughout Walcott's early work, numerous poems also show the influence of Neruda, notably "The

Star-Apple Kingdom." But the most extended treatment of the Spanish Caribbean is the section of *Midsummer* titled "Tropic Zone," composed in an old mansion converted to a hotel in the high-rise beach neighborhood of El Condado in San Juan, Puerto Rico, where Walcott stayed while giving a series of readings at the University of Puerto Rico in 1982. The hotel, called Hostería del Mar, is a short walk up the beach from the Puerto Rico Convention Center.[26]

"Tropic Zone" comprises eight numbered one-page poems. The first two sections play with the poetic possibilities of the new place (Puerto Rico is never named and often seems to become Spain or Cuba) and with the alien language of the Spanish Caribbean—in Walcott's accustomed trope of the interpenetration of nature and word: "This is my ocean, but it is speaking / another language" (XLIII, i). The speaker resists the sea as a noun spelled "*el mar.*" A sparrow chirps to him that a "walk on the beach should teach you our S's / as the surf says them." On the street outside the hotel, everything is still text: "The boulevards open like novels / waiting to be written" (XLIII, i).

Like Walcott's morning constitutional past the hotel, the poem appears to be a daily exercise, developing familiar themes; yet history begins to give it contours it could not have had at "home." Here, unlike the sea-grape-strewn beaches of St. Lucia, "history will pierce your memory like a migraine." In "Tropic Zone" and the other Spanish Caribbean poems, many military and political references evoke this history, references relatively absent in Walcott's poems of the English Caribbean.[27] In the opening section, the hotel's vines resemble "olive green infantry / over from Cuba." A white dory on the beach has been " 'shot / for being a gringo.' " In the second section, " 'the wrong done to our fathers' / weeps along empty streets" (XLIII, ii). Despite sentries in front of the palace, "Blue skies convert all genocide into fiction," a conversion, familiar, as we have seen, in the later *The Arkansas Testament* and *The Bounty.*

But it is the third section of "Tropic Zone" that opens up the Spanish heterotopia aesthetically and historically by evoking the murals in national palaces all over Latin America.

Above hot tin billboards, above Hostería del Mar,
wherever the Empire has raised the standard of living
by blinding high rises, gestures are made to the culture

of a remorseful past, whose artists must stay unforgiving
even when commissioned. If the white architectural mode is
International Modern, the décor must be the Creole's.
(XLIII, iii)

In its subsequent treatment of the murals, "Tropic Zone" explores the sites
of postcolonial identity formation and exploitation by state and commercial
apparatuses. Walcott's technical prowess, though it may also trivialize the
history in question, allows him to squeeze every popular postcolonial trope
into his verses, ending by dismissing them all in a touristic gesture:

> in a terra-cotta lobby with palms, a local jingle
> gurgles of a new *cerveza*, frost-crusted and golden,
> right next to a mural that has nationalized Eden
> in vehement acrylics, and this universal theme
> sees the golden beer, the gold mines, "the gold of their bodies"
> as one, and our two tropics as erogenous zones.
> A necklace of emerald islands is fringed with lace
> starched as the ruffles of Isabella's bodice,
> now the white-breasted Niña and Pinta and Santa María
> bring the phalli of lances penetrating a jungle
> whose vines spread apart to a parrot's primal scream.
> Then, shy as the ferns their hands are bending, stare
> fig-nippled maidens with faces calm as stones,
> and, as is the case with so many revolutions,
> the visitor doubts the murals and trusts the beer.
> (XLIII, iii)

The hotel commissioned this mural to decorate its bar with a version of
a jungle Eden convergent with local histories, in the style, judging by the
description, of Henri Rousseau more than of Diego Rivera or Oruzco.
The artist's revolutionary, "unforgiving" stance is what makes him com-
missionable. The mural must depict a revolutionary history in order to sell
beer, whose gold evokes the other golds of a pre-Columbian golden age, of
metals in the earth, and of golden skin. (The metonymies, though not the
particular images, are reminiscent of the several golds in Bishop's magical
"Santarém.") The "universal theme"—the multinational beer jingle—sees
these as one "and our two tropics as erogenous zones" (not only the

Tropics of Cancer and Capricorn but also the Anglophone and Hispanic Caribbean). From corporation headquarters, that is, from the perspective of the North, the tropics as playground, as escape from drudgery, are billed as erogenous zones, not only in travel posters but also in this mural with its "fig-nippled maidens."[28]

This is a recipe for refusing if not annihilating the migraine of history—the cycle of co-optation, commercialization, and consumption, the nationalization of Eden, and the beer blotting out the "revolution," which is given the lie by that very metonymic chain. If the story is of a fall into commodification, it is the visitor himself who has fallen, who doubts the revolutions, just as he does genocides and all the rest of history as victimization; he prefers or at least trusts the beer, which has reached him by such a suspicious concatenation.

These versions of Latin America are predigested, but Walcott does not pass them off as anything *but*. As ever, he is as interested in scenery that folds up as he is in scenery that is "natural." Among sunstruck plazas and equestrian statues out of a Chirico painting, the speaker comments,

> And that's how it was
> in the old scenarios, a backdrop for the hectic
> conscience of the gringo with his Wasp's rage at tedium,
> but now in the banana republics, whose bunches of recruits
> look green in fatigues, techniques of camouflage
> have taught the skill of slitting stomachs like fruits,
> and a red star without a sickle is stitched to a flag.
> (XLIII, iv)

Just as in "Signs," where historical loss and atrocity become a film shoot, so here the speaker unabashedly treats history as movie cliché:

> At the movies, I still love it when gap-toothed bandidos laugh
> in growling pidgin, then grin at the sudden contradiction
> of roses stitching their guts. In colonial fiction
> evil remains comic and only achieves importance
> when the gringo crosses the plaza, flayed by the shadows of fronds.
> (XLIII, iv)

This nod to genre movies and fiction fits into the touristic cynicism of the sequence, yet it places readers in an odd position. Can the poem stand as a critique of Graham Greene-ish uses of the developing world as a backdrop for northern melodramas if the speaker says, "I still love it"?[29] Or should we insist that texts incorporate their own correctives so that readers are left with nothing to do but with the comfortable certainty that this is (or is not) a right-minded text? Should we insist that distances between authors and unreliable, even unsavory, narrators be clearly marked? Given that the chief texts of interest to critics of advocacy over the past thirty years have been the wrongheaded ones—whether *Heart of Darkness* or *Robinson Crusoe* or, more lately, Elizabeth Bishop's "In the Waiting Room"—must we ask that authors clarify what they are satirizing and what endorsing so that we would all know whether Conrad or Defoe or Bishop was a "racist" or not?

Such demands, of course, are unrealistic, and yet Walcott's musings in these Puerto Rican poems are troubling. Do tropical settings as backdrops for *yanqui* psychodramas reveal a lamentable ignorance of tropical realities, of the tropics as a place where people really live? Or is the tone not more often that of condescension toward the "snoring peon" (XLIII, iv), the tacky pseudorevolutionary mural, the corrupt dictator, and so on?[30] We get the easy barb aimed at the "gringo with his Wasp's rage at tedium," but, throughout "Tropic Zone," we also get ready-made scenery and cliché Latin Americanisms presented without a tone that might guide us through the layers of irony. Only, possibly, at the closing of the sequence does the author orientate us so that we understand that evil is portrayed as comic in "colonial fiction," only taking on importance, in such texts, when a North American life is in danger.

Both *Midsummer* and, to some extent, its thematic and formal successor *The Bounty* are books of exercises, brilliant watercolors of "scenic" subjects—seascapes, plazas, old forts—where Walcott plays on accustomed tropes of the scene in question. These occur as nature/culture inversion ("stones crawling toward language" [*M* IX]); as self-referential commentary on the problems of writing, in the style of Lowell ("everything I read / or write goes on too long. Ah, to have / a tone colloquial and stiff" [IX]); or as Rorschach blot, allowing curious chains of associations—in "Tropic Zone," associations and images branching from Puerto Rico into other Hispanic image caches—of Cuban revolutionaries, Spanish flamenco, or Guatemalan poverty.

Keeping in mind this idea of Walcott's heterotopia as a historical incursion into a home field normally denuded of history—a home field of "sacramental stasis"—I would like to turn to a last juxtaposition of the Anglophone and Hispanophone New Worlds in his poems. Even while Walcott cites Whitman, St.-John Perse, and Pablo Neruda, among others, as Adamic poets, to be admired for their courage in transcending linear history, Neruda, particularly, reminds him of what history can mean to poets. Walcott's ambivalent stance between aesthete and political poet indeed invites comparison with Neruda's early work. Neruda had been called, as he tells it (*Twenty Poems* 12), a kind of Theocritus, admired for his love poems until, after his confrontation with Chilean strongman Videla and his subsequent flight to the hinterlands to avoid imprisonment, he began to write the poems of the vast *Canto General*, in which he was severely critical of the governments of both Latin America and the United States. Walcott borrows heavily from these poems in the early "The Star-Apple Kingdom," with whole sections seeming almost lifted out of "The United Fruit Company" and other poems of *Canto General*:

> And while they prayed for an economic miracle,
> ulcers formed on the municipal portraits,
> the hotels went up, and the casinos and brothels,
> and the empires of tobacco, sugar, and bananas.
> (*SAK* 50)

Walcott's position of fidelity to "the people," however, is more problematic than Neruda's was. Walcott's movement from love poet to engaged poet, unlike Neruda's, is accompanied by both a refusal of history and an inability to exorcise its force. In "The Star-Apple Kingdom," the speaker stands accused of lacking revolutionary commitment. He tells how "Revolution," in the form of a beautiful woman—"the darker, the older America"—demanded his action, but he wanted only peace, "a revolution without any bloodshed":

> he wanted a history without any memory,
> streets without statues,
> and a geography without myth. He wanted no armies
> but those regiments of bananas, thick lances of cane,
> and he sobbed, "I am powerless, except for love."
> (51)

So the Revolution abandons him. His response is another denial, a peaceful aestheticism, a reversion to pleasure, and a turn to metaphor, ecstasy, and filial love: "He slept the sleep that wipes out history, / he slept like the islands on the breast of the sea, / like a child again in her star-apple kingdom" (54).

He wakes up, now committed, it seems, though not to Revolution: "he was a bride under lace, remarrying his country" (56). He returns to his country, to the obligation he repudiated, feminized and infantilized by both bond and vow. "Nature," in the form of the ocean, receives him: fluid, chaotic, and apolitical. (Despite the title of one of Walcott's poems, the sea, here at least, is *not* history.)

Where will the new commitment lead? In the space of the poem, it leads to an allegory of the failure dooming any retrieval of roots. The islands become turtles—that species that migrates across the Atlantic every year, constituting proof of the Gaia concept, the former unity of the continents.[31] The turtles yearn for Africa, "lemmings drawn by magnetic memory / to an older death" (56). They are certain to drown or to be eaten, with "sea eagles circling them." He cries out to the turtles "as one screams at children / with the anger of love," and miraculously the predators recede. In the silence that ensues, "Star-apples rained to the ground" (57). This sublime conclusion, where star-apples fall like sugar plums in a "silence that lasted for half an hour" and yet a "single second, a seashell silence resounding / silence" (59) is troubling in a poem that sets out to grapple with moral and historical questions. The turn toward the aesthetic "obsession," away from the "responsibility," to use the terms of "Sea Grapes," is echoed in the fairy-tale music of "that single second, a seashell silence." The poem climaxes in a global, unaccountable happiness, where the perspective draws back to encompass the "creak of light"

> between rich and poor, between North and South,
> between white and black, between two Americas.
> (57)

The woman's wrinkled face smiles, and the subject of the poem eats his breakfast egg, "crack[ing] the day open" (58).

The argument *against* history, of which this is one of a great many instances in Walcott, keeps open the dialogue *with* history. The poet retains both models—history as time and history as myth—but explores them only in the latter model's terms.[32] Oppositions in Walcott, such as "responsibility" versus "obsession" in "Sea Grapes" or "grenades" versus "star-apples" in "The Star-Apple Kingdom," are ultimately inert, since the poet only casts them in terms of the latter, aesthetic figures. The oppositions themselves constitute his "one theme," the "expedition" he sets out on in poem after poem.

"The Fortunate Traveler" 's parlaying of individual selfishness and disengagement into the global consequences of failure to love is an unusual moment for Walcott. By far, the greater part of his poetry acts out the gesture we see in "The Star-Apple Kingdom," not building toward apocalyptical prophecy but disappearing into textuality, that simultaneous mourning of presence and embrace of metaphor most characteristic of his work, whether in its ludic or dramatic modes.

I have pointed in this chapter to more than one kind of "transport" in Walcott's poems: first, the metaphorical displacement, the turning so strongly to metaphor that its ground in the world slips away; second, transport in the sense of ecstasy, if not in the collective rocking of the bus passengers listening to Bob Marley, in "The Light of the World," then in the sense of a rhetorical thickness relished even while interrogated; and, finally, the physical, geographic sense of "transport." Of these three, given the coordinates of subject position I mentioned at the outset of this chapter, I must return to geography. If the European poet is permitted to seek ekstasis from Europe, heading south for inspiration, escape, and pleasure, why may not the Caribbean poet travel? No one begrudged the English Romantics their flight to the Mediterranean. The reverse migration, from south to north, has had different consequences and has been burdened with different expectations. The commitment of fidelity to island realities continues to constrain the Caribbean poet's situation. Walcott has interiorized this constraint in many of his poems. I have suggested here a dialoguism in those poems, in which the poet creates a speaker who argues with his own demons of duty and who, since he can never silence those voices, makes poetry out of that conversation.

The "Flight" that so often figures in Walcott's poems, whether in "The Schooner *Flight*," "The Fortunate Traveler," *Omeros*, or other works, is a flight toward an expression unencumbered by the demand to witness, a flight from the political to the personal, from the collective to the individual, from teleology to myth. Perhaps fortunately, it is incomplete. The very movement toward surfaces that Walcott's poems both perform and thematize constitutes a form of witness—not raw, not transparent, not a *testimonio*—but a faithful witness to misrepresentation, to the troubled, inevitable gap between life and the poem.

Wandering, then, is staked out with signs, with characters.

MICHEL BUTOR, "Travel and Writing"

Travel and Difference
Lyn Hejinian and Nathaniel Mackey

An article in *Writer's Digest* advises "travel poets" as follows: "To compose publishable travel verse, you need to depict a scene, a site or a person in a manner that you otherwise would not have employed were you back home" (Bugeja 12). The author recommends Pound's "The Garden" and "In a Station of the Metro" as touchstones. In the same article, poet Jim Barnes advises not to take tours or travel in a crowd. "I find in Paris, that to know Paris you have to get away from the crowded spots and take the side streets" (13). Keep a journal, he and Karen Swenson advise. "My poetry," Barnes says, "comes from the things I perceive with the five senses. If I am writing about a place, I must absolutely be in, or have been in, that place" (14).

Compare this advice, with its assumptions of a stable subject, a describable object, and a straightforward mimetic project, to the more linguistic and programmatic travel writings of Raymond Roussel, who never left his trailer or train car and of whom Michel Leiris wrote, "It seems likely that the outside world never broke through into the universe he carried within him, and in all the countries he visited, he saw only what he had put there in advance, elements which corresponded absolutely with that universe that was peculiar to him" (qtd. in Ashbery, introd. xi. I discuss Roussel at greater length in my chapter on John Ashbery).

Obviously myriad peculiar sites lie between these two compass points of the expressivist and the linguistic. The expressivist or subjective turn—the personal poem written in response to an experience—characterizes the work of most of the contents of most poetry anthologies and literary quarterlies. None of the poets discussed in this book, however, have been naïve expressivists; all problematize subject-object relations; none assume that "out there" offers a key to representation. The difference in the two poets discussed next lies, then, not only in their deliberate (if inevitably partial) repudiation of the expressivist mode set out in the *Writer's Digest* version of poetry, but also in their linguistically more disjunctive poetics, their heightened sense of the gap between words and the world, and, incidentally, in their small-press provenance, as opposed to the mainstream publishing world of, say, Lowell, Bishop, Walcott, and Ashbery. Thematically, they have chosen to pursue questions usually raised in the provinces of literary theory or in studies of culture, nationality, and ethnicity, questions concerning the tenuousness of identity and the constructedness of the subject, complicated by the trope, as well as by the literal experience, of travel. Although Lyn Hejinian and Nathaniel Mackey are involved in different poetic projects, their travel poems are similar in that they map, across a landscape both geographic and linguistic, the expedition to locate an elusive and estranged identity.

Translation and Lyn Hejinian's *Oxota*

The poems of *Oxota: A Short Russian Novel* are written "after" Pushkin's *Evgeny Onegin*. Some of them apparently transliterate Pushkin, but most are tangential responses, takes, or riffs on experiences of travel. These are the poems of a North American woman, traveling in Russia, who is associated with "language" poetry. In her critical book *The Language of Inquiry*, Hejinian writes that *Oxota* concerns

> unsettlement and disorientation; its milieu, the Soviet Union, is for a Westerner perhaps exotic, but in the "novel" it is the narrator who becomes exoticized; she becomes estranged from the markers of self and incapable of self-location. Curiously, though this theme of dislocation or disorientation might seem to be generic to "travel literature" and hence somewhat inevitable in *Oxota*, it is also very much a Russian theme [here Hejinian cites numerous Russian novelists, from Dostoevsky and Gogol to Nabokov]. (210)

The "language" affiliation is problematic in Hejinian, since *Oxota*, like the poet's better-known *My Life*, is often autobiographical, not to mention descriptive, coherent, and poignant. Nevertheless, an antisubjective stance announces itself in the book's very first poem: "There is no person. . . . / There is relationship but it lacks simplicity" (11; ellipsis added).[1] This is in fact "language" poetry in an exacerbated sense, first because *Oxota* is a book about the hunt for language and, second, because the poems actually discuss linguistic incidents, problems of language and especially of translation. Hejinian's frequent references to grammar underscore the linguistic dimension of difference. What does an English speaker do in a country where "even 'it' is irregular" (164); where "there are constant predicates and variable subjects" (70); where "there are prepositions everywhere in the possessive / The of of one and the of of all, a difference to infinity" (223); where even the dangling pipe on the gas stove is "in a prepositional state / for, not for, off, on" (221); and where "the neighbors themselves were little more than pronunciation" (248)? The grammar of language is inextricable from the grammar of life and culture. This country has "[m]onstrous prepositions," and, in the same poem, "two sullen men in blue fish / I wonder why their plurals are the same as their possessives" (147). "Form subjugates every experience," as Hejinian writes (76), in an immediate regard: linguistic form subjugates and subordinates the world around the traveler, so that she finds herself vulnerable in the negotiating of difference, lost in translation.

A poet who writes that "Form subjugates every experience" would seem to demand a formal rather than a thematic treatment. Nevertheless, it is difficult *not* to address the theme of that sentence since it permeates the 270 travel poems or "chapters" of *Oxota*. Other formulations of this idea include

"[S]peech doesn't guarantee an object" (138); "The mere mood of our words was producing content" (79); and "We have words, and their things must remain in abeyance" (187). In one of three different poems titled "Truth," Hejinian writes, "Truth is not a likeness—not of depicted sense" (281), a statement that begins to spell out the difference in the approach to representation under discussion here. "Truth" has to be something besides a correspondence, something, as it happens, suggested in the book's title. Toward the end of *Oxota*, the meaning of that Russian word finally appears:

> It's characteristic of a Russian novelist to reveal some lack of confidence in the
>   relationship between words and their things
> . . . .
> How many alternatives there must be
> How many patient comparisons await fulfilling
> Unextracted paradoxes . . .
> It was Zina who called it *oxota*
> The hunt
> . . . .
> But this lack of confidence often culminates in a single instant of ignorance
> And that instant, Akadii said, might correspond to what you have called
>   paradise
> (278; ellipsis added)

Oxota, then, is a writer's hunt, a hunt across text more than territory, but instead of arriving at a "Eureka" moment as the writer finds the mot juste, the hunt ends in an "instant of ignorance"—not a pejorative here, since that instant *"might correspond to what you have called* paradise" (emphasis added), a phrase indicating the double tentativeness of the equation at both the Russian and the English ends of the language transaction. The hunt is staged within a welter of "alternatives," "comparisons," and "paradoxes," where the relations between words and things are deeply unstable. Because the object of the hunt remains elusive, the hunt continues: the hunt for a common idiom, a "faithful" translation, a successful relation between sign and referent, and ultimately a ground of understanding between English and Russian—all of these objects, finally, mythical. Given these definitions of *oxota*, it is necessarily also, as Hejinian shows in another late chapter, a hunt through the pages of a dictionary.

At the most quotidian level, the poems are chapters in a book of culture studies, each study revealing a different misreading. Sometimes a poem illustrates a Russian misreading of U.S. contemporary culture, ethnicity, or literature:

> Sergei asked about nigger music
> You mean, I said—Black
> And I see you're pink, he raged then—yes, is that your color?—and maybe
>   yellow too—it disgusts me—it's like chicken fat
> He was pleased with that
> Sergei says you're a racist, Mitya told me later—he heard you calling niggers
>   black
> Niggers?
> As Faulkner says—it's a literary word, respectful, yes?
> (34)

Other instances concern gender:

> I was asked to explain the phrase sex kitten and the term pussy
> . . . .
> He asked which women prefer?
> (36)

And socioeconomic systems:

> There's an infinite line in Moscow, Masha said . . . to enter McDonald's
> And meanwhile people are turning to chalk in the cold
> Have you been there?
> It's just cutlets!
> (241; ellipsis added)

Insofar as some of these "errors" and slippages are more linguistic than referential, the poems of *Oxota* occupy themselves with difficulties of translation back and forth between the two languages. They constitute linguistic and semantic gaffes and faux pas, evoking the shape changing as well as the vulnerability and ineffectuality travel entails. This meditation on translation is perhaps the most dominant theme of *Oxota*, both in the grammatical and in the semantic and cultural senses. "Comparisons are frequent in language situations" (158), Hejinian writes: "both awake and asleep the process of translating matter into memory continued" (30). And it does continue, through the hundreds of episodes to follow. Some instances are external, specific, and referential:

> A circle of ice—there's no single English word for it—a certain very clear
> and thick lens of ice that forms on a window after a sequence of many
> partial meltings and subsequent freezings
>
> (262)

This reminds one of Edward Sapir's claim, now disputed, that the Eskimos have hundreds of words for snow, a situation whereby the referential world of one culture generates vocabulary lacking in the other culture, so that the visitor searches in vain for a correspondence.

Other instances are "errors" in translation on the part of the host:

> About something which is nothing, for example, we can say
> We can say he is . . . he is don't-sew-a-sleeve-to-a-cunt
> Fixed white
> (16)

When the American poet's friend bids farewell, "I adore you, my cunt, said Dimitrii in English" (192).

On a more theoretical level, Hejinian states her "preference for difference" in the first poem of *Oxota*; the preference is prominent in several poems where linguistic and affective pressures of travel shape both identity and the process of representation. The desire for difference, however, is frustrated by travel's failure to make good on its promise of access to interiors, destinations, and arrival. This is "Chapter Sixty-Three" in its entirety:

> Goodbye, America, which I have never seen
> I float forever in my paper boat
> A paper flicker, no telephone
> If there would be phone, there would be love
> No taken distance—but there's only difference
> Description of it is a form of waiting
> But the time deteriorates
> I remember how it was, and what a fine memory of it was forming
> Or that was the anticipation
> Cold was imminent and my sense of it merely deferred

The climate was inexact and inert
With the person disappeared the person's obsequiousness
The person now morose or immune
It's afloat in its intimations
(73)

The paper boat the speaker floats in—an image carried even into the last line's "afloat in its intimations"—suggests both the traveler's vulnerability, bidding farewell to her homeland, and the vulnerability of representation itself, the poem folded up to make a paper boat and set afloat, as Li Po was said to have done with his poems, to drift like "a paper flicker," frail and doomed to perish. ("Chapter 127" suggests that the poem is a "A Vulnerable Apparatus" [142].) In "Chapter Sixty-Three," the pathos, weakness, fragility, even impossibility of the poetic project are set out lyrically—and conventionally, given the pentameter and alliteration of the "float forever" line—before the concepts of "distance" and "difference" are introduced in the fifth line.

The description of difference serves as a way of filling the time, distance, and painful absence suggested in "If there would be phone [instead of paper], there would be love" and "Description of it is a form of waiting." The poem traces a process of translating into memory, as if into a travel diary, a particular yet still indistinct experience. The poet remembers the experience and watches the memory of it coalescing but, as "the time deteriorates," sees that the memory may not be at issue so much as the hope attached to it, the transference infusing it, before it is formulated or set down in writing. With its pathos of farewell at the outset, the poem is subdued not only for traditional reasons—separation from a loved one and unease in a cold and indeterminate place—but also for less traditional reasons: the paratactic metacommentary on representation, fraught to the same degree with difficulty and failure. The poem mourns, in other words, the irretrievability of the experience it is called on to represent. As time passes and decays, that experience recedes and becomes resistant, immune to description and irreducible: "afloat in its intimations," too many to contain.

The sense I attribute to the poem so far may not account for a style as far from the *Writer's Digest* version of representation as one could wish, even while Hejinian has followed the *letter* of that law, depicting "a scene, a site or a person in a manner that you otherwise would not have employed were you back home." Bob Perelman writes that "*Oxota* does not display any larger wholes: the line is a provisional unit, always ending without a period" (74), but Perelman's focus on the paratactic unit ignores longer arcs: travel arcs, thematic arcs, and obviously the arc of the Russian surroundings. Moreover, lines without periods have been a modernist convention—even more in European than in American poetry—for almost a century. The openness of the line, its provisionality, should encourage a reading for "larger wholes," rather than shorter or smaller ones.

Perelman goes on to say that

> *Oxota* demonstrates one way parataxis operates in a context of scarcity. In the West, overloads of objects, viewpoints, schools, channels, typefaces, marketing strategies create pressure which can make the sequential coherence and drama of the novel seem like Victorian coincidence. In the world of *Oxota*, on the other hand, there is not enough of anything: chickens, paper, phones, living spaces are constantly being sought; connection itself becomes a luxury, and metaphorical extravaganzas fill the gaps between things. (75)

Perelman speaks here of cultural difference, surely the chief difference Hejinian herself pursues in these poems. The old-world scarcity means a prizing of continuity and connection, while the American glut and overload make continuity and connection passé and suspect, producing among middle-class, educated writers the desire to subvert them. Perelman, or for that matter Hejinian, may not put it this way, but in my reading of Perelman's comment, textual *dis*continuity is an American luxury. Saying as much neither disparages discontinuity nor prescribes realism, as Frederic Jameson does, as the literary mode appropriate for third-world writing.[2] The stylistic and referential discontinuities of contemporary bourgeois culture, rather, are necessary and inevitable, but they contrast with the discontinuities forced on one by travel—discontinuities of language, food, manners, values, climate, geography, and time zones. Consider Hejinian's "Chapter 186," which reads in part,

> Discontinuity is self-contained—that's an effect of nationalities
> But an idea is not ours
> Nor while moving certainly, absolute
> A horde, and I had to admit I was not an occupant

But the doorman permitted me, after an argument, to come in
Why not—he shook my hand
Mayakovsky, he said
I knew the marvel, the state of being hard to know
(204)

Discontinuity is an effect of crossing borders in this poem, but, despite the elliptical constructions and grammatical quirks ("absolute" / "A horde"), we find something literal and familiar in "I had to admit I was not an occupant" and in the events and reflections following that admission. The exchange with the doorman is, after all, narrative and dialogue. A thematic arc controls the poem, which begins and ends with a reflection on border crossing and difference. In the last line, the poet sees herself with the same wonder with which the other sees her: as different, "hard to know."

The preference for difference, as suggested earlier, runs constantly into the broken promise of travel, its failure to offer arrivals (a failure to provide a way "to know Paris," in the *Writer's Digest* directive). This broken promise appears not only in the form of monoculture—for example, the Moscow McDonald's somehow serves the same American meat—but also in the sense of nonarrival at the other culture or place. Hejinian writes in "Chapter 187" that "I could only move, even naming in place." Difference tells the traveler she is moving, and difference, in linguistics, *is* information, but "naming" is stranded here:

> Most days and nights there was no particular point and so no direction from
> there
> I could only move, even naming in place
> Probably that's why I couldn't sleep—I was always sleeping away
> Then we often ate no matter how late
> Noodles, soft scallions, and salt
> Pickled stalks
> I wandered in trust with nothing to tell
> Nothing, but it wanted its figurative form
> Just time in the kitchen with spoons, flames, and steams
> Nobody's business, nobody's narration
> We just scurried in our socks
> We could only have pleasure as we changed

But I wondered if it was rude to read the dictionary then
And it was always more different in the morning
(205)

"[N]o particular point" refers both to a compass point for getting our bearings and to a purpose. The first sense is metaphor for the second ("no particular point and so no direction"): the traveler is both unmoored and purposeless in this place. The compass disorientation becomes more important when we consider that for this speaker, just as distance is difference, a direction or a sense of direction constitutes perspective and identity. One of the poet's Russian friends says, "I have no sense of direction. . . . / One absolutely must have a sense of direction if one's to hate the West" (137; ellipsis added). Pointlessness, then, is a continuity of the poem: from the first lines to the wandering "with nothing to tell," the torpor and "sleeping [and slipping] away" of time, the tedium, and the blandness of the food. Another continuity is the domesticity, the images of stasis and the warmth of indoors: kitchens, time to sleep, late meals, stocking feet. Finally, as in virtually all the *Oxota* poems, there is the stated problem of translating the "nothing to tell" into the "figurative form" it requires. "Just time in the kitchen" is "nothing" in the sense that we say "nothing" to mean inconsequential. Moreover, we have "nothing to tell" if the experience has not yet been enfigured. It cannot be told on its own account; it can be told only when the language for it appears.

"There's only difference," Hejinian says in "Chapter Sixty-Three," and here, "it was always more different in the morning." Distance, as travelers attest, *creates* difference both in time and in space: in the course of a day, the sensitivity to difference diminishes as one accustoms oneself, whereas waking to it afresh defamiliarizes it anew. "We could only have pleasure as we changed" argues for travel as a mode of defamiliarization, of keeping life fresh. One travels, in part, to avoid being enslaved by convention or numbed by routine. The pleasure lies in change, but change requires translation. Pleasures of the domestic, of security, of warmth—all that one loses on leaving home—are only restored when one makes the complete change to the new place and translation ceases. We enjoy and suffer travel by breaking down the self, but to sustain defamiliarization entails further change. Again, distance constitutes difference: "habit is a dynamic only in everyday time / The further away the more aestheticized habits become" (138).

Subjectivity is constituted and identity provisionally established through difference from others and from one's surroundings. The self's instability may be conveniently ignored until affective or cognitive problems arise to call it to one's attention or until one moves from the space that has nurtured the self to a space that begins to dismantle it. "Chapter 253," like "Chapter Sixty-Three," is a poem of farewell that articulates this dismantling process, exploring the work farewells can do:

> Certainly I, more than anyone else, was made for parting, since parting to me
>   is a sort of non-being becoming aware of itself
> A real appearance in a real disturbance
> Not the one with not the other in the very place around the stairwell or onion
> Not waiting
> The thousand tints for difference
> Hints
> Milks
> Pinks
> Procrastinations will gleam, yearning for keeping
> The arrival of disappearance—awake, in sight
> Everything was before—returning our famous *glasnost* metaphor
> The light ground, what's seen in its grains
> The old grannies were out, conspiring over space
> And I agree, Arkadii said—they're always right[3]
> (272)

Parting from a place, as from a dear person, means parting with some part of oneself. Thus put, it is a familiar sentiment and a familiar experience, but for Hejinian, parting is "non-being becoming aware of itself," so instead of a presence becoming absence, here an absence, extant from the beginning, becomes aware of its own presence. One becomes aware at the moment of parting that the subject was *always already* a fiction, but the "disturbance" of parting raises nonbeing into a "real appearance." The cultural component of this, the almost anthropological emphasis pursued in these poems, appears in the phrase "The thousand tints for difference," which, with its free-associative riffs on "tints"—"Hints / Milks / Pinks"—invokes not only the multidimensionality but also the synesthesia of difference. The colored tints become psychological hints, then nutritive milks, and then colors (or flowers) again, with a largely phonetic and visual rather than semantic link.

Of the many commentaries on identity offered through these poems, consider this line: "The coincidence of experiences occurring with experiences already had produced identity—but it spills" (101). In such lines, we see that Hejinian's objections to the subjective are not the same as those of other poets and critics of our time. Adrienne Rich's late poem "In Those Years," for example, retrospectively bemoans the self-centeredness of the poetry of her time, suggesting that while the "great dark birds of history" flew over them, poets were "reduced to *I*," having "lost the meaning of *we*" (4). One understands the complaint and its application to U.S. culture, but for Hejinian, "I" represents a different kind of mistake, one that concerns the moment of composition as much as the moment of experience: in addition to ignoring the "we" of social movements and history, personal poetry interferes with the process of representation. The jazz pianist Bill Evans once compared jazz improvisation to Zen brush painting on thin rice paper; one has to be utterly absorbed in the process, for the moment of self-consciousness is the moment at which the process is spoiled. Hejinian's metaphor is similar:

> If language is like a river, it's like a melting one whose ice is weak
> If you pause while crossing to say "I" you'll fall in
> (264)

"I," in this context, is not only an indulgence and a distraction; it is also an intervention counterproductive to the process of representation, that is, counterproductive to the hunt, a process that should not end. The subjective emphasis dooms the hunt. To "succeed" in finding something (to match a sign and a thing) is torpor, then stasis. To stop the hunt, then, is to waste it: "The truth that is halted is squandered" (282), Hejinian writes in the last of the three poems titled "Truth," part of the short "Book Eight."

In the "Coda" that ends the book, while the poet asserts the primacy of language over the nonlinguistic world unequivocally, the unresolved poetic question remains how to represent, how to keep that hunt going, by *which* linguistic or literary generic means:

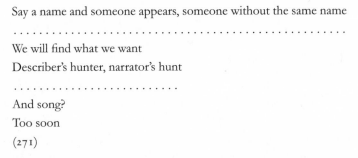

Say a name and someone appears, someone without the same name

. . . .

We will find what we want
Describer's hunter, narrator's hunt

. . . .

And song?
Too soon
(271)

The first line above suggests a lack of correspondence between sign and referent. The hunt's necessity ("The hunt must accomplish necessity" [187]) is the calling up of the world by words, but what responds to that calling, and what form should the calling take? The hunt has been the "Describer's hunt" and the "narrator's hunt" but not yet the singer's. To take these genres one by one, in "Chapter 144: Description," the poet writes: "My description gives my face in space, my story changes it / All narration is set with change" (159). The poet has resisted creating a narrative, though one might not expect to find the reasons (or the ambivalence about them) so clearly set out as they are earlier in the book:

> However there is a danger that life, being narrated, will turn into an "ad-
> venture" and every adventure moves inexorably towards resolution—
> but how can I say I don't like adventure?
> I think now of the startling antiquity of the sensation that *this is happening*.
> (124)

The generic distinctions are difficult to maintain in the poetry. Hejinian's work is by turns narrative and lyric, though seldom in either case for longer than a line or two. She can sustain description, however, through several lines. But why is it "[t]oo soon" for song? "Too soon" suggests, first, that the traveler is as yet insufficiently fluent to sing in the foreign language, since she is still at the stage of translating from her own; second, that as yet no closure or rite of passage has occurred to celebrate with song; and third, that she is still on the track of signs, still engrossed, indeed lost, in the enfiguring sense, to the point where that sense dominates all others.

All this serves to highlight the primacy of language, but which language— that is, which rhetoric, which discourse? It also highlights the primacy of form, but which form? To say it is too soon for song is an assertion with a history: the assertion accounts not only for Hejinian's immediate situation in *Oxota*—absorbed in the "hunt," in translation, and not (yet) empowered or *inclined* to sing—but also for her poetics: prose lines with few echoes of verse forms, following the American poets, at least since Williams, who have preferred prose rhythms and prose virtues to lyric models in their poetry. If it is too soon for song in this sense, the statement is part of a century-long disenchantment with enchantment. Enchantment (as *melos*) struggles against that prosaic repression but has not staged, in print poetry, a substantial comeback to date.[4]

But genre, while certainly reflective of Hejinian's concern in phrases such as "Form subjugates every experience," is only one facet of the larger problem of how to represent. "Oxota" is a hunt for an idiom, a ground, and a relation; a bridge between the two worlds of the traveler. Those two worlds are Russia and America, but they are also the worlds of sign and referent. Through the interstices of unfaithful translation (the only possible kind), the traveler can pursue her preference for differences, particularly, as it turns out, differences set up within the self. In the midst of her meditations on identity, she is exoticized not merely to her Russian hosts and fellow writers but to herself. Travel confers in *Oxota* not arrival or understanding but a dispersion of the self amid the pleasure and plenitude of its signs.

Nathaniel Mackey and the Compass of *Strick*

Nathaniel Mackey's recording of *Strick: Song of the Andoumboulou* 16–25 is the continuation of the long open-ended poem *Song of the Andoumboulou* whose installments have appeared in numerous journals and in two of his books, *Eroding Witness* and *School of Udhra*.[5] While alluding in its title to its inspiration, the West African Dogon "Song of the Andoumboulou," *Strick* is not itself a song; in fact, both its prosody and its "raspiness," to use Mackey's term, resist the transcendence we associate with song.[6] *Strick*'s interest lies instead in three areas: First, it comments on millennial poetic concerns about roots and the linguistic detours, deferrals, and dead ends involved in the root-seeking process. Second, it enacts a struggle between the scribal and the oral, between signing and singing, presenting an important inversion of our accustomed perception of literature as mimetic and referential and music as formal and combinatory. Third, *Strick* is a specimen of the inclusive American "world poem"—with its precedents in Whitman, Pound, Williams, and Duncan—as it appears in cross-cultural poetic encounters of the late twentieth century.

This last point—the world poem as it might or must be written today—requires comment. In the *Cantos* or in *Paterson*, no matter how much incoherence is allowed or included, no matter how many languages, collages, or intertexts are involved, the poet still stands at the center in Rapallo or Pisa or Paterson. Whitman witnesses and wanders through a varying landscape, but it is always the landscape of America sung into existence. In the last decades of the twentieth century, as I suggest in the introduction to this book, a figure-ground reversal of "home" and "elsewhere" occurred in which travel and displacement have become the norm against which the stability of home increasingly seems an aberration. Bearing this reversal in mind is helpful when considering the subjective and geographic drift of a work such as *Strick*.

"Strick" is defined as flax or hemp just before it has passed through the hackle that separates the fleshy matter from the fiber so that the latter may be woven into rope or string. The travelers in *Strick* are trying to find connective strands that are widely dispersed and do not often cohere; these strands are nonetheless gathered up in the hope of shaping a tentative cultural continuity. Both Lyn Hejinian's traveler and the travelers in Mackey's poem find themselves "thumbing" reference books, looking for alphabets, cues, and signs to guide themselves through an alien referential world. The project of *Strick* is not so much to sing as it is to sift, to hackle, to search for what is usable, and not to leave out the "erroneous" turns or turnarounds along the way. There is no moment when the traveler looks out, sees, and describes, no moment that is not overcome with the shifting and reorienting processes of subjectivity.

To return briefly to the somewhat impoverished "expressivist" and "linguistic" opposition at the beginning of this chapter, we should note that American poetry seen as "ethnic" has been usually relegated to the first of these categories, if only because, in the past half century of the critique of objectivity, academics and general readers alike have realized the importance of knowing, in a given text, who is speaking. Obviously crucial questions—Is it a woman or man? Is he or she black or white?—have, however, a way of reinforcing a view of the text as a vehicle for an experience, recorded and written by a witness, in which mediation and the constructedness of discourse are not, or not as often, called into question. Of numerous critics who have noticed this problem, Charles Bernstein writes,

> [W]hile I welcome the challenge of multiculturalism as it has entered U.S. arts and education in the past decade, I continue to find many of its proponents more interested in reinforcing traditional modes of representation than in allowing the heterogeneity of forms and peoples that make up the cultural diversity of the Americas to transform poetic styles and personal and group identities. Yet it is hardly surprising that static conceptions of group identity represented by authentic spokespersons continue to ride roughshod over works and individuals whose identities are complex, multiple, mixed, confused, hyperactivated, synthetic, mutant, forming, or virtual. ("Poetics" 3)[7]

All of the latter adjectives characterize the narrators of Nathaniel Mackey's *Song of the Andoumboulou*. Indeed, Mackey himself occupies a problematic place in contemporary poetry. An African American poet whose essays on mid- to late-century African American poetry and Black Mountain poetry are collected in his critical book *Discrepant Engagement*, Mackey writes poems usually featured in anthologies of formally experimental rather than identitarian writing. Because such oppositions organize texts and syllabi, and because it matters *where* we find and read poetry, I note the following comment from Douglas Messerli's introduction to *From the Other Side of the Century: A New American Poetry 1960–1990*, where Messerli explains that his principle for inclusion has nothing to do with subject position and everything to do with experimentation:

> Poets of great talent whose writing has more to do with cultural, social, and political subjects than the more formally-conceived poems in this volume, must recognize the specific focus of this anthology. (12)

Given Mackey's presence in other anthologies of postmodern poetry, I take this remark, and this distinction, as representative. As Bernstein suggests, it is important to problematize the conservative representational model to which African American poetry has often been consigned. Certainly, in Mackey's case, that model could hardly be more inappropriate. The distinction Messerli and other anthologists make risks obscuring the role that linguistically experimental writing can have in exploring differences in identity.

The topic here is travel, but that thread is inextricable from the music that surrounds, imbues, and often overwhelms *Strick*.[8] Musicians Royal Hartigan and Hafez Modirzadeh collaborated with Nathaniel Mackey in creating a work that juxtaposes, on the one hand, contemporary improvised jazz and traditional musics of Iran, India, China, the Philippines, and West Africa and, on the other, a poetic speech that gestures toward roots even as it frustrates the comforts of rootedness. Words and music refer to each other in *Strick*, raising questions as to the referential dimensions of music in a work of poetry concerned with versions of collective identity.

The traveling narrators of *Strick* frequently allude to the mythical site of an aboriginal collective, what they call the "one we Ouadada" (Song 18) or the "collective kiss we called Ouadada" (Song 20), yet the poem's shifting terrains, mythologies, and frames of reference complicate any settled sense of identity. From the beginning of *Strick*, music, geography, and history present themselves as three dimensions of displacement. One hears first the sand-and-sea hiss of the drummer's hands stroking the snare drumhead, followed by Mackey's two-stress lines: "They were drédging the seá / coúnting the sánd / Pounded rócks into grável / paid a dóllar a dáy."[9] At these words a voiced tenor saxophone comes in, sung through without a mouthpiece, sounding somewhat like an Australian didgeridoo, and echoing that purpose of singing the land into being.[10] The spoken lines mention flamenco strings and the oud—placing us at the two ends of the Mediterranean. Then, as if to fill out the map, come the place names, the geographic sites of this plaintive and melismatic moan: "The same cry taken up in Cairo, Córdoba, north Red Sea near Nagfa, Muharak." The contours of that cry—its linguistic, geographic, and musical permutations—are traced in the succeeding songs of *Strick*, with the travelers searching for the "one we Ouadada" that lies beyond memory. This is a quest for home. While *Strick*'s travelers often suspect home as illusory, the music nevertheless continually invokes the "we," both in its melodies and instrumentation and in the narrator's commentary *about* the music. In the last segment of Song 20, Mackey reads,

No such we the where we knew
Pres's people an illusion
music said was no illusion
Ruse it behooved us beware of.

Empirically, for these travelers, no "we" as yet exists. (And if, in the era of Pres—saxophonist Lester Young—a viable collectivity surrounding jazz existed, it is not so now.) And yet the "music said [that the *we*] was no illusion." Music's trustworthiness, however, is called into question often in *Strick*, not alone for its geographic confusions. "[M]usic said" also can be read as an instance of an elided subject, common in these songs: not, in other words, that music spoke but that "music [he] said was no illusion." The characters and geographic locales are more unstable and insubstantial than the strains of ouds, the "cuts" on the radio, and other musical currents that shape the travelers' experience. The "Ruse," in this latter reading, is not the music but the wished-for collective foundations.

As in Allen Ginsberg's trans-U.S. travel poems, recorded music complements the journey, though in Ginsberg radio music heard en route was the emanation of a hegemonic, political intelligence. Mackey's travelers are more postmodern in their listening modes as well as in their technology. They listen—in trains, cars, or buses—to musical tracks they can change or play back. If they do not know where they are or even how they are traveling—and they usually do not—they do know what they are hearing. Indeed the limitlessness of their options muddies the vision of a coherent journey, despite the travelers' urge toward coherent, foundational signs.

The travelers are repeatedly confused about their mode of transportation and, still more, about their location. At one moment "it was a train we were on," and, at another, they "wondered was it even a train we were on / if it was was it going the right way." The places of *Strick* are not predefined or given but arise and are named out of events, sometimes of pain or duress but most often of music. The fact that subjective and musical rather than geographic markers indicate the places the travelers try to fathom seems to confuse them pleasurably. When "a Brazilian cut" comes on, at the opening of Song 21, and "Paulinho's voice [Paulinho da Costa, the Brazilian percussionist and singer] lit our way," the travelers are not in Brazil but in Andalusia. Indeed, all ten of these songs trace the Mediterranean coast. In the same song, the poet says, "It was a train in Southern Spain we were on" and yet "It was a train outside Sao Paolo, on our way to Algeciras." The route to Spain via Brazil marks a viable New World line of inquiry, but the mode of cohering is musical rather than chronological or geographic.

Frequently, in *Strick*, as in the poetry of John Ashbery, the travelers realize either that they have not moved at all or that they are moving in the wrong direction. At the precise moment of expressing their determination not to be turned around, they are turned around:

> This while on our way to Ouadada
> vowed we'd let nobody turn us around
> thought we saw Dadaoua.
> (Song 20)

"Dadaoua," an anagrammatic "turning around" of "Ouadada," echoes also the "real" city, Ouagadougou "D.C.," where, unintentionally, they do arrive in the last song of *Strick* (Song 25).[11] But this latter is the violent city, "Mothered in blood," where they began their journey. At every stop but this, a conductor had cried "Not yet." Why had he not said it this time? the travelers wonder.

> Throughout it all a buzzing drum at our backs
> again it was a train we were on
> Outside the window came a sign read "Ouar"
> we scratched our heads
> no such stop on the schedule we read
> no such where
> (Song 25)

Knowing Mackey's anagrammatic plays—"sihg," for example, as somewhere between *sigh* and *sing* (and, of course, *sign*)—we can view "Ouar," while not the "one we Ouadada," as nevertheless *our*(s). The *a* that troubles the usual spelling is a convention of the French prefixes established in *Ouadada*, *Ouagadougou* (often spelled *Wagadougou*), and *Ouab'da*. Ouar, though not "on the schedule," is uncannily familiar, as is Ouagadougou "D.C."—"our" nation's capital. It is familiar in part for its scene of devastation, like that depicted in the first song of *Strick*. The scene of catastrophe and enslavement, with its "charred bodies," is here recapitulated in the "bombed origins." Song 25, if the most prophetic and apocalyptical of the songs ("End-of-the- / world augury, new world omen"), is also the one most burdened with a traveler's and a roots-seeker's moral:

> we the dismembered
> winced. Inasmuch as what we want
> was unreal there it stood, "four

times fallen asleep" not even

                                close,

     came to where they'd always been.

At the moment of arrival, the travelers wince, knowing that what they wanted was unreal, that what they will find is "not even close," and that their return must be to "where they'd always been."

One important irony in *Strick* is that, while this spoken text seems to invoke the primacy of the oral, it is in fact obsessed with the scribal. The obsession exists partly at the sentence level, with the many wordplays, and partly at the thematic level: the concern with illegible, blank, or unobtainable books (travel guides) that one requires to make sense of where one is going and, especially, to guide one along the road to the collective, to the "one we."[12]

On the oral side, the "Song" of the larger poem's title takes up the vocal trope of the American long poem, seen (or heard) in Whitman's *Song of Myself*, Pound's *Cantos*, and Ginsberg's *Howl*. (Of these—for its fragmentation, its wide frame of reference, its prosody, and its journey themes—the "Song of the Andoumboulou" is closest to the *Cantos*.) Lawrence Kramer points out in his work on nineteenth-century music and poetry that "poets traditionally call poetry song when they want to represent it as vision, epiphany, or prophecy" (2). "Song of the Andoumboulou 1" begins with "The song says the / dead will not / ascend without song," lines that identify the poem as performative, ceremonial, and elegiac. Poetry is generally seen as approaching the source of creation when it unites with musical harmony, yet music, conversely, seems to aspire to the condition of writing.[13] Both the referential concreteness of music and the deferring play of writing (poems as, often, less mimetic than music) are important to consider when looking at *Strick*, which is clearly not a referential narrative "accompanied" by music. Musical meaning may be inexact, but, particularly in traditional and sacred music, it need not be nonpredicative or unlocalized.

While we must acknowledge the oral and musical tropes in this sequence, then, and the attraction of "a life sought beyond the letter" (Song 23), *Strick* nevertheless revels in the pull of the scribal. Song 23, after mentioning "the beginningless book," now seen as "more scroll than book," struggles etymologically away from the scribal with the next apposition: "Talismanic strum." If we work backwards from "scroll," it takes us to Old French *escroe* and thence to Germanic *skraudh*, parent both of *shred* and *shroud*. "Strum," while moving toward the trope of music, retains the shredlike nuance of "scroll": it derives from Old High German *thrum*, a fabric remnant, the extra fringe trimmed off and discarded from the loom's edge. We must think, again, in both cases, of the meaning of "strick," the mass of plant matter from which the valuable fiber, strong enough to be woven into rope or a *textus*, must be extricated. All these etymologies lead away from the aural toward the letter. The metaphors of music struggle with the stasis and weight of the book, as they do with those named, fixed points on the map.

Strick is a work of ontopology, of sites of the self and their construction. It is also, to borrow a coinage of Lévi-Strauss, a work of entropology; Mackey's travelers, in their journeys through vanished or vanishing cultures, illegible palimpsests, and lost languages, share dreams of an early oneness: "Dreamt articulation, dreamt wordless rapport, dreamt entanglement" (Song 18). Music, as an experience in which, like a stretched skin, the self vibrates as Other, seems to offer this promise. Music, as a return to a mystical or prenatal oceanic state, is the condition the travelers of *Strick* often seek, even though or *because*, they say, "we'd been that way before" (Song 18).

And yet *Strick*'s gesture is to reject nostalgia. The numerous rejected "we's" of Song 18 ("No we of romance . . . no nation's we") are strongly antinostalgic. The book thumbed in Song 23, "if it was a book," is "the book of having once been there . . . all wish to go back let go." Even given the infusion of *nostos* throughout the poem, of the need for a viable Ouadada, the principal thrust is antinostalgic. The book so often mentioned (but never cited) is also "no book of a wished else / the where we thumbed," rejecting the attachment of genealogical hopes to travel.[14] If those hopes are evoked anywhere, it is in the music—the long sinuous *nay* notes, the resonant *bendir*—and the referential dimensions of those scales and rhythms: the musical symptom of the aftermath of trauma, which is also its memory, and the continuity of a mournful Andalusian/Arab voice across the Mediterranean.[15]

To consult again the compass of *Strick*: the first song sets out the theme of the dreadful having already happened, of a long-accustomed loss: "what song there was," "what *where* we had left," "what *we* they exacted," "what plot there was" are all phrases of *Strick*'s "what-sayer," indicating meagerness, an entropic, desolated universe. Yet, though countertranscendent elements in both voice and music beleaguer the songs, a deeply qualified hope pervades them: "We knew there was a world somewhere / How to get there no / Would we get there no" (Song 20).

By the end of *Strick*, in Song 25, after a history as much of beating and ruin as of singing and lovemaking, the travelers face unreadable horizons on every side, especially on the *in*side, where pronouns, traces of identity effects, have proliferated beyond any hope for articulable identity. Arriving at an outside commensurable with their inmost desires, they are forced to reflect that "inasmuch as what we want was unreal / there it stood." Their "genetic letter," like the illegible book so often thumbed in *Strick*, presents an "inaccessible alphabet." The place itself is as bewildered as the travelers—and the song raises some doubt whether it *is* a place. (Twice the narrator asks, "Was it a place?") The narrator's name, like his DNA, and like all the letterless "books," is a cipher ("Hollow be my name"). But a deferred and finally failed arrival is only a failure if the traveler cannot shape his own desire. The mobile element is, as usual, not the geographic but the subjective world. On a trackless road, the travelers, like that Beckett narrator who ends *The Unnameable* with "I can't go on. I'll go on," neigh like horses and head "pa'l monte"—that is, in a last echo of Latin American folk music, "for the hills."[16]

Tout récit est un récit de voyage. (All stories are travel stories.)

MICHEL DE CERTEAU, *L'Invention de Quotidien*

Epilogue
The Trouble with Travel

The argument against travel presented in the first chapter of this book takes several forms. One is the Emersonian critique that sees in travel a vain search for qualities that can be found only in oneself; another is the insistence that travelers pay home its due, that they be faithful to the community; and a third is the moral objection to Western travelers imposing themselves—their technologies, their values, and their discursive systems— on the rest of the world.

From the traveler's standpoint, yet another argument against travel exists, springing from late-capitalist melancholy: the sense that the world— flattened by communications and polluted with industrial effluvia—no longer has much to offer. Claude Lévi-Strauss remarks early in *Tristes*

Tropiques, "The first thing we see as we travel round the world is our own filth, thrown into the face of mankind" (38) and spells out the gloomy implications:

> [C]ivilization has ceased to be that delicate flower which was preserved and painstakingly cultivated in one or two sheltered areas of a soil rich in wild species which may have seemed menacing because of the vigor of their growth, but which nevertheless made it possible to vary and revitalize the cultivated stock. Mankind has opted for monoculture; it is in the process of creating a mass civilization, as beetroot is grown in the mass. Henceforth, man's daily bill of fare will consist only of this one item. (38)

But has the world flattened? Is the reservoir of wildness and strangeness, cultural or natural, exhausted or even exhaustible, given a perceiving subject who can maintain, through psychic or geographic motility, the sense of a freshness deep down things? Putting the burden on the subject, as the present book has done, is not to ignore leveling forces in the modern world, whether in communications, industry, and commerce or in liberal philosophy and politics, but, taking those forces into account, to ask whether we need to treat the world as despoiled because of them. To see, from an airplane, the forest or ocean stretching from horizon to horizon is to realize that it is the human being who is the figure against the ground of the non-human, and to wonder if the current version of our impact on the planet is not exaggerated. What suspicion could be more heretical? We know that our information—from the vantage point of the ground or the airplane—is incomplete. We know we cannot see all the effects of global warming, deforestation, and acid rain, but that is just the point: how and what we see will always be partial and contingent. We cannot wait for all the information to be in; we must in the meantime see the world in its variety and strangeness. All times are belated times. Lévi-Strauss comments at length on the troubled position of the ethnographer who, no matter when arriving, arrives too late. But he goes on to point out that even the objects of the ethnographic study are blighted with belatedness: the Nambikwara people seemed to feel that the "real" Nambikwara had died off long ago, that the present Nambikwara were mere shadows of what once had been.

In light of this mirage of belatedness, and in light of the fact that *no* Nambikwara exist now, nor ever will again, can we now say that the world has arrived at the human monoculture Lévi-Strauss also dreaded? Languages have disappeared, never to return. Whole cultures—those Lévi-Strauss commemorated and mourned and countless others—have vanished. Yet, among the thousands of cultures and languages that remain, we are as far from sameness as we have ever been. Despite the World Trade Organization and other leveling forces, the current political and cultural situation is virtually defined by conflicts based on ethnic, religious, and national difference. Precisely because the world has grown smaller, differences are foregrounded and societies interact, often abrasively, in terms of culture and identity.

Thus to Elizabeth Bishop's question, "Should we have stayed at home, / wherever that may be?" one must continue to answer no or, at the very least, not necessarily. Of course, Bishop's "wherever that may be" has already answered the question for us in this wise, but America today offers additional political and cultural reasons why the answer should be no. Travel may sometimes narrow the mind wonderfully, but staying home is deadlier. If the world is not yet a monoculture, home often is, perhaps particularly home in the United States, with its much-vaunted but suspiciously monochrome heterogeneity. Ask United States college students what they know about France, particularly in the age of "freedom fries." Or note the results of the 2002 *National Geographic* study, in which out of ten nations, U.S. students (ages eighteen to twenty-four) came in second to last (Mexico was last; Sweden was first) in their ability to identify nations on the globe. Most could not locate France, England, or Japan; 30 percent could not find the Pacific Ocean, and 11 percent could not locate the United States. All of the other participants could better identify the U.S. population than Americans could. Most of the young Americans estimated U.S. population at between one and two billion.[1]

Recent test results on young Americans' "self-esteem," in contrast, are off the charts. A discussion of the apogee of American hegemony in the time of the apogee of American geographic and cultural ignorance, like the topic of globalization and the threat of monoculture, lies beyond the scope of this book, whose focus has been poetry and the individual subject in flight, but the vagaries and versions of the traveling subjects discussed here occur under the pressure of precisely those larger issues.

We live in a time of insistence on the personal, even while we have great difficulty naming what it means. In discussing the destabilizing yet liberatory properties of travel, I argue for a view of the personal in which continuities favored at a given time—those of race, gender, or nationality, for example—are deeply complicated by a proliferation of other continuities, newfound, unsuspected, often unnamable, that proceed from the terrain one crosses, the passages one undertakes.

For the writers discussed in this book, poems are actions, not solutions. The poem's action is very often to shake free from the continuities that narrative and expository prose so often insist on. This is not good news for many contemporary classrooms, since unthematizable poems are often left off the syllabus. It remains good news for readers excited by the transgressive and the transfigurative, by language that speaks to us at levels just beneath that of reference, offering a sense, doggedly specific, of what it is like to be alive and, always, en route.

Pascal, after making his famous remark that all the trouble of the world is due to one's inability to stay in one's room, added that our mortal condition was so unhappy that once we gave it all our attention, nothing could console us except *divertissement*, which leads us away from ourselves and thus brings us to ruin. Neither Pascal nor Emerson thought that a movement away from the "self" could be productive. Insofar as they conceived of a self one departs from and returns to, they were mistaken. While a voyage, colonial or postcolonial, is notoriously a voyage inward, it is also an escape from the self. This seeming paradox is resolved when we understand that the self abandoned is not the self found, that while there is no return from losing one's way, losing is always finding something else, a new configuration of the self.

Shout it on the rooftops

And rite it on the sky

His name is Derek Walcott

e mus get dat Nobel Prize

MIGHTY PEP (ALOYSIUS BROUET), St. Lucian

Calypso Monarch, 1989

Appendix A

The Nobel and Travel

In "Does It Matter Why Walcott Won the Prize?" Raoul Grunquist argues that writers perceived as universalist win Nobel prizes. By now academic readers are accustomed to the view that universal humanism constitutes a hegemonic will to deform, depreciate, or erase difference. In Grunquist's view, the Swedish Academy has more or less "universalized" laureates such as Wole Soyinka (Nobel, 1986) and Nadine Gordimer (Nobel, 1991). In Soyinka's case, this has meant rhetorically subordinating his African root-edness and foregrounding his universal perspectives. In a phrase from the Academy secretary, Soyinka was commended for his "poetic plays that are deeply rooted in the African soil but have universal perspectives." Grunquist calls our attention to this latter qualification. Gordimer was similarly appropriated and homogenized, her writing seen as "of very great benefit to humanity" (qtd. in Grunquist 152).

The Nobel discourse celebrating Walcott reveals a similar pattern, according to Grunquist. Walcott's exile status and dislocations between Boston and the Caribbean islands were transformed into popular sagas of the modern exile. Boundary demarcations along racial and geographic lines, abundant in the press releases, projected Walcott as a hybrid containing a Third World representative and a First World inhabitant, a transgressor of boundaries, and a restless traveler between many centers and cultures. Thus, the Caribbean poet was turned into the alter ego of postmodern Western man, an isolated, solitary, postcolonial figure in an increasingly disoriented cultural environment that provoked Western imagination (Grunquist 153). In other words, the Swedish Academy, and implicitly many of the public at large, place the supreme value on Walcott as a universalist who can speak to all. Regionally, by contrast, his function is reduced to that of an inspired cultural worker.

In an essay titled "The Rise of Gabriel García Márquez and Toni Morrison," Dane Johnson makes a similar argument, suggesting that these two novelists (Nobel, 1982 and 1993, respectively) were chosen for their "universal and timeless appeal" (129). Johnson's, like Grunquist's, horror of the universal apparently stems from the view of universalizing as something done *to* the writers in question: she refers to "the profound transformation *visited upon* authors like Morrison and García Márquez by a reception that reads 'universally'" (153; emphasis added). But Johnson goes beyond this, suggesting that these two writers are really political conservatives at the service of a white Euro-American hegemony, that they are complicit with the "system of literary evaluation and concept of cultural difference that still exclude cultural forms that do not adhere to Western ideas of high art." Both writers, after all, are "easily exportable into a world literary marketplace that desires classic stories from exotic places" (131). Further, she argues, they are "in many ways 'conservators of culture' that is never exactly theirs," and "the 'pastness' of their stories . . . makes them safer in the present for the politically conservative metropolitan" (153).

Leaving aside the fact that metropolitans are a good deal less politically conservative, as a rule, than rural or tribal constituencies, the problem with Grunquist's and Johnson's treatments of the Nobel institution and its selection process is that the language under analysis can be read even more persuasively just the other way around. The very language the Academy uses, and which Grunquist rightly points to as exoticizing, can be seen as consistently emphasizing difference rather than universalism. Yes, the dichotomies are there—and how can the Academy ignore them in a poet such as Walcott who has taken them as his themes from his earliest work right up to the present? In "A Far Cry from Africa," he asks, "I who am poisoned with the blood of both, / Where shall I turn, divided to the vein?" and uses those same iambics to ask, in the last line of that poem, "How can I turn from Africa and live?" These early questions perhaps too easily set up a crude dichotomy that Walcott critics have examined ever since. Walcott indeed may be accused of exploiting (or simply exploring) this dichotomy throughout his work.

Thus the Swedish Academy's key terms that Grunquist points to for the three Nobel laureates in his discussion—"universalism" for Soyinka, "humanity" for Gordimer, and "multiculturalism" for Walcott—are indeed important but important also, especially the last of these three, for the shift they trace. At a time when the American academy places a high value on difference, the Swedish Academy is hardly out of step. Far from the Academy having a universalist bias, the ingredient for a Nobel laureate is difference. Walcott's formal and thematic conservatism are there for anyone to see, but these are precisely what the Nobel foundation tried to overlook. For Nobel purposes, he must be made to seem subversive—if not a Rigoberta Menchú, then at least a Solzhenitsyn. One does not win a Nobel prize for universality; one wins it by identification with a people, by representing the local.[1] That *Omeros* mixes styles, vernaculars, and traditions, that its strands include Homer, Poe, Mayakovsky, Melville, and the Beatles, is practically an embarrassment for the Swedish Academy. Soyinka has little truck with postmodern pastiche, nor did Solzhenitsyn or Pablo Neruda or Gabriela Mistral or Miguel Angel Asturias. Asturias had to live in Paris because his life was in danger in his native Guatemala: that is Nobel material.

No one—neither a nation nor a Nobel committee—seems to want a primarily linguistic or "experimental" poet as spokesperson. (Consider the U.S. poet laureates from Frost till the present, particularly now that each poet is allowed a very short tenure—Rita Dove, Robert Pinsky, Robert Hass, Billy Collins, and others, and then consider what chance an even more famous figure such as John Ashbery might have of being selected.) Committees want theme, not play. In his essay "The Muse of History," rejecting the apparent differences between the two great Francophone Caribbean poets St.-John Perse and Aimé Césaire (particularly the racial difference: one white, one black), Walcott points out the similarity of their visionary rhetoric and their repudiation of the historical. Language, he insists in that essay as throughout his poetry, is the real empire. Walcott's scandal is the scandal of the universal. The Swedish Academy had to sidestep that to praise the Caribbean locus and emphasis in Walcott's voluminous work.

Appendix B

Writing the Land

The trope of the unrecuperability of travel sites, of the recourse to maps and the deferral of territories, appears often in the poetry of Ashbery and Walcott and occasionally in that of Bishop, Snyder, and Hejinian. Practically rampant in Walcott, it often seems a way both of posing and of eluding the questions of geography and history. In Ashbery's poems, more obviously than for the other poets, the earth/text conflation, each term concealing or disappearing into the other, seems part of a wider postmodern consensus, the idea that our reality is constructed, woven, a *textus*. Examples from these five poets follow.

Verandahs, where the pages of the sea
are a book left open. . . .
I begin here again,
begin until this ocean's
a shut book
(*AL* 3; ellipsis added)

the eternal summer sea
like a book left open.
(*AL* 150)

Far from streets seething like novels with their century's sorrow
(*B* 21)

the travel book,
its paragraphs like windows from a train.
("The Fortunate Traveler," *FT* 96)

Too rapid the lightning's shorthand . . .
. . . .
too slow the stones crawling toward language every night
(*M* IX)

[In England,] the fields, not their names, were the same
(*M* XXXV)

children lie torn on rubble for a noun
(*M* XXII)

The right verb leapt like a fish from its element,
the tadpole wriggled like an eager comma,
and the snake coiled round its trunk in an ampersand.
(*M* XXIV)

and the beach close like a book
behind me with every footmark.
(*O* 295)

I followed the sea-swift to both sides of this text;
her hyphen stitched its seam.
(*O* 319)

the shale-like speckle of stanzas,
and the seam like a stream stitching its own language
. . . .
the verb in the earth, the nouns in the stones, the walls
. . . .
these heat-cracked stanzas.
("Reading Machado," *B* 43)

I was considering a syntax the color of slate.
(*B* 56)

ornate cyrillics of gesturing fronds.
(*B* 70)

[The light] falls
and folds over the last word of a wave.
(*B* 76)

breakers that foam from the page
(*B* 77)

like commas
in a shop ledger gulls tick the lined waves
. . . .
Sea-light on the cod barrels writes: *St. Thomas*
. . . .
tidal couplets of lament
(*TH* 3)

their street of letters
(*TH* 4)

A panel of sunrise
on a hillside shop
gave these stanzas
their stilted shape.
("Cul de Sac Valley," *AT* 9)

JOHN ASHBERY

It is the erratic path of time we trace
On the globe, with moist fingertip, and surely, the globe stops;
We are pointing to England, to Africa, to Nigeria;
And we shall visit these places, you and I, and other places,
Including heavenly Naples, queen of the sea, where I shall be king and you will be
      queen.
. . . .
It is too late to go to the places with the names (what were they, anyway? just
      names).
("And You Know," *ST* 57–58)

And we finger down the dog-eared coasts
("The Skaters," *RM* 44)

the coast stammered with unintentional villages
(*Tennis* 11)

dark, squishy footprints in the slush
Take over our notion of a country as a map would
("Winter Weather Advisory," *AG* 67)

the veiled
Shapely masses of this country you are the geography of
("Something Similar," *Shadow Train* 23)

Today is cooler or warmer than yesterday, and it all works itself out into a map, projects, placed over the other real like a sheet of tracing paper, and these two simultaneously become what is going on.
("The New Spirit," *TP* 18)

ELIZABETH BISHOP

"The Map" uses this trope in its entirety, but especially such lines as the following:

The names of the seashore towns run out to sea,
the names of the cities cross the neighboring mountains
. . . .
these peninsulas take the water between thumb and finger
like women feeling for the smoothness of yard-goods
(*Complete* 3)

LYN HEJINIAN

the neighbors themselves were little more than pronunciation
(*Oxota* 248)

the dangling pipe on the gas stove is in a prepositional state
for, not for, off, on
(*Oxota* 221)

two sullen men in blue fish
I wonder why their plurals are the same as their possessives
(*Oxota* 147)

GARY SNYDER

old ghost ranges, sunken rivers, come again
    stand by the wall and tell their tale,
walk the path, sit the rains,

grind the ink, wet the brush, unroll the
    broad white space:

lead out and tip
the moist black line.
(*MR* 9)

NOTES

Preface: Points on a Personal Compass

1. "Traveler, there is no road—one makes the road by walking" (Machado 138).

Roots and Routes: The Trouble with Travel

1. See, for example, Rey Chow's "Where Have All the Natives Gone?" in which a search committee finds a Chinese candidate insufficiently Chinese.

2. These three paragraphs appear in somewhat different form in Gray, "Literature, Difference, and the Land of Witness," 59–60.

3. See Pratt, as well as various works on the colonizing gaze—for example, Buzard, Mulvey, and Urry.

4. Katie Mills, examining vocabularies of travel among U.S. subcultures, finds that critical theory has just as often used the travel metaphor in precisely the opposite way, where theories of subversion read "like the typical road story of rebellion and escape. Racist patriarchy (the story goes) immobilizes and paralyzes the heroic Other, who, in turn ultimately enlivens the pale white world by his or her status as a 'cultural outlaw.'" Thus, mobility is not the privilege of dominant power only. Moreover, "the stasis of reification becomes as threatening as any other effect of capitalism."

5. U.S. tourism abroad has dropped even more drastically since September 11, 2001.

6. Said elsewhere argues for a much wider range of possibilities and for much greater malleability for the traveling subjectivity. In "Identity, Authority, and Freedom: The Potentate and the Traveler," he writes that one "should be able to discover and travel among other selves, other identities" (17). "The image of the traveler depends not on power, but on motion, on a willingness to go into different worlds, use different idioms, and understand a variety of disguises, masks, and rhetorics. . . . Most of all . . . the traveler crosses over, traverses territory, and abandons fixed positions, all the time" (18). It is difficult to square these views with those quoted from *Orientalism* and "Representing the Colonized."

7. A good argument may be made that this is a New World phenomenon, but I use "Americans," at least in this section, to mean people born in the United States. I suggest cultural neoteny not as a scientific proposition but as an explanatory principle.

8. In *Orientalism*, Said says, "Perhaps the most important task of all would be to undertake studies in contemporary alternatives to Orientalism, to ask how one can study other cultures and other peoples from a libertarian, or a nonrepressive and nonmanipulative perspective" (24). If we take Said in his early-Foucauldian mode, the undertaking of such studies should be impossible within the constraints of the existing system of discourse.

9. Baudrillard makes a similar observation regarding travel, photography, and the ignorance that Lévi-Strauss stops short of recommending: "The only trick here . . . is to be ignorant of how one's subjects live. This gives them an aura of mystery, a savagery, which the successful picture captures" (*The Transparency of Evil*, 152).

10. Among the few critical books on twentieth-century travel (not to be confused with the hundreds of travel accounts, for which see the bibliography in Kowalewski) are MacCannell, Kaplan, Urry, and Clifford's work in general.

11. Lowell's and Ashbery's centrality is clear, yet if we shift from terms of critical acclaim to terms of visibility to a broad American public, we would have to substitute Robert Frost and perhaps Maya Angelou as choices for the most "popular" poets of the mid- and late century, respectively. Both have read at presidential inaugurations, both have commanded the highest reading-circuit fees, and both are seen as populist poets. People who do not read poetry are likely to have heard of both these poets and not to have heard of either Lowell or Ashbery.

12. Rorty says, "[One] should try to abjure the temptation to tie in one's responsibilities to other people with one's relation to whatever idiosyncratic things or persons one loves with all one's heart and soul and mind" ("Trotsky" 42). This thesis is explored at greater length in Rorty's book *Contingency, Irony, and Solidarity*.

Falling off the Round, Turning World: Elizabeth Bishop's *Tristes Tropiques*

1. Many American poets have traveled. I mention Bishop and Crane as poets whose, or one of whose, principal poetic topoi was travel.

2. In 1951, while on a freighter trip around South America, Bishop suffered a violent reaction to a cashew fruit she had bought in the market at Rio de Janeiro. Because of this accident, from which she recovered in a few days, she ended up staying in Brazil for nearly twenty years, most of that time with her companion Lota de Macedo Soares, whom she had met in New York nine years earlier.

3. This and all subsequent quotations from Elizabeth Bishop's poetry are from *The Complete Poems: 1927–1979*.

4. Most of Elizabeth Bishop's commentators have addressed her alleged reticence and withholding of emotion. Doreski argues of "Crusoe in England" that

"a stern aesthetic forbids . . . tropes of sentimentality" (133). Shetley's chapter on Bishop is titled "Elizabeth Bishop's Silences." Paz subtitled his tribute to Bishop "The Power of Reticence." Travisano praises the Brazil poems for being "mostly impersonal," for not making "the jungle a symbol for inner turmoil," and indeed for showing "that poems can have depth and resonance without emotional turmoil" (134). Though Bishop's work, like much American poetry of her time, became both more direct and more explicit over the years, the license to write with autobiographical openness was one she approached with caution.

5. The "we" or "us" in Bishop also requires investigation. Why is it that "we are determined to rush / to see the sun the other way around?" Of course, not everyone *is* so determined. Kaplan refers to Bishop's "we" as a particular "cast of historical agents" (7). "We," less dramatically, consists of those who have the money to sail or fly to Brazil and those who regard travel as either a status enhancer or a psychological necessity. These are not coterminous groups. Millions of Americans—perhaps hundreds of millions—have enough money to travel to Brazil but no inclination. Millions cannot find Brazil on a world map.

6. In addition to the many examples from Ashbery and Walcott that I catalogue in Appendix B, consider the following from James Merrill, where Merrill seems to be thinking of Bishop's "The Map":

> The countries are violet, orange, yellow, green;
> Names of the principal towns and rivers, black.
> A zipper's hiss, and the Atlantic Ocean closes
> Over my blood-red t-shirt from the Gap.
> "Self-Portrait in Tyvek™ Windbreaker," *Collected Poems* 669

7. The only other candidate for inclusion in the genre of map-reading poems is "Poem" from *Geography III*.

8. A few years later, Bishop remarks, in her jacket blurb for Lowell's *Life Studies*, "As a child, I used to look at my grandfather's Bible under a powerful reading-glass. The letters assembled beneath the lens were suddenly like a Lowell poem, as big as life and as alive, and rainbow-edged. It seemed to illuminate as it magnified; it could also be used as a burning-glass" (Schwartz and Estess 285).

9. Regarding "Brazil, January 1, 1502" and, to a lesser extent, "Over 2,000 Illustrations and a Complete Concordance," see Matos on a kind of writing whose main purpose is to retrace others' journeys: "Thus a double focus is created: a journey made by somebody in the past is duplicated by a contemporary traveler, and a prior text is articulated with a present narrative. The old journey serves, that is, both as pretext and pre-text" (219). Matos has in mind prose accounts such as Tim Severin's books on the track of the Argonauts, Ulysses, and Sinbad or Bernard Levin's *Hannibal's Footsteps*.

10. An additional insight into the complicity of tourist and conquistador is offered by Anne Colwell, who notices the meaning inherent in the comma in the line "came and found it all, not unfamiliar": "'not unfamiliar' modifies not the soldiers' finding a version of lovers' bowers but our experience and the speaker's with the soldiers'. The experience is what is 'not unfamiliar'" (142).

11. Bishop wrote during the emergence of the "bossa nova," the new beat, created most famously by Antonio Carlos Jobim, whose most famous song, second only to "The Girl from Ipanema," was "Desafinado," that is, "Out of Tune."

12. See also Spivak, 66. See also Said regarding the Orientalist and the Oriental: "the former *writes* about, whereas the latter *is written* about" (*Orientalism* 308).

13. The images of the African women do not figure in the earlier version of this account, which appears in Bishop's prose memoir "The Country Mouse," where young "Elizabeth" glances only at the cover of *National Geographic*—at the margins and the date—and experiences the trauma she describes, of realizing she is a "human being" (*Collected Prose* 33).

The February 1918 issue of *National Geographic* mentioned in the poem does not contain the images Bishop describes, an interesting point for a poet who insisted so much on veracity and literalism. She writes to Frank Bidart from Ouro Preto (July 2, 1971) that when she went to the library to look up that issue of the magazine, she found it concerned Alaska and "the Valley of the Thousand Smokes" and decided she could not use it. She remembered an earlier issue that had made "a more relevant impression" on her and used that instead without changing the date. She tells Bidart that she "was sure the *New Yorker* would 'research' this . . . but apparently they are not quite as strict as they used to be" (*One Art* 546). See also her interview with George Starbuck: "Something's wrong about that poem and I thought perhaps that no one would ever know. . . . My memory had confused two 1918 issues of the *Geographic*" (Starbuck 318).

14. Bishop wrote "Crusoe in England" while she was translating Brazilian poetry for her 1972 anthology. Among the poems she translated was Carlos Drummond de Andrade's "Infancy," which contains the lines "I read the story of Robinson Crusoe, / the long story that never comes to an end," and which ends, "I didn't know that my story / was prettier than that of Robinson Crusoe" (*An Anthology* 87).

15. Millier offers a brief survey of how Bishop's poem revises Defoe's novel (447–50).

16. James Merrill may be the only critic who has acknowledged the comic tone, when he calls the poem the "longest, funniest, and finally bleakest of these late narratives" (254).

17. This is not to say that undiluted pleasure is foreign to Bishop's other travel

poems. An early echo of this pleasure can be heard in "Pleasure Seas," with its repetition of "happy" and "happily" (196).

18. In fact, Bishop does not use the word "merge" but "conflux" and "coming together." While eventually, out to sea, the two streams become indistinguishable, they do not *mix* at Santarém. I owe to Carmen Oliveira the information that the pH composition of the Tapajos and the Amazon is such that, as the *Voices and Visions* film on Bishop shows, the two rivers flow side by side, in full contact, each maintaining its distinct color. One might apply this observation metaphorically to argue that Bishop makes things converge when they really do not, whether referring to the races and ethnicities in "Santarém" or to the *National Geographic* articles in "In the Waiting Room."

19. Most critics associated with postmodern poetry today would be unlikely to map postmodern poetry on *either* of these poets; they might choose, instead, Charles Olson or Gertrude Stein. But Longenbach takes "postmodern" literally: the generation that followed Eliot, Pound, Williams, and Stein, extending but often contesting their poetics.

Interlude. Travelers and Tourists: From Bishop to Lowell

1. Kalstone discusses Bishop's influence on Lowell at length in *Becoming a Poet*. More recently, see Shetley, who comments, "Bishop's work offers the possibility of a poetry without rhetoric, without the inflation of Lowell's apocalyptic mode . . . at the same time that it remains true to an ideal of exacting craft" (36).

2. In the summer of 1957, Bishop and Lota, on a prolonged visit to New York, visited Lowell in Castine. Lowell was drinking heavily and may have made amorous advances; Lota and Bishop cut the visit short (see Laskin 292). Lowell drove them to the Bangor airport, came back to Castine, and wrote much of *Life Studies*. On that visit Bishop invited Lowell to Brazil, insisting that Hardwick and baby come too, which they did in 1962.

3. Yet another draft reads, "Wholly Atlantic / you combed this seaboard north and south / for room to live." Years later, Bishop used some of the diction in the poem ("rode," "star," "anchor," "drift") in "North Haven," her elegy to Lowell.

4. Von Hallberg's argument has since been thoroughly documented in *The Cultural Cold War*, by Frances Stonor Saunders, who demonstrates that the CIA spent staggering sums on the Congress of Cultural Freedom, which supported particularly those artists deemed decadent by the Soviets, such as the composers Stravinsky and Schoenberg, and the painters Pollock, Motherwell, and Rothko. Stephen Spender, Dwight McDonald, and Irving Kristol all served as editors of the CIA-funded journal *Encounter*. The CIA argument was that an individual's

behavior or integrity was not compromised if no one knew that he or she was benefiting from CIA support.

5. The picture of Lowell as pacifist and draft resister is complicated by that of Lowell the elitist. Lowell's privileged upbringing may have made him particularly susceptible to the influence of the Agrarians, who were his tutors and whose antiurban, anticapitalist program contained racist and classist elements. For an account of Lowell's political conflicts and swervings, see Axelrod, "Robert Lowell and the Cold War."

Fear of Flying: Robert Lowell and the Trope of Vulnerability

1. In using the term "vulnerable," I refer to Harold Bloom's phrase the "trope of vulnerability," which he coined to characterize (and to disparage) Lowell's poetry. Bloom complains, "I am left uncertain as to whether I am not being moved by a record of human suffering, rather than by a making of any kind" (*Lowell* 1).

2. In a letter to Bishop, Lowell expressed his concern over how little he knew of Latin American literature or culture (Mariani 307). Keith Botsford, the Congress of Cultural Freedom's representative in South America, claimed to have tried to educate Lowell in this area, as well as to introduce him to the leading Argentine writers, but Lowell, Botsford said, showed little interest.

3. See also "Liberty and Revolution, Buenos Aires" (*History* 147).

4. See Bidart's notes to Lowell's *Collected Poems*, 1060.

5. Lowell's *Collected Poems* has recently appeared, and reviewers have been quick to notice that these problems—not only multiple published versions of poems but also poems made out of parts from two or three earlier poems—are, inevitably, unsolved. Bidart and Gewanter have chosen not to print *Notebook* at all. See, for one of the earliest reviews, Anthony Lane (86).

6. Lowell even writes "south of the South" in *Notebook* (103).

7. Lowell's remarks in his two essays on John Crowe Ransom indicate his ambiguity on the question of "honest speech": he had praised Ransom's poems as having "the distinction of good conversation," saying Ransom wrote poetry in "the language of one of the best talkers" (*Collected Prose* 19). In the second essay, however, he regrets that Ransom had abandoned "pretty rhymes" to write "honest" essays (25), then praises him again for his "unpainted" poetic language, "not far removed" from prose (27). Lowell maintains the ambivalence in his own poems, notably in his last, "Epilogue" (*DD*).

8. After Bishop had entertained Lowell and Hardwick for several weeks in Brazil, Lota commented, "They aren't interested in things or places much, are they? Just people and books" (qtd. in Goldensohn 187).

Interlude. Dandies and Flaneurs: American Poetry and the Center-Margin Debate

1. Without dismissing all pre-9/11 poetry as B.S. (Before September 11, 2001), as Lawrence Ferlinghetti has done, one can say that American poetry has not *generally* occupied itself with portraying historical disaster, or any collective as opposed to "personal" trauma, despite conspicuous individual poems by Whitman, Jarrell, Brooks, Lowell, Ginsberg, Rich, and so on and despite the work of a few poets— for example, Muriel Rukeyser, Yusef Koumounyakaa, and Michael Harper—who have consistently written poems about and against war. The phrase "poetry of witness" refers almost always to the poetry of Eastern Europe and Latin America, sometimes Africa or China. Carolyn Forché's anthology *Against Forgetting: Twentieth-Century Poetry of Witness* deals mainly with those parts of the world; it does round up occasional poems by Cummings, Pound, George Oppen, Levertov, and others but only finds a significant body of American "witness" poetry in the sections on the civil rights era and the Vietnam and Korean wars. Bruce Murphy has gone so far as to suggest that American poets, embarrassed at the irrelevance of poetry in the United States and envious of its revolutionary importance among their oppressed peers in China, Latin America, and Eastern Europe, actually hunger for surveillance ("The Exile of Literature").

2. The only reason to qualify this silence with "almost" is the publication of Jahan Ramazani's book on postcolonial Indian poetry.

3. Some titles that reflect this concern include Shetley's *After the Death of Poetry*, Perelman's *The Marginalization of Poetry*, and Epstein's much earlier article "Who Killed Poetry?" See also, reacting to Epstein, Hall's *Death to the Death of Poetry*.

4. Perloff points out that Jameson and other Marxist critics (she no doubt means the Jameson of "Third World Literature in the Era of Multinational Capitalism") seem to believe that "the 'marginalized' have the right (perhaps even the duty) to use what would otherwise be considered well-worn clichés because these groups have hitherto been denied all access to poetic speech" ("Janus-Faced" 207).

The Great Escape: John Ashbery's Travel Agency

1. The "dicks" lines follow: "[T]here are so many other, nicer things to be doing! Sleeping while the navigator / is poised, adrift, and sucking each other's dicks is only one. / Travel is another" (*FC* 184).

2. The *en abime* of the phrase comes into English most famously from Jacques Derrida, for whom—as *mise en abime*—it depicts the view into the abyss created by infinite recursion, as in the example of the cover of a Quaker Oats box, where a Quaker holds a Quaker Oats box showing a Quaker holding . . . and so *ad infinitum.*

3. Sawyer-Laucanno recounts this period in Ashbery's life in *The Continual Pilgrimage* (233–60).

4. Foucault's first book was *Death and the Labyrinth: The World of Raymond Roussel*; Ashbery wrote the preface to the English edition. Roussel's techniques, using arbitrary sequences of homonyms and homophones to generate his novels and plays, are discussed in great detail in his *How I Wrote Certain of My Books*, which includes the same preface (here an introduction) by Ashbery.

5. See also the passenger in Walcott's "The Fortunate Traveler," whose privilege allows him to avert his gaze from misery: "for everywhere that earth shows its rib cage / and the moon goggles with the eyes of children, / We turn away to read" (*FT* 90).

6. Or as Nerval says in another context: "I have already lost, kingdom after kingdom, province after province, the more beautiful half of the universe, and soon I will know of no place in which I can find refuge for my dreams; but it is Egypt that I most regret having driven out of my imagination, now that I have sadly placed it in my memory" (qtd. in Said, *Orientalism* 100).

7. In the poem, Ashbery's is the situation of several privileged postwar poets: consider James Merrill's search for and securing of habitations away from the patria, Merrill-Lynch. And consider William Burroughs in Tangiers or Mexico City, far from the empire of Burroughs adding machines, the basis of the family's fortune.

8. Freud writes, "I had long seen clearly that a great part of the pleasure of travel lies in the fulfillment of these early wishes, that it is rooted in dissatisfaction with home and family" ("Disturbance" 246–47).

9. See Van Den Abbeele, who quotes Montesquieu regarding the view from a tower: "Quand j'arrive dans une ville, je vais toujours sur le plus haut clocher ou la plus haute tour, pour voir le tout ensemble, avant de voir les parties; et, en la quittant, je fais de meme, pour fixer mes idées" ("Montesquieu" 67). ("When I arrive in a town, I always climb the tallest clock or the highest tower, in order to see everything at once before seeing it in parts; when I am ready to leave, I do the same thing again, to fix my ideas.") Montesquieu sees three different views of a city: the initial, elevated view; the sight of the parts seen up close and singly in the order of the tourist itinerary; and then, a repetition of the first view to fix it in mind.

10. Among many contemporary examples, consider The Lonely Planet Journeys list, which features titles such as *Lost Japan* ("a backstage tour") and *Islands in the Clouds* ("remote and beautiful . . . a region rarely noticed by the rest of the world").

11. As an example of our increasing acceptance of staged authenticity in tourism, consider the Lascaux caves. After the discovery that the pictures on the

caves' walls had begun to disintegrate due to the condensation caused by human breath, the drawings were x-rayed, photographed, and carefully reproduced in new caves built for the purpose. Tourists now see the "Lascaux Caves" rather than the Lascaux Caves with no appreciable difference (see Matos 221). Similar replicas of touristic/historical sites may be seen all over the world—ancient tombs in China or Egypt, for example.

12. Any of the doggerel couplets of "Variations" reveal travel rhetoric as banal sublimity:

> Gazing at the alps was quite a sight
> I felt the tears flow with all their might

> A climb to the Acropolis meant a lot to me
> I had read the Greek philosophers you see
> (*DDS* 25)

13. Of Ashbery's many rhetorics, politics is largely phased out after *Flow Chart*. In that book, one finds passages such as the following: "Latest reports show that the government / still controls everything but that the location of the blond captive / has been pinpointed thanks to urgent needling from the backwoods constituency" (14). On the map-territory problem, especially the view of cities as texts, *Flow Chart*'s first lines seem to echo the early "Rivers and Mountains": "Still in the published city but not yet / overtaken by a new form of despair" (3).

14. Shoptaw provides a helpful reading of these lines by suggesting an elliptical clause, so the line should read, "On the secret map [that] the assassins / Cloistered" (77), a reading that restores *cloister* to its transitive function. Still, dropping *that* gives us the idea of the assassins gathering on the map, an odd but interesting reading for the rest of the poem.

15. So many instances occur in Ashbery where reality, as in *Three Poems*, "works itself out into a map" or where, as in "The Skaters," the coast is dog-eared like a book whose pages we finger as we follow it that I have relegated a catalogue of them to Appendix B, along with their parallels in Elizabeth Bishop's "The Map, " some instances from Lyn Hejinian and Gary Snyder, and many examples from Derek Walcott, a poet whose fascination with the map-territory problem reaches extremes.

16. Train references in other Ashbery poems include the following: "We know that we are en route in a certain sense, and also that there has been a hitch somewhere: we have as it were boarded the train but for some unexplained reason it has not yet started" ("The System," *TP* 18); "The train is waiting / in the little enclosed yard. My only duty / now is to thank all those who put up with me / and trusted me so long." ("No Good at Names," *HL* 28); "There was nothing to do except

wait / for another train, yet this one still stayed at the platform" ("Film Noir," *HL* 43); "some got off at the next-to-last stop; / others, less fortunate / were lost on the trail. ("In Vain, Therefore," *HL* 80); "All along I had known what buttons to press, but don't / you see, I had to experiment, not that my life depended on it, / but as a corrective to taking the train to find out where it wanted to / go" (*FC* 123); "I see I am as ever / a terminus of sorts, that is, lots of people arrive in me and switch / directions but no one moves on any farther" (*FC* 127); "a pleasant dinner / and a frozen train ride into the exhaustible resources" (*Chinese Whispers* 85).

In *Flow Chart*, the book-length poem that charts Ashbery's writing career and critical reception, the poet uses the train metaphor to reveal his role as travel agent, ticket agent, and conduit for poetry.

17. See Chatwin's *Songlines* regarding the Australian Aboriginal idea of singing the land into existence and of locating land through song.

18. Costello, in her article "John Ashbery's Landscapes," remarks that Ashbery "is very fond of window views, which mark the negotiation between mental and environmental landscapes" (63).

19. Perhaps the only other late-twentieth-century poem in English by a major poet to be commissioned in this way is Philip Larkin's "Going, Going," solicited and underwritten by a British government environmental agency.

20. Ashbery explains in a 1984 interview that he lifted the title of *Houseboat Days* from an issue of *National Geographic* (following a practice of Elizabeth Bishop and Marianne Moore), whose cover reads

> "Houseboat Days in Old Kashmir" or "in the Vale of Kashmir" or something like that and I sort of liked the kind of homely, old-fashioned sound of the phrase "Houseboat Days." Also, although I didn't choose it because of a list of things I liked about it, had I done so, probably one would have been the idea of both being on the move and being stationary in one's home—which is sort of what life is like. (qtd. in Sloan 6)

Shooting the Gulf: Three Beat Questions of Travel

1. See particularly Freud, "Disturbance," and Porter (188–201).

2. Note the contrast between the turbulence of air travel as metaphor for neurosis, as seen in Lowell's flight poems, and the literal groundedness of Snyder's humbler mode of travel as metaphor for a spiritual and psychological stability.

3. All quotations from Ammons's *Tape for the Turn of the Year* are from the original tape, titled "Today," at Cornell University. The first transcription onto typing paper from the "Today" tape, with a few changes, was titled *Fugue*; the final,

published version was *Tape for the Turn of the Year.* On the original tape, each dated entry bears the same "Today" title and no page numbers.

4. All that remains of this passage in the published version (*Tape for the Turn of the Year*) are the lines "what's the way home?" and "what's wrong / with these excitements, shows: / excursions" (28).

The Problem of Witness: The Travels of Derek Walcott

1. See Appendix A for a discussion of the critical commentary on Walcott's 1992 Nobel.

2. Should the argument need to be made, Walcott has stated, "I am primarily, absolutely a Caribbean poet" ("What" 33). Walcott lived and worked in St. Lucia and Trinidad for decades before he left to the United States in 1981 to begin teaching in Boston. On a trip to England he carried with him, as he says in *Another Life*, the images of the seaport Castries, making of his heart an ark, "a ship within a ship within a ship, a bottle where this wharf, these rotting roofs, this sea, sail, sealed in glass" (108). He has described *Omeros* as a thank-you note to the people of St. Lucia. Of his home islands he has said, "I feel very needed. In the Caribbean, meeting people anywhere . . . I feel as if I could speak for them" (Montenegro 214). He dedicated his Nobel Prize money to funding repairs to the Trinidad Theater Workshop, which he founded; setting up a Caribbean poetry prize; and, most ambitious, establishing the Rat Island Foundation, off the coast of St. Lucia, dedicated to development of the arts.

3.   Shout it on the rooftops
And rite it on the sky
His name is Derek Walcott
e mus get dat Nobel Prize
(Mighty Pep [Aloysius Brouet], St. Lucian Calypso Monarch)

Note also that the central square of Castries, St. Lucia, formerly Columbus Square, is now Walcott Square.

4. Parallel examples abound of writers from many nations, not all developing countries. Fenton mentions the Vosnesensky poem in which Gauguin travels from Montmartre to the Louvre by a detour through Java, Tahiti, and the Marquesas. Seamus Heaney's course is similarly instructive: "from Belfast and Dublin via county Wicklow, from Ulster to Stockholm via California and Harvard" (Fenton 40). Here the individual history of one poet is the collective history.

5. *Midsummer* has no page numbers, only poems numbered by roman numerals.

6. While I concentrate here on only a few, Walcott has written many poems of guilt at privilege and of privileged perspective, particularly his early work. See,

for example, "Mass Man" (*The Gulf* 48), where Walcott is the privileged boy, the literary celebrity, not black enough for the locals, who find he cannot even dance. The blacks also exclude Shabine in "The Schooner *Flight*." The poem "The Gulf" provides another example, as indeed does the book title, the "Gulf" suggesting the gap between poet and people.

7. In "The Spoiler's Return," the insects—lice, vermin, bedbugs, and fleas—are positive figures for the social satirist (the poem's narrator), whose sting on the "cleft arse" of society "reminds Authority man is just meat" (*FT* 69). They return in *The Bounty*, where gnats, cockroaches, termites, and locusts appear as the poet's critics, from whose attacks he hopes to find the strength to turn.

8. In an earlier poem, his envy of "backward" religion is unqualified. Watching island churchgoers in "Return to D'Ennery: Rain," he says to himself, "You are less than they are, for your truth / Consists of a general passion, a personal need" (*GN* 8). And the Creole poet-sailor Shabine says, "I from backward people who still fear God" (*SAK* 18).

9. These third-world photo-essay images occur in other Walcott poems; for example, in *Another Life*, Chapter 6, part ii, their description, as in "The Fortunate Traveler," may betray an undertone of contempt:

> At Anse-la-Raye,
>
> moving among pot-stomached, dribbling, snotted,
>
> starved, fig-navelled, mud-baked cherubim,
>
> the French priest strolls down to the pier.
>
> (37)

The use of "cherubim" suggests something incongruously "cute" about the children's misery. As elsewhere in Walcott, the poem has no obviously unreliable narrator to indicate satirical intent.

10. But both Shabine and Spoiler invoke literary and high-culture antecedents. Shabine mentions Aleksandr Blok; Spoiler catalogues satirists, including Quevedo, Martial, Juvenal, Pope, Dryden, Byron, and Swift.

11. Victorian historian, novelist, and traveler James Anthony Froude's presence asserts itself repeatedly in Derek Walcott's work, as it does in that of other modern Caribbean writers. The key passage, from Froude's *The English in the West Indies*, is quoted in Walcott's early essay "What the Twilight Says" and in "Air," a poem from *The Gulf*. It is paraphrased, twenty-five years later, in the first poem of *Midsummer*: "that island known / to the traveler Trollope, and the fellow traveler Froude / for making nothing. Not even a people" (I, i). Finally, it appears in his Nobel acceptance speech: "No people there, in the true sense of the word?" ("Antilles" 67–68). V. S. Naipaul, in *The Middle Passage*, quotes the passage in full: "They [the islands] were valued only for the wealth which they yielded, and society there has never assumed any particularly noble aspect. There has been splendour and luxurious living, and

there have been crimes and horrors, and revolts and massacres. There has been romance, but it has been romance of pirates and outlaws. The natural graces of life do not show themselves under such conditions. There has been no saint in the West Indies since Las Casas, no hero unless philonegro enthusiasm can make one out of Toussaint. There are no people there in the true sense of the word, with a character and purpose of their own" (167).

12. The sail-page appears again in *The Bounty*: "a page that my right hand steers— / a small sail making for Martinique or Sicily" (34).

13. Compare this to the swarmings in "The Fortunate Traveler."

14. I am indebted to Rei Terada's treatment of this poem in *Derek Walcott's Poetry: American Mimicry*, to which I enthusiastically refer the reader.

15. An early version of the poem reads "tourists" instead of "transients."

16. Rilke's passage follows: "[O]ur task is so deeply and passionately to impress upon ourselves this provisional and perishable earth, that its essential being will arise again 'invisibly' in us. We are the bees of the invisible. We frantically plunder the visible of its honey, to accumulate it in the great golden hive of the invisible" (letter to Polish translator Witold von Hulewicz, qtd. in notes, Rilke 133).

17. In my chapter on Lyn Hejinian and Nathaniel Mackey, I cite Douglas Messerli's remarks, from the introduction to his anthology of late-twentieth-century American poetry, concerning this schism between "cultural, social, and political" poetry and the "more formally-conceived poems in this volume" (34). One may contrast Messerli's linguistically experimental emphasis with the thematic and ethnic bases for selection of post-1950 poets in the *Norton Anthology of Modern Poetry*; of the six poets born after 1950, Marjorie Perloff has noted, four are women and all are minority writers. ("Why" B7). The contrast sharpens if we turn to *Norton*'s alternative, the Oxford *Anthology of Modern American Poetry*, which Perloff also reviews, pointing out that "[o]f the twenty-five poets born after 1946 who are included, twenty-one are poets of color" ("Janus-Faced" 212).

18. In *Midsummer*, Walcott uses Bishop's map-territory metaphor, as if answering "The Map": "we had crossed into England— / the fields, not their names, were the same" (xxxv). See Appendix B for many instances of such metaphors, particularly in Walcott and Ashbery.

19. The casuarina, a leafless tree, plays a large part also in "The Schooner *Flight*," where the sailor Shabine sings back to the casuarinas, as here the poet talks back to them.

20. The title poem of *The Arkansas Testament* offers one of these meanings: "a breeze turned the leaves of an aspen / to the First Epistle of Paul's / to the Corinthians" (108), the biblical passage that is incidentally the source of the refrain in "The Fortunate Traveler."

21. Walcott's *Tiepolo's Hound* continues the trope of trees and mobility—"we, as

moving trees, must root somewhere" (160)—and extends the problem of roots to language: "Our tribes were shaken like seeds from a sieve. / Our dialects, rooted, forced their own utterance" (157).

22. The echoes of this theme are practically innumerable throughout Walcott, but to mention three relatively recent ones: in *Tiepolo's Hound*, the poet writes, "There is no history now, only the weather" (71); in his Nobel acceptance speech, he refers to "that seriousness that comes only out of a culture with four seasons" ("Antilles" 72); and, in a talk at City College, New York, regarding the four seasons, he observes: "If you don't have these marking the year, you don't have stages of maturity, and in a sense you don't have 'time.'" One of the effects of this timelessness and historylessness, Walcott adds, is the impossibility of dating a writer or of labeling him or her "postcolonial" or "commonwealth." Beyond this theme, Walcott's poems contain many descriptions of the tropics as static and torpid. In *Midsummer* the poet depicts Puerto Rico as an island where "things topple gradually," where "only a mare's tail switches," and where "a sacramental stasis" finally brings sleep (XLIII, viii).

23. The term *heterotopia* owes something to Michel Foucault (*"Des espaces autres"*), for whom heterotopias, unlike utopias, are actual spaces that contest and invert known cultural sites. Foucault's examples are various, but they include places linked to deviance, flight, and the changing of functions. For Foucault, the ship or boat is "the heterotopia *par excellence*" (27). See also Axelrod, "Heterotropic Desire."

24. Walcott comments (as I quote in the chapter "Dandies and Flaneurs"), "the [U.S.] poet is almost crying out for the society to be hostile to him—or her, I mean both him and her—to repress him, to take notice, to imprison him, to pay attention in a sense" (Montenegro 213). See also Bruce Murphy's view that American poets, stung by poetry's marginality, envy poets in totalitarian regimes ("Exile").

25. This is the last line of *Omeros*: "When he left the beach the sea was still going on" (325).

26. I am grateful to Lowell Fiet of the University of Puerto Rico, Rio Piedras, English Department for an account of Walcott's time in Puerto Rico.

27. Walcott offers no explanation why St. Lucia should be treated as a history-less island compared to Puerto Rico. Puerto Rico was settled more than a century earlier by the Spanish and was the site of clashes, during three hundred years, between the Spanish and their enemies, the imperial upstarts the English, French, and Dutch—a more visible and storied history than that of the smaller and more peripheral St. Lucia, perhaps. Or perhaps history elsewhere can be more easily experienced without personal association, while history at home is constraining and burdensome.

28. Another comparison with Bishop's narrators suggests itself. In "Arrival at

Santos," the speaker thinks only of bargains in the free port; in this section of "Tropic Zone," the traveler thinks of sex and alcohol, two of the Caribbean's strongest touristic suits.

29. I mention Greene for his well-known settings, but Greene himself objected to novelistic treatments of the developing world where that world takes on importance only as it impinges on the "gringo."

30. These clichés are the more puzzling in that Puerto Rico is hardly a banana republic. It has U.S. economic support and, compared to most Latin American nations, a stable government and relatively high income levels.

31. Note *The Star-Apple Kingdom*'s epigraph from Lafcadio Hearn, where Hearn refers to "a geological dream, a vision of the primeval sea: the apparition of the land as first brought forth, all peak-tossed and fissured and naked and grim, in the tremendous birth of an archipelago" (1).

32. An excellent discussion of Walcott's lengthy and complex treatments of this opposition may be found in Tejumola Olaniyan's *Scars of Conquest/Masks of Resistance*. For the two terms mentioned, Olaniyan prefers to substitute "history as culture" versus "history as politics."

Travel and Difference: Lyn Hejinian and Nathaniel Mackey

1. All quotations of Lyn Hejinian's poetry are from *Oxota: A Short Russian Novel.*

2. See Jameson, "Third World Literature in the Age of Multinational Capitalism."

3. "Arkadii," mentioned in many of the poems, is Leningrad poet Arkadii Dragomoshchenko, whom Hejinian met during her first visit to the Soviet Union in 1984, whose work she has translated, and to whom her book *The Guard* is dedicated. She discusses his work in *The Language of Inquiry*. Arkadii's comments in the various *Oxota* poems take on more interest when one realizes that his poetry has something in common with that of U.S. language poets, such as, as Hejinian explains, "an involvement with the epistemological and perceptual nature of language-as-thinking, a belief that poetic language itself is an appropriate instrument for exploring the world, an interest in the linguistic layering of the landscape" (*Language* 173).

4. Too long a footnote would be required here to cover the emergent recent alternatives to a hundred years of personal, yet stylistically antiromantic, free verse constituting America's mainstream. The spoken word movement, cowboy poetry, and the new formalists are the most visible groups to have returned to the lyrical in the more obvious verse senses of rhyme, rhythm, and musical language.

5. *Song of the Andoumboulou* 1–7 appeared in *Eroding Witness*, 8–15 in *School of Udhra*. Songs 16–25 (together titled *Strick*) are listed in the works cited.

6. As Mackey has explained, in Dogon mythology the Andoumboulou are an earlier, flawed form of human being, an unviable rough draft. They are invoked at the time of Dogon funeral ceremonies. "My understanding of it is that the Andoumboulou become relevant in a ritual that is marking death and mortality, the failure of human life to sustain itself indefinitely, because they are figures of frailty and failure" (O'Leary 36).

7. For a case in point, especially on the "complex, multiple . . . synthetic, mutant" poetic text, see my discussion of the poet Jay Wright in "In the Name of the Subject."

8. I take up the musical elements of *Strick* at greater length in "'Beyond the Letter,'" the source of much of this section on Mackey.

9. Approaching this text as heard unfortunately requires a certain violence in quoting. While American poetic practice after William Carlos Williams, at least, has generally entailed breaking lines against syntax, most poets read their work aloud with grammatical logic, regardless of visual lineation. Respecting the latter at some times and not at others is awkward, so—chiefly because it is often important *not* to visualize lines on a page—I indicate not Mackey's written but his spoken line breaks (i.e., pauses) with slashes, following the spoken contours. These spoken lines are usually of uneven syllabic count and with two stresses per (heard) line. I also italicize words *heard* as emphasized in Mackey's reading.

10. See Chatwin, *Songlines*, for a full treatment of this practice.

11. Ouagadougou is a city in Burkina Faso (formerly Upper Volta) in Mossi country. "D.C." is not part of its name. "Ouagadougou D.C." certainly suggests a code for a stateside trip by bus and train.

12. The scribal turn is still more obvious at the graphic level, in the poet's play with spelling, as in "Razz, with an e on the end, a way of spelling" (Song 20),

> sing less what
>
> he did than sihg, anagrammatic sigh,
>
> from *war the male ruse* to *"were" the*
>
> *new ruse*
>
> (Song 23)

and "that words be would, would words" (Song 18); with writerly puns and slippages ("limb" or "limp," "plain" or "plane," "mute" or "moot"); and with lineation on the page.

13. Many instrumental works have been written as glosses on poetic texts. Lawrence Kramer discusses some of these, including Liszt's renditions of Dante

and Goethe and Debussy's "Prelude to the Afternoon of a Faun," written to elucidate Mallarmé's poem, which is arguably less referential than Debussy's music.

14. *Strick*'s "book," so often "thumbed," the idea of land as text, and the idea of a home to which it is too late or too difficult to return—all these echo the lines in Countee Cullen's 1927 poem "Heritage": "Africa? A book one thumbs / Listlessly, till slumber comes" (104).

15. The Persian nay is a six-tone flute. The bendir is a Turkish frame drum.

16. *Monte*, a word that appears in many Latin American and particularly Afro-Cuban song lyrics, can be translated as the woods, the wilderness, or the mountains. A wild, timeless space outside society, it often has sacred overtones. Piedra argues that it comes from the Dogon word *muntu* (116). A ready example of its use in song choruses is "El Carretero," now widely known from the recording of the song by the Buena Vista Social Club.

Epilogue: The Trouble with Travel

1. National Geographic Education Foundation, "National Geographic–Roper 2002 Global Geographic Literacy Survey," 14 Apr. 2004 <http://www.nationalgeographic.com/geosurvey/highlights.html>.

Appendix A: The Nobel and Travel

1. Early in the writing of this book, I had noted that V. S. Naipaul, winner of the Booker Prize and the lucrative David Cohen Award, had been nominated for the Nobel but was unlikely ever to win it, precisely because he is seen as a renegade who has failed to represent the developing world favorably. However, in October 2001, Naipaul won the Nobel Prize. Paul Gray plausibly suggests that the Nobel committee misread Naipaul's *The Enigma of Arrival*, thinking the author was condemning Europe rather than extolling it.

WORKS CITED

Akhmatova, Anna. "I Heard a Voice," "I Am Not One of Those," and "Requiem." *Twentieth-Century Russian Poetry: Silver and Steel.* Ed. Albert G. Todd and Max Hayward. New York: Doubleday, 1993. 173–74, 180.

Ammons, A. R. *Garbage.* New York: Norton, 1993.

———. *Selected Poems.* New York: Norton, 1986.

———. *Sumerian Vistas.* New York: Norton, 1987.

———. *Tape for the Turn of the Year.* Ithaca: Cornell UP, 1965.

———. "Today." First vers. of *Tape for the Turn of the Year.* Typed on adding-machine paper roll. Special Collections. #14/12/2665. Box #98. Ithaca, NY: Cornell University Library.

Anderson, Benedict. *Imagined Communities: Reflections on the Origin and Spread of Nationalism.* New York: Verso, 1983.

Appiah, Kwame Anthony. "The Multiculturalist Misunderstanding." *New York Review of Books* 44.15 (1997): 30–36.

Ashbery, John. *And the Stars Were Shining.* New York: Noonday, 1995.

———. *April Galleons.* New York: Penguin, 1984.

———. *Can You Hear, Bird?* New York: Farrar, 1995.

———. *Chinese Whispers.* New York: Farrar, 2002.

———. *The Double Dream of Spring.* New York: Ecco, 1976.

———. *Flow Chart.* New York: Knopf, 1992.

———. "Frank O'Hara's Question." *Book Week.* 25 Sept. 1966: 6.

———. *Hotel Lautréamont.* New York: Knopf, 1993.

———. *Houseboat Days.* New York: Viking, 1975.

———. Introduction. *How I Wrote Certain of My Books.* By Raymond Roussel. Ed. Trevor Winkfield. Boston: Exact Change, 1995.

———. *Rivers and Mountains.* New York: Ecco, 1962.

———. "Second Presentation of Elizabeth Bishop." *World Literature Today* 51 (1977): 8–11.

———. *Self-Portrait in a Convex Mirror.* New York: Penguin, 1972.

———. *Some Trees.* New Haven: Yale UP, 1956.

———. *The Tennis Court Oath.* Middletown: UP of New England, 1962.

———. *Three Poems.* New York: Ecco, 1970.

———. *A Wave.* New York: Viking, 1984.

Auden, W. H. *Collected Shorter Poems, 1927–1957.* New York: Random House, 1966.

Augé, Marc. *Non-Places: Introduction to an Anthropology of Supermodernity.* Trans. John Howe. London: Verso, 1995.

Axelrod, Steven Gould. "Heterotropic Desire in Elizabeth Bishop's 'Pink Dog.'" *Arizona Quarterly* 60.3 (2004): 61–81.

———. "Robert Lowell and the Cold War." *The New England Quarterly* (September 1999): 339–61.

———. *Robert Lowell: Life and Art.* Princeton: Princeton UP, 1978.

Baldwin, James. *Giovanni's Room.* New York: Dell, 1956.

Bammer, Angelika, ed. *Displacements: Cultural Identities in Question.* Bloomington: Indiana UP, 1994.

Baudelaire, Charles. "Le Voyage." *Flowers of Evil.* Ed. Jackson Matthews and Marthiel Matthews. New York: New Directions, 1955. 133–44.

———. "N'Importe Où Hors du Monde. Any Where Out of the World." *The Parisian Prowler* (Le Spleen de Paris, Petits Poèmes en Prose). Trans. Edward K. Kaplan. Athens: U of Georgia P, 1989. 119–120.

Baudrillard, Jean. *Simulations.* Trans. Paul Foss, Paul Patton, and Philip Beitchman. New York: Semiotext(e), 1983.

———. *The Transparency of Evil: Essays on Extreme Phenomena.* Trans. James Benedict. London: Verso, 1993.

Bedient, Calvin. "Derek Walcott: Contemporary." *Parnassus* 9 (1981): 31–44.

Behdad, Ali. *Belated Travelers: Orientalism in the Age of Colonial Dissolution.* Durham: Duke UP, 1994.

Bellamy, Joe David, ed. *American Poetry Observed: Poets on Their Work.* Urbana: U of Illinois P, 1984.

Benítez-Rojo, Antonio. *The Repeating Island: The Caribbean and the Postmodern Perspective.* Trans. James E. Maraniss. 2nd ed. Durham: Duke UP, 1996.

Berger, John. *And Our Faces, My Heart, Brief as Photos.* New York: Pantheon, 1984.

Bernstein, Charles. *A Poetics.* Cambridge: Harvard UP, 1992.

———. "Poetics of the Americas." *Modernism/Modernity* 3.3 (1996): 1–23.

Bishop, Elizabeth. *Brazil.* Ed. *Life* magazine. New York: Time, 1962.

———. *The Collected Prose.* New York: Farrar, 1984.

———. *The Complete Poems, 1927–1979.* New York: Farrar, 1979.

———. *One Art: Letters, Selected and Edited.* Ed. Robert Giroux. New York: Farrar, 1994.

———, ed. *An Anthology of Twentieth Century Brazilian Poetry.* Middletown: Wesleyan UP, 1972.

Bloom, Harold, ed. *Modern Critical Views: Elizabeth Bishop.* New York: Chelsea, 1985.

———, ed. *Modern Critical Views: John Ashbery.* New York: Chelsea, 1985.

————, ed. *Modern Critical Views: Robert Lowell*. New York: Chelsea, 1987.

Borges, Jorge Luis. "The Lottery in Babylon." *Labyrinths: Selected Stories and Other Writings*. Ed. Donald A. Yates and James E. Inby. New York: New Directions, 1962. 30–35.

————. "On Rigor in Science." *Dreamtigers*. Trans. Mildred Boyer and Harold Morland. New York: E. P. Dutton, 1970.

Bowles, Paul. *The Sheltering Sky*. New York: Ecco, 1949.

Brathwaite, Kamau. *The Arrivants: A New World Trilogy*. Oxford: Oxford UP, 1992.

Breslin, Paul. "'I Met History Once, But He Ain't Recognize Me': The Poetry of Derek Walcott." *TriQuarterly* 68 (Winter 1987): 168–83.

Brown, Stewart, ed. *The Art of Derek Walcott*. Mid Glamorgan, Wales: Seren, 1991.

Bugeja, Michael J. "Poets Abroad." *Writer's Digest*. September 1998: 12–14.

Burnett, Paula. *Derek Walcott: Politics and Poetics*. Gainesville: UP of Florida, 2000.

————. "Hegemony or Pluralism? The Literary Prize and the Post-Colonial Project in the Caribbean." *Commonwealth* 16.1 (1993): 1–20.

Butor, Michel. "Travel and Writing." *Mosaic* 7 (Fall 1974): 1–16.

Buzard, James. *The Beaten Track: European Tourism, Literature, and the Ways to "Culture," 1800–1918*. New York: Oxford UP, 1993.

"By Many Hands." *Three Hundred Things a Bright Boy Can Do*. London: Sampson, 1911.

Caesar, Terry. *Forgiving the Boundaries: American Travel Writing*. Athens: U of Georgia P, 1995.

Cavafy, C. P. "Ithaca." *Complete Poems*. Trans. Rae Dalven. New York: Harcourt, 1961. 34–36.

Certeau, Michel de. *L'Invention de Quotidien: Arts de Faire*. Paris: 10/18, 1980.

Césaire, Aimé. *Notebook of a Return to My Native Land*. In *Aimé Césaire: The Collected Poetry*. Trans. Clayton Eshelman and Annette Smith. Berkeley: U of California P, 1983.

Chamoiseau, Patrick, Raphael Confiant, and Jean Bernabé. *Éloge de la Créolité*. Édition bilingue francais/anglais. Trans. M. B. Taleb-Khyar. Baltimore: Johns Hopkins UP, 1990.

Chatwin, Bruce. *The Songlines*. In *In Patagonia / The Viceroy of Ouidah / The Songlines*. New York: Quality Paperback, 1977. 365–659.

Chow, Rey. "How (the) Inscrutable Chinese Led to Globalized Theory." *PMLA* 116.1 (2001): 69–74.

————. "Where Have All the Natives Gone?" *Displacements: Cultural Identities in Question*. Ed. Angelika Bammer. Bloomington: Indiana UP, 1994.

Clifford, James. "Notes on Travel and Theory." *Inscriptions* 5 (1989): 177–89.

————. *The Predicament of Culture: Twentieth-century Ethnography, Literature, and Art.* Cambridge: Harvard UP, 1988.

————. *Routes: Travel and Translation in the Late Twentieth Century.* Cambridge: Harvard UP, 1997.

Colwell, Anne. *Inscrutable Houses: Metaphors of the Body in the Poems of Elizabeth Bishop.* Tuscaloosa: U of Alabama P, 1997.

Conrad, Joseph. *Heart of Darkness.* Ed. Robert Kimbrough. New York: Norton, 1988.

Corn, Alfred. "A Magma of Interiors." *Contemporary Poets.* Ed. Harold Bloom. New York: Chelsea, 1986. 235–44.

Costello, Bonnie. "John Ashbery's Landscapes." *The Tribe of John: Ashbery and Contemporary Poetry.* Ed. Susan M. Schultz. Tuscaloosa: U of Alabama P, 1995.

————. *Elizabeth Bishop: Questions of Mastery.* Cambridge: Harvard UP, 1991.

Creeley, Robert. *The Collected Poems: 1945–1975.* Berkeley: U of California P, 1982.

————. Foreword. *Death and Fame: Poems, 1993–1997.* By Allen Ginsberg. New York: HarperFlamingo, 1998. xv–xvi.

————. *Life and Death.* New York: New Directions, 1998.

————. *So There: Poems 1976–83.* New York: New Directions, 1998.

Cucullu, Lois. "Trompe l'Oeil: Elizabeth Bishop's Radical 'I'." *Texas Studies in Language and Literature* 30.2 (1988): 246–71.

Cullen, Countee. *My Soul's High Song: The Collected Writings of Countee Cullen.* Ed. Gerald Early. New York: Anchor, 1991.

Curry, Renée R. "Augury and Autobiography: Bishop's 'Crusoe in England.'" *Arizona Quarterly* 47.3 (1991): 71–91.

Damon, Maria. *The Dark End of the Street: Margins in American Vanguard Poetry.* Minneapolis: U of Minnesota P, 1993.

Derrida, Jacques. "Différance." *Margins of Philosophy.* Trans. Alan Bass. Chicago: U of Chicago P, 1982. 1–27.

————. "The Violence of the Letter: From Lévi-Strauss to Rousseau." *Of Grammatology.* Trans. Gayatri Chakravorty Spivak. Baltimore: Johns Hopkins UP, 1974. 101–40.

Diehl, Joanne Feit. "Bishop's Sexual Politics." *Elizabeth Bishop: The Geography of Gender.* Ed. Marilyn May Lombardi. Charlottesville: UP of Virginia, 1993. 17–45.

Donoghue, Denis. Rev. of *The Fortunate Traveler. The New York Times Book Review.* 3 January 1982: 5.

Doreski, C. K. *Elizabeth Bishop: The Restraints of Language.* New York: Oxford UP, 1993.

Edelman, Lee. "The Geography of Gender: Elizabeth Bishop's 'In the Waiting Room.'" *Contemporary Literature* 26.2 (1985): 179–96.

Eliade, Mircea. *The Myth of the Eternal Return.* Trans. Willard R. Trask. Princeton: Princeton UP, 1954.

Eliot, T. S. *Selected Poems.* London: Faber, 1941.

Ellison, June. "A Short History of Liberal Guilt." *Critical Inquiry* 22 (Winter 1996): 344–71.

Emerson, Ralph Waldo. "Self-Reliance." *Emerson's Prose and Poetry.* Ed. Joel Porte and Saundra Morris. New York: Norton, 2001. 120–36.

Epstein, Joseph. "Who Killed Poetry?" *Commentary* 86.2 (1998): 13–20.

Eshleman, Clayton. *Antiphonal Swing: Selected Prose, 1962–1987.* Kingston, NY: McPherson, 1989.

Fenton, James. "The Orpheus of Ulster." *New York Review of Books.* 11 July 1996: 37–41.

Ferlinghetti, Lawrence. "Poetry as Prophecy." 16 Oct. 2001. pbs.org/newshour/bb/poems/july-deco1/ferlinghetti.

Forché, Carolyn. *Against Forgetting: Twentieth-Century Poetry of Witness.* New York: Norton, 1993.

Foucault, Michel. *Death and the Labyrinth: The World of Raymond Roussel.* Trans. Charles Ruas. Garden City: Doubleday, 1986.

———. "*Des espaces autres.*" Lecture delivered in 1967. *Architecture-Mouvement-Continuité* (1984); *Dits et Écrits, Vol. 4.* Paris: Editions Gallimard, 1994. Rpt. as "Of Other Spaces." Trans. Jay Miskowiec. *Diacritics* 16 (Spring 1986): 22–27.

———. *The History of Sexuality, Vol. 2: The Use of Pleasure.* New York: Vintage, 1990.

———. *The History of Sexuality, Vol. 3: The Care of the Self.* New York: Vintage, 1988.

———. "On the Genealogy of Ethics: An Overview of Work in Progress." *The Foucault Reader.* Ed. Paul Rabinow. New York: Pantheon, 1984. 340–72.

Fountain, Gary, and Peter Brazeau, eds. *Elizabeth Bishop: An Oral Biography.* Amherst: U of Massachusetts P, 1994.

Fredman, Stephen. *Poet's Prose: The Crisis in American Verse.* 2nd ed. Cambridge: Cambridge UP, 1990.

Freud, Sigmund. "A Disturbance of Memory on the Acropolis." *The Standard Edition of the Complete Psychological Works of Sigmund Freud.* Vol. 22. Trans. James Strachey. London: Hogarth, 1964. 239–48.

———. "Mourning and Melancholia." *The Standard Edition of the Complete Psychological Works of Sigmund Freud.* Vol. 19. Trans. James Strachey. London: Hogarth, 1961. 225–80.

———. "The 'Uncanny.'" *The Standard Edition of the Complete Psychological Works of Sigmund Freud.* Vol. 27. Trans. James Strachey. London: Hogarth, 1917–1919. 219–52.

Frost, Robert. *The Poetry of Robert Frost: Collected Poems, Complete and Unabridged.* Ed. Edward Lathem. New York: Holt, 1975.

Froude, James Anthony. *The English in the West Indies, or The Bow of Ulysses.* London: Longmans, 1888.

Fussell, Paul. *Abroad: British Literary Traveling between the Wars.* New York: Oxford UP, 1980.

Gadamer, Hans-Georg. *Warheit und Methode.* Tübingen: Mohr, 1975.

Gangel, Sue. Interview with John Ashbery. *American Poetry Observed.* Ed. Joe David Bellamy. Urbana: U of Illinois P, 1984.

Gingell, Susan. "Returning to Come Forward: Dionne Brand Confronts Derek Walcott." *Journal of West Indian Literature* 6.2 (1994): 43–53.

Ginsberg, Allen. *Collected Poems, 1947–1980.* New York: Harper, 1984.

———. *The Fall of America.* San Francisco: City Lights, 1972.

———. *Howl.* San Francisco: City Lights, 1956.

———. *Planet News.* San Francisco: City Lights, 1971.

Goldensohn, Lorrie. "The Body's Roses: Race, Sex, and Gender in Elizabeth Bishop's Representations of the Self." *Elizabeth Bishop: The Geography of Gender.* Ed. Marilyn May Lombardi. Charlottesville: UP of Virginia, 1993. 70–90.

Gray, Jeffrey. "Ashbery's 'The Instruction Manual.'" *The Explicator* 54.2 (1996): 117–20.

———. "'Beyond the Letter': Identity, Song, and *Strick*." *Callaloo* 23.2 (2000): 621–39.

———. "Bishop's 'Brazil, January 1, 1502.'" *The Explicator* 54.1 (1995): 36–39.

———. "Derek Walcott's Traveler and the Problem of Witness." *Callaloo* 28.1 (2005).

———. "In the Name of the Subject: Some Recent Versions of the Personal." *Personal Effects: The Social Character of Scholarly Writing.* Ed. Deborah Holdstein and David Bleich. Logan: U of Utah P, 2001. 51–76.

———. "Literature, Difference, and the Land of Witness." *Profession 2002.* New York: MLA, 2002. 51–62.

———. "Memory and Imagination in *Day by Day*." *The Critical Response to Robert Lowell.* Ed. Steven Gould Axelrod. London: Greenwood, 2000. 224–38.

Gray, Paul. "October Surprise." *Smithsonian.* Dec. 2001: 106–7.

Gray, Rockwell. "Travel." *Temperamental Journeys: Essays on the Modern Literature of Travel.* Ed. Michael Kowalewski. Athens: U of Georgia P, 1992. 33–52.

Grunquist, Raoul. "Does It Matter Why Walcott Received the Prize?" *Research in African Literature* 25 (1994): 151–57.

Hall, Donald. *Death to the Death of Poetry.* Ann Arbor: U of Michigan P, 1994.

————. "Robert Lowell and the Literature Industry." *Georgia Review* 32.1 (1978): 7–12.

Hamilton, Ian. *Robert Lowell: A Biography*. New York: Random, 1982.

Harrison, Virginia. *Elizabeth Bishop's Poetics of Intimacy*. New York: Cambridge UP, 1993.

Hassan, Ihab. *Selves at Risk: Patterns of Quest in Contemporary American Letters*. Madison: U of Wisconsin P, 1989.

Heaney, Seamus. "Current Unstated Assumptions About Poetry (1)." *Critical Inquiry* 7 (Summer 1981): 645–51.

Hejinian, Lyn. *The Language of Inquiry*. Berkeley: U of California P, 2000.

————. *Oxota: A Short Russian Novel*. Great Barrington, MA: The Figures, 1991.

Hemingway, Ernest. *The Sun Also Rises*. New York: Scribner, 1926.

Herd, David. Interview with John Ashbery. *Onward: Contemporary Poetry and Poetics*. Ed. Peter Baker. New York: Lang, 1996.

Hirsch, Edward. "An Interview with Derek Walcott." *Contemporary Literature* 20.3 (1979): 279–92.

Holden, Jonathan. *Style and Authenticity in Postmodern Poetry*. Columbia: U of Missouri P, 1986.

Hollander, John. "Elizabeth Bishop's Mappings of Life." *Modern Critical Views: Elizabeth Bishop*. Ed. Harold Bloom. New York: Chelsea, 1985.

hooks, bell. "Representations of Whiteness in the Black Imagination." *Black Looks: Race and Representation*. Boston: South End, 1992. 165–78.

Howard, Richard. "John Ashbery." *Modern Critical Views: John Ashbery*. Ed. Harold Bloom. New York: Chelsea, 1985.

Hugo of St. Victor. *The Didascalicon: A Medieval Guide to the Arts*. Trans. Jerome Taylor. New York: Columbia UP, 1961.

Iyer, Pico. *Video Night in Kathmandu and Other Reports from the Not-So-Far-East*. New York: Vintage, 1988.

Jameson, Frederic. *The Political Unconscious*. Ithaca: Cornell UP, 1981.

————. *Postmodernism, or the Cultural Logic of Late Capitalism*. Durham: Duke UP, 1991.

————. "Third World Literature in the Era of Multinational Capitalism." *Social Text* 15 (1986): 65–88.

Jehlen, Myra. "Response to Peter Hulme." *Critical Inquiry* 20 (Autumn 1993): 187–91.

Johnson, Alexandra. "Geography of the Imagination." *Christian Science Monitor*. 23 Mar. 1980: 24–25.

Johnson, Dane. "The Rise of Gabriel García Márquez and Toni Morrison." *Cultural Institutions of the Novel*. Ed. Deirdre Lynch, et al. Durham: Duke UP, 1996. 129–56.

Kalaidjan, Walter. *Languages of Liberation: The Social Text in Contemporary American Poetry.* New York: Columbia UP, 1989.

Kalstone, David. *Becoming a Poet.* New York: Farrar, 1989.

———. *Five Temperaments.* New York: Oxford UP, 1977.

Kaplan, Caren. *Questions of Travel: Postmodern Discourses of Displacement.* Durham: Duke UP, 1996.

Kinzie, Mary. " 'Irreference': The Poetic Diction of John Ashbery, Part I: Styles of Avoidance." *Modern Philology* 84 (1987): 267–81.

———. " 'Irreference': The Poetic Diction of John Ashbery, Part II: Prose, Prosody, and Dissembled Time." *Modern Philology* 84 (1987): 382–400.

Koethe, John. "The Absence of a Noble Presence." *The Tribe of John: Ashbery and Contemporary Poetry.* Ed. Susan Schultz. Tuscaloosa: U of Alabama P, 1995. 83–90.

Kowalewski, Michael, ed. *Temperamental Journeys: Essays on the Modern Literature of Travel.* Athens: U of Georgia P, 1992.

Kramer, Lawrence. *Poetry and Music: The Nineteenth Century and After.* Berkeley: U of California P, 1984.

Kulisher, Eugene M. *Europe on the Move: War and Population Changes, 1917–47.* New York: Columbia UP, 1948.

Lane, Anthony. "The Fighter: Rereading Robert Lowell." *The New Yorker.* 9 June 2003: 80–89.

Larkin, Philip. "Going, Going." *Collected Poems.* New York: Noonday, 1993.

Laskin, David. *A Common Life: Four Generations of American Literary Friendship and Influence.* Hanover, NH: UP of New England, 1994.

Lawrence, D. H. *Sea and Sardinia.* London: Penguin, 1999.

Lazer, Hank. "Charles Bernstein's *Dark City:* Polis, Policy, and the Policing of Poetry," *American Poetry Review* 24.5 (1995): 35–44.

Leed, Eric J. *The Mind of the Traveler: From Gilgamesh to Global Tourism.* New York: Basic, 1991.

Levin, Bernard. *Hannibal's Footsteps.* New York: Random, 1988.

Lévi-Strauss, Claude. *Tristes Tropiques.* Trans. John and Doreen Weightman. New York: Atheneum, 1984.

Lodge, David. *Paradise News.* London: Penguin, 1993.

Logan, William. "The Fatal Lure of Home." *The New York Times Book Review.* 29 June 1997: 11.

Lombardi, Marilyn May, ed. *Elizabeth Bishop: The Geography of Gender.* Charlottesville: UP of Virginia, 1993.

Longenbach, James. "Elizabeth Bishop and the Story of Postmodernism." *Southern Review* 28.3 (1992): 469–84.

———. *Modern Poetry after Modernism.* New York: Oxford UP, 1997.

Lowell, Robert. *Collected Poems.* Ed. Frank Bidart and David Gewanter. New York: Farrar, 2003.

———. *Collected Prose.* Ed. Robert Giroux. New York: Farrar, 1987.

———. *Day by Day.* New York: Farrar, 1977.

———. *The Dolphin.* New York: Farrar, 1973.

———. *For Lizzie and Harriet.* New York: Farrar, 1973.

———. *For the Union Dead.* New York: Farrar, 1964.

———. *History.* New York: Farrar, 1973.

———. *Imitations.* New York: Farrar, 1961.

———. *Life Studies.* New York: Farrar, 1959.

———. *Notebook.* New York: Farrar, 1970.

———. *Notebook, 1967–68.* New York: Farrar, 1969.

———. *A Reading.* Recording. 8 December 1976. Caldman TC1569, 1978.

Lyotard, Jean-Francois. *The Postmodern Condition: A Report on Knowledge.* Trans. Geoff Bennington and Brian Massumi. Minneapolis: U of Minneapolis P, 1988.

MacCannell, Dean. *Empty Meeting Grounds: The Tourist Papers.* London: Routledge, 1992.

———. *The Tourist: A New Theory of the Leisure Class.* 2nd ed. New York: Schocken, 1989.

Machado, Antonio. *Antología Poética.* Navarra: Salvat Editores, 1971.

Mackey, Nathaniel. *Discrepant Engagement: Dissonance, Cross-Culturality, and Experimental Writing.* Cambridge: Cambridge UP, 1993.

———. *Eroding Witness.* Urbana: U of Illinois P, 1984.

———. *School of Udhra.* San Francisco: City Lights, 1993.

———. "Song of the Andoumboulou: 16." *River City* 14.2 (1994): 41–45.

———. "Song of the Andoumboulou: 17." *New American Writing* 2 (Summer/Fall 1993): 36–40.

———. "Song of the Andoumboulou: 18." *The Poetry Project Newsletter* 149 (Apr./May 1993): 8–9.

———. "Song of the Andoumboulou: 19." *The World* 49 (Apr. 1994): 104–6.

———. "Song of the Andoumboulou: 20." *Fourteen Hills* 2.1 (1995): 83–96.

———. "Song of the Andoumboulou: 21 and 22." *apex of the M* 1 (Spring 1994): 32–36.

———. "Song of the Andoumboulou: 23, 24 and 25." *Sulfur* 34 (Spring 1994): 43–54.

———. *Strick: Song of the Andoumboulou.* With Royal Hartigan and Hafez Modirzadeh. Spoken Engine, 1995.

Mariani, Paul. *The Lost Puritan: A Life of Robert Lowell.* New York: Norton, 1994.

Matos, Jacinta. "Old Journeys Revisited: Aspects of Postwar English Travel Writing." *Temperamental Journeys: Essays on the Modern Literature of Travel.* Ed. Michael Kowalewski. Athens: U of Georgia P, 1992.

McGann, Jerome. "Contemporary Poetry, Alternate Routes." *Politics and Poetic Value.* Ed. Robert von Hallberg. London: U of Chicago P, 1987. 253–76.

McIrwin, Michael. Rev. of *Seventh Circle* by Maggie Jaffe. *Rain Taxi* 4.2 (1999): 31.

Merrill, James. Afterword. *Becoming a Poet.* By David Kalstone. New York: Farrar, 1989.

———. *Collected Poems.* Ed. J. D. McClatchy and Stephen Yenser. New York: Knopf, 2001.

Merrin, Jeredith. "Elizabeth Bishop: Gaiety, Gayness, and Change." *Elizabeth Bishop: The Geography of Gender.* Ed. Marilyn May Lombardi. Charlottesville: UP of Virginia, 1993. 153–74.

———. *An Enabling Humility: Marianne Moore, Elizabeth Bishop, and the Uses of Tradition.* New Brunswick: Rutgers UP, 1990.

Merwin, W. S. *Travels.* New York: Knopf, 1993.

Messerli, Douglas, ed. *From the Other Side of the Century: A New American Poetry, 1960–1990.* Los Angeles: Sun and Moon, 1994.

Michaux, Henri. *A Barbarian in Asia.* San Francisco: New Directions, 1986.

Millier, Brett. *Elizabeth Bishop: Life and the Memory of It.* Berkeley: U of California P, 1993.

Mills, Katie. "Traveling Theory Blues: Race, Gender, and the Metaphors of Critical Theory." Unpublished paper. 1994.

Milosz, Czeslaw. *The Witness of Poetry.* Cambridge: Harvard UP, 1983.

Mintz, Sidney W., and Sally Price. *Caribbean Contours.* Baltimore: Johns Hopkins UP, 1985.

Monga, Luigi. "Hodoeporics?" *Annali d'italianistica* 14 (1996): 5.

Montenegro, David. "An Interview with Derek Walcott." *Partisan Review* 57.2 (1990): 202–14.

Mulvey, Laura. *Visual and Other Pleasures.* Bloomington: Indiana UP, 1989.

Murphy, Bruce F. "The Exile of Literature: Poetry and the Politics of the Other(s)," *Critical Inquiry* 17.1 (1990): 162–73.

———. "Verse versus Poetry." *Poetry* 177.3 (2001): 279–86.

Naipaul, V. S. *A Bend in the River.* New York: Vintage, 1989.

———. *In a Free State.* New York: Vintage, 1984.

———. *The Middle Passage.* Harmondsworth, UK: Penguin, 1969.

———. *The Mimic Men.* London: Penguin, 1967.

Nelson, Cary, ed. *Anthology of Modern American Poetry.* New York: Oxford, 2000.

Neruda, Pablo. *Canto General.* Trans. Jack Schmitt. Berkeley: U of California P, 1991.

————. *Twenty Poems.* Trans. James Wright and Robert Bly. Madison, Minn.: Sixties Press, 1967.

O'Hara, Frank. *Collected Poems.* Ed. Donald Hall. Berkeley: U of California P, 1995.

Olaniyan, Tejumola. *Scars of Conquest/Masks of Resistance: The Invention of Cultural Identities in African, African-American, and Caribbean Drama.* Oxford: Oxford UP, 1995.

O'Leary, Peter. "An Interview with Nathaniel Mackey." *Chicago Review* 43.1 (1997): 30–46.

Olson, Charles. "Projective Verse." *Charles Olson: Selected Writing.* Ed. Robert Creeley. New York: New Directions, 1996. 15–30.

Packard, William, ed. "Craft Interview with John Ashbery." *The Craft of Poetry: Interviews from the* New York Quarterly. New York: Paragon, 1987. 111–32.

Parker, Robert Dale. *The Unbeliever: The Poetry of Elizabeth Bishop.* Chicago: U of Illinois P, 1988.

Paz, Octavio. "Elizabeth Bishop, or the Power of Reticence." *World Literature Today* 51.1 (1977): 15–16.

Perelman, Bob. *The Marginalization of Poetry: Language, Writing, and Literary History.* Princeton: Princeton UP, 1996.

Perloff, Marjorie. "Empiricism Once More." *The Uses of Literary History.* Ed. Marshall Brown. Durham: Duke UP, 1995. 51–61.

————. "Janus-Faced Blockbuster." Rev. of *The Oxford Anthology of American Poetry*, ed. Cary Nelson. *Symploke* 8.1–2 (2001): 205–13.

————. "Why Big Anthologies Make Bad Textbooks." *Chronicle of Higher Education.* 16 Apr. 1999: B6–B7.

Piedra, José. "Through Blues." *Do the Americas Have a Common Literature?* Ed. Gustavo Pérez Firmat. Durham: Duke UP, 1990. 107–29.

Pinsky, Robert. *Poetry and the World.* New York: Ecco, 1988.

Plimpton, George, ed. Interview with John Ashbery. *The Paris Review Interviews.* New York: Viking, 1989. 389–412.

Pollack, Frederick. "Poetry and Politics." In *Poetry after Modernism.* Ed. Robert McDowell. Browneville, OR: Story Line, 1991. 5–55.

Porter, Dennis. *Haunted Journeys: Desire and Transgression in European Travel Writing.* Princeton: Princeton UP, 1991.

Pratt, Mary Louise. *Imperial Eyes: Travel Writing and Transculturation.* New York: Routledge, 1992.

Proust, Marcel. *Remembrance of Things Past, Vol. 3: The Captive, the Fugitive, and Time Regained.* Trans. C. K. Moncrieff, Terence Kilmartin, and Andreas Mayor. New York: Random House, 1981.

Ramazani, Jahan. *The Hybrid Muse: Postcolonial Poetry in English*. Chicago: U of Chicago P, 2001.

Rasula, Jed. *The American Poetry Wax Museum: Reality Effects, 1940–1990*. Urbana: NCTE, 1996.

Rich, Adrienne. *Dark Fields of the Republic*. New York: Norton, 1995.

Rilke, Rainer Maria. *Sonnets to Orpheus*. Trans. M. D. Herter Norton. New York: Norton, 1942.

Rorty, Richard. *Contingency, Irony, and Solidarity*. Cambridge: Cambridge UP, 1989.

———. *Philosophy and Social Hope*. New York: Penguin, 1999.

———. "Trotsky and Wild Orchids." *Wild Orchids and Trotsky: Messages from American Universities*. Ed. Mark Edmundson. Harmondsworth, UK: Penguin, 1993. 29–50.

Rotella, Guy. *Reading and Writing Nature: The Poetry of Robert Frost, Wallace Stevens, Marianne Moore, and Elizabeth Bishop*. Boston: Northeastern UP, 1991.

Roussel, Raymond. *How I Wrote Certain of My Books*. Ed. Trevor Winkfield. Boston: Exact Change, 1995.

Rushdie, Salman. "My Unfunny Valentine." *The New Yorker*. 15 Feb. 1999. 28–29.

Sacks, Peter. *The English Elegy: Studies in the Genre from Spenser to Yeats*. Baltimore: Johns Hopkins UP, 1985.

Said, Edward. *Culture and Imperialism*. New York: Vintage, 1994.

———. "Identity, Authority, and Freedom: The Potentate and the Traveler." *Transition* 54 (1991): 4–19.

———. *Orientalism*. New York: Vintage, 1978.

———. "Reflections on Exile." *Out There: Marginalization and Contemporary Cultures. Documentary Sources in Contemporary Art 4*. Ed. Russell Ferguson, et al. New York: NMCA; and Cambridge, MA: MIT P, 1990. 357–66.

———. "Representing the Colonized: Anthropology's Interlocutors." *Critical Inquiry* 15 (Winter 1989): 205–25.

Sarup, Madan. "Home and Identity." *Travelers' Tales: Narratives of Home and Displacement*. Ed. George Robertson, et al. London: Routledge, 1994.

Saunders, Frances Stonor. *The Cultural Cold War: The CIA and the World of Arts and Letters*. New York: New Press, 1999.

Sawyer-Laucanno, Christopher. *The Continual Pilgrimage: American Writers in Paris, 1944–1960*. New York: Grove, 1992.

Schultz, David. *John Ashbery: An Introduction to the Poetry*. New York: Columbia UP, 1979.

Schultz, Susan. "Impossible Music." *Postmodern Culture* 2.2. (1992): 1–8.

Schwartz, Lloyd, and Sybil P. Estess, eds. *Elizabeth Bishop and her Art*. Ann Arbor: U of Michigan P, 1983.

Shapiro, David. *John Asbery: An Introduction to the Poetry*. New York: Columbia UP, 1979.

Shetley, Vernon. *After the Death of Poetry: Poet and Audience in Contemporary America*. Durham: Duke UP, 1993.

Shklovsky, Victor. "Art as Technique." *Russian Formalist Criticism: Four Essays*. Trans. Lee T. Lemon and Marion J. Reis. Lincoln: U of Nebraska P, 1965. 3–24.

Shoptaw, John. *On the Outside Looking Out*. Cambridge: Harvard UP, 1994.

Sloan, Benjamin. "*Houseboat Days* and 'Houses Founded on the Sea': An Example of Emerson as Source for Ashbery." *Notes on Contemporary Literature* 23.3 (1993): 5–6.

Snyder, Gary. *The Back Country*. New York: New Directions, 1968.

———. *Earth House Hold*. New York: New Directions, 1969.

———. *Mountains and Rivers without End*. Washington, D.C.: Counterpoint, 1996.

———. *No Nature*. New York: Pantheon, 1993.

———. *Rip-Rap and Cold Mountain Poems*. San Francisco: Four Seasons, 1969.

Spires, Elizabeth. "The Art of Poetry XXVII: Elizabeth Bishop." *Paris Review* (Summer 1981): 56–83.

Spivak, Gayatri. "Questions of Multiculturalism." *The Postcolonial Critic*. Ed. Sarah Harasym. New York: Routledge, 1990.

Starbuck, George. " 'The Work!': A Conversation with Elizabeth Bishop." *Elizabeth Bishop and her Art*. Ed. Lloyd Schwartz and Sybil P. Estess. Ann Arbor: U of Michigan P, 1983. 312–30.

Stewart, Susan. "The State of Cultural Theory and the Future of Literary Form." *Profession 93*. New York: MLA, 1993. 12–15.

Terada, Rei. *Derek Walcott's Poetry: American Mimicry*. Boston: Northeastern UP, 1992.

Tillinghast, Richard. "Damaged Grandeur: The Life of Robert Lowell." *Critical Responses to Robert Lowell*. Ed. Steven Gould Axelrod. Greenwood, 1999.

Todorov, Tzvetan. *On Human Diversity*. Cambridge: Harvard UP, 1993.

Travisano, Thomas J. *Elizabeth Bishop: Her Artistic Development*. Charlottesville: UP of Virginia, 1988.

Trinh Minh-ha. "Other than Myself / My Other Self." *Travelers' Tales: Narratives of Home and Displacement*. Ed. George Robertson, et al. London: Routledge, 1994. 9–26.

Urry, John. *The Tourist Gaze: Leisure and Travel in Contemporary Societies*. London: Sage, 1990.

Van Den Abbeele, George. "Montesquieu *Touriste*, or a View from the Top." *L'ésprit Créateur* 35.3 (1985): 64–74.

———. *Travel as Metaphor: From Montaigne to Rousseau.* Minneapolis: U of Minnesota P, 1992.

Vendler, Helen. "Domestication, Domesticity and the Otherworldly." *Modern Critical Views: Elizabeth Bishop.* Ed. Harold Bloom. New York: Chelsea, 1985.

Villers de L'Isle-Adam, Auguste. *Axel.* Englewood Cliffs: Prentice-Hall, 1970.

von Hallberg, Robert. "Tourists." *American Poetry and Culture, 1945–1980.* Cambridge: Harvard UP, 1985. 62–92.

Walcott, Derek. *Another Life.* New York: Farrar, 1973.

———. "The Antilles: Fragments of Epic Memory." *What the Twilight Says: Collected Essays.* New York: Farrar, 1998. 65–84.

———. *The Arkansas Testament.* New York: Farrar, 1987.

———. *The Bounty.* New York: Farrar, 1997.

———. "The Caribbean: Culture or Mimicry?" *Journal of Interamerican Studies and World Affairs* 16.1 (1974): 3–13.

———. *The Castaway and Other Poems.* London: Cape, 1965.

———. *Collected Poems.* New York: Farrar, 1986.

———. *The Fortunate Traveler.* New York: Farrar, 1981.

———. *The Gulf.* London: Cape, 1969.

———. *In a Green Night.* London: Cape, 1962.

———. Lecture. City College, New York City. 19 November 1999.

———. *Midsummer.* New York: Farrar, 1984.

———. "The Muse of History." *What the Twilight Says: Collected Essays.* New York: Farrar, 1998. 36–64.

———. *Omeros.* New York: Farrar, 1990.

———. *Sea Grapes.* New York: Farrar, 1976.

———. *The Star-Apple Kingdom.* New York: Farrar, 1979.

———. *Tiepolo's Hound.* New York: Farrar, 2000.

———. "What the Twilight Says: An Overture." *What the Twilight Says: Collected Essays.* New York: Farrar, 1998. 3–35.

Weinberger, Eliot. *American Poetry Since 1950: Innovators and Outsiders.* New York: Marsilio, 1993.

Wolff, Janet. "On the Road Again: Metaphors of Travel in Cultural Criticism." *Resident Alien: Feminist Cultural Criticism.* New Haven: Yale UP, 1995. 115–34.

Wolosky, Shira. "Representing Other Voices: Rhetorical Perspective in Elizabeth Bishop." *Style* 29.1 (1995): 1–17.

Yeats, William Butler. *The Collected Poems.* New York: Macmillan, 1956.

Bishop, Elizabeth (*continued*)
unempowered, 25; and years in
Brazil, 110–11. Works: "Arrival at
Santos," 36, 37, 39–40, 46, 50, 55,
153, 262–63 (n. 28); "The Bight,"
52; *Brazil*, 37, 39; "Brazil, January
1, 1502," 31, 32, 34, 36–39, 40,
48, 75, 251 (n. 9); "The Burglar of
Babylon," 27; "Cirque d'Hiver," 29;
A Cold Spring, 31; *The Complete Poems
1927–1979*, 28; "Crusoe in England,"
29, 48–54, 55, 57, 118, 252 (n. 14);
"The End of March," 60; *Geography
III*, 31, 44, 48; "In the Waiting
Room," 30, 34, 44–48, 50, 69, 70–71,
85, 207, 253 (n. 18); "Jerónimo's
House," 59; "The Map," 20, 28–31,
32, 48, 57, 194, 247, 257 (n. 15);
North and South, 24, 44; "North
Haven," 87; "Over 2000 Illustrations
and a Complete Concordance,"
31–36, 38, 41, 251 (n. 9); "Pleasure
Seas," 253 (n. 17); *Questions of Travel*,
31, 36, 39, 44; "Questions of Travel,"
12, 26–27, 34, 38, 41–44, 57, 149,
171; "Santarém," 27, 48, 54–59, 60,
205, 253 (n. 18)
Blackburn, Paul, 146
Blackwood, Caroline, 66, 79, 80
Bloom, Harold, 100, 101, 103, 254
(n. 1)
Bly, Robert, 146
Borges, Jorge Luis, 124, 126, 143
Botsford, Keith, 254 (n. 2)
Bougainville, Louis-Antoine de, 23
Bowles, Paul, 4
Brand, Dionne, 180
Brathwaite, Kamau, 180
Breslin, Paul, 179

Bronk, William, 146
Brouet, Aloysius, 239
Burnett, Paula, 180, 183
Burroughs, William, 146, 256 (n. 7)
Butor, Michel, 212

Caesar, Terry, 9–10, 23
Campbell, Joseph, 100, 137
Cavafy, C. P., 170
Certeau, Michel de, 234
Césaire, Aimé, 180, 187, 242
Chamoiseau, Patrick, x–xi
Chatwin, Bruce, ix, 258 (n. 17)
Chow, Rey, 161, 249 (n. 1)
Clifford, James, 1, 2, 5
Colwell, Anne, 32, 39, 252 (n. 10)
Condé, Maryse, 180
Confiant, Rafael, x
Congress of Cultural Freedom, 66, 68,
73, 253–54 (n. 4), 254 (n. 2)
Conrad, Joseph, 47, 183, 207
Corman, Cid, 146
Corn, Alfred, 103
Correa de Araujo, Lili, 61
Costello, Bonnie, 28, 44, 59, 258 (n. 18)
Crane, Hart, 24
Creeley, Robert, 21, 95, 145, 147,
170–77. Works: "Desultory Days,"
174–77; "The Dogs of Auckland,"
173; *Hello: A Journal, February
29–May 3, 1976*, 171; "Histoire de
Florida," 172; *Life and Death*, 171,
172–73; "Poem for Beginners,"
170–71; *So There: Poems 1976–83*, 171,
173; "Wellington, New Zealand,"
171
Crusoe, Robinson, 49, 117–18, 207,
252 (n. 14)
Cucullu, Lois, 44

Cullen, Countee, 265 (n. 14)
Curry, Renée, 51

Damon, Maria, 93–95, 102
defamiliarization, 14
Defoe, Daniel, 48, 49, 51, 53, 207
Derrida, Jacques, 13, 46, 130, 137, 161, 255 (n. 2, bottom)
Diderot, Denis, 23
Diehl, Joanne Fiet, 51
Donne, John, 24
Doreski, C. K., 250–51 (n. 4)
Dragomoshchenko, Arkadii, 263 (n. 3)
Drummond de Andrade, Carlos, 252 (n. 14)
Duncan, Robert, 226

Edelman, Lee, 44
Eliade, Mircea, 153–54
Eliot, T. S., 53, 253 (n. 19)
Emerson, Ralph Waldo, 6, 13, 20–21, 23, 27, 42, 176–77, 179, 234, 237
Epstein, Joseph, 255 (n. 3)
Eshleman, Clayton, 41, 146
ethnicity, as product of travel, 12–13
Europe on Five Dollars a Day, 65, 147
Evans, Bill, 223

Fenton, James, 259 (n. 4)
Ferlinghetti, Lawrence, 255 (n. 1, top)
Fiet, Lowell, 262 (n. 26)
Forché, Carolyn, 255 (n. 1)
Foucault, Michel, 12, 111, 256 (n. 4), 262 (n. 23)
Freud, Sigmund: on infantile oceanic consciousness, 136; on oedipal travel, 113; on travel as critique of home, 147–48. Works: "A Disturbance of Memory on the Acropolis," 16, 174, 175, 256 (n. 8); "Mourning and Melancholia," 54; "The Uncanny," 16, 47, 85, 113
Frost, Robert, 138–39, 158, 164, 166, 250 (n. 11)
Froude, James Anthony, 187, 203, 260–61 (n. 11)
Fussell, Paul, 162

Gadamer, Hans-Georg, 60
geography, as textuality, 121, 123–25, 126, 158–59, 243–48
Ginsberg, Allen, 19, 21, 58, 109, 146, 147, 148–58, 229, 231; "Angkor Watt," 152–53; "The Change: Kyoto-Tokyo Express," 153; Death and Fame, 176; The Fall of America, 154–57; "Galilee Shore," 152; "Heat," 152; Howl, 146; "The Moments Return," 152; "Patna-Benares Express," 152; "Siesta in Xbalba," 145, 151; "Thru the Vortex West Coast to East 1965–1966," 155; "Wichita Vortex Sutra," 154; "Zigzag Back thru These States 1966–1967," 155
Goldensohn, Lorrie, 51
Gordimer, Nadine, 239–40, 241
Gray, Paul, 265 (n. 1, bottom)
Gray, Rockwell, 4
Greene, Graham, 207, 263 (n. 29)
Grunquist, Raoul, 239–41
Guatemala, writers of, 1–2

Hall, Donald, 92, 255 (n. 3)
Hardwick, Elizabeth, 64, 66, 68, 80, 91
Harrison, Virginia, 9, 25–26
Hartigan, Royal, 228
Heaney, Seamus, 259 (n. 4, bottom)
Hearn, Lafcadio, 263 (n. 31)

Heart of Darkness (Conrad), 47, 183, 207
Hecht, Anthony, 6
Hejinian, Lyn, 22, 99, 226, 247, 257
    (n. 15), 263 (n. 3). Works: *My Life*,
    214; *Oxota*, 213–25
heterotopia, 203, 207–8, 262 (n. 23)
Holden, Jonathan, 101–2
Hollander, John, 6–7, 44
hooks, bell, 5
Howard, Richard, 102, 103, 109, 110,
    145, 150
Hugh of St. Victor, ix

Illich, Ivan, 73
irony, 114–15, 116, 120–21. *See also*
    parody, in John Ashbery
It's a Wonderful Life, 115, 176
Iyer, Pico, 15

Jameson, Frederic, 16–17, 122, 219,
    255 (n. 4)
Jarrell, Randall, 6, 28
Jeffers, Robinson, 164
Jehlen, Myra, 28
Jobim, Antonio Carlos, 252 (n. 11)
Johnson, Dane, 240

Kalaidjan, Walter, 97–100, 102
Kalstone, David, 253 (n. 1)
Kaplan, Caren, 7–10, 23, 58, 251 (n. 5)
Keelan, Mary, 73
Kerouac, Jack, 146
Kincaid, Jamaica, 180
Koch, Kenneth, 150
Koethe, John, 96, 103
Kramer, Lawrence, 231, 264–65 (n. 13)

Larkin, Philip, 258 (n. 19)
Laskin, David, 63, 92

Lazer, Hank, 100, 102
Leed, Eric, 10
Leiris, Michel, 111–12
Levertov, Denise, 146
Levin, Bernard, 251 (n. 9)
Lévi-Strauss, Claude, 14, 24, 26–27, 43,
    44, 45, 46, 60, 154, 232, 234–36
Li Po, 218
Lodge, David, 4
Lonely Planet Journeys, 256 (n. 10)
Longenbach, James, 26, 59, 96
Lowell, Robert, 21, 49, 54, 110,
    145, 180, 207, 213; admiration of,
    for Bishop and her travels, 64;
    ambivalence of, toward Ransom,
    254 (n. 6); Bishop's influence on,
    253 (n. 1); "breakthrough" of, 59,
    64; changing reputation of, 63; and
    Congress of Cultural Freedom, 66,
    68; and emergence of trope of travel,
    67–68; friendship of, with Bishop
    and Walcott, 19; letters from Bishop
    to, 49, 54; as "mainstream," 18, 88,
    92–95, 104; as pacifist, 254 (n. 5,
    top); as "political poet," 89–92; as
    reluctant internationalist, 18, 68,
    254 (n. 2); and translation style,
    146–47; and travel as trauma, 79–80;
    and trope of travel, 67–68. Works:
    "America from Oxford," 90–91;
    "Beyond the Alps," 64; "Buenos
    Aires," 67, 68–69; "Christmas," 84–
    85; *Day by Day*, 86, 158; *The Dolphin*,
    73, 75, 81, 90–91; "Dropping South:
    Brazil," 67, 68, 69–71, 73, 74, 76, 77,
    79, 81, 83; "During a Transatlantic
    Call," 87; "Eight Months Later,"
    77; "Epilogue," 27, 158; "Eye and
    Tooth," 67, 88; "Flight," 83–84;

construct," 8; as "off the beaten track," 113–14; as pursuit of archaism, 39; social relations of, 115. *See also* travel

transport, 127, 190, 191, 210

travel: banality of, 114; as betrayal, 2, 6–8, 10, 179–81, 196–98, 203; and composition, 135–36; as critique of home, 146, 147–58; and defamiliarization, 15; as deferral of signification, 109–10; as destabilizing, 3–6, 14–15, 25, 151–52; etymology of, 3; as figure for spiritual path, 110; as frightening, 152; as guilt and remorse, 128–29, 130–31, 133, 170–71, 174–77; as illusory, 108, 137, 139, 228, 229; as infantile, 109, 121, 127, 150; as mass displacement, 4–5; and music, 155–57, 226, 228–29, 232; and poetics, 15; as quest for difference, 217–25; as release from obligation, 109, 179–81; as textuality, 121, 123–25, 126, 158–59, 243–48; as "transport," 127, 190, 191, 210; and the uncanny, 16; after World War II, 17, 65. *See also* Freud, "The Uncanny"

Travisano, Thomas, 28, 31, 250–51 (n. 4)

Trinh Minh-ha, 5

Tristes Tropiques (Lévi-Strauss), 24, 26–27, 154, 234–36. *See also* Lévi-Strauss, Claude

Van Den Abbeele, George, 13, 256 (n. 9)

Vendler, Helen, 46, 103

von Hallberg, Robert, 6, 65, 68, 99, 145, 253 (n. 4)

Wakowski, Diane, 95

Walcott, Derek, 32, 173, 213; and apophasis, 200; and argument against linear view of history, 199, 202, 203, 209–10; on the Caribbean as static, 187; and geography as text, 158, 194, 243–46; and Hispanic Caribbean, 202–8; and the mourning of presence, 193, 194–98, 199; and the Nobel Prize, 178–79, 180, 239–42, 259 (n. 2); and poetic excess, 188; as tourist in his native country, 189; on travel as betrayal, 171, 175, 179–81, 196–98, 203; as traveler, 179–81; and universalism, 198–99. Works: "Air," 260 (n. 11); *Another Life*, 179, 182, 259 (n. 2), 260 (n. 9); *The Arkansas Testament*, 198, 203, 204, 261 (n. 20); *The Bounty*, 21, 196, 198–99, 204, 207, 260 (n. 7), 261 (n. 12); "The Bounty," 195; "Cantina Music," 203; *The Capeman*, 179; "The Caribbean: Culture or Mimicry?" 43; "Central America," 203; "Crusoe's Island," 15; "The Divided Child," 178; "Elsewhere," 200–202; "A Far Cry from Africa," 178, 186, 241; *The Fortunate Traveler*, 203; "The Fortunate Traveler," 182–85, 210, 256 (n. 5), 261 (nn. 13, 20); "French Colonial. 'Vers de Société,'" 203; "The Gulf," 182, 259–60 (n. 6); "Homecoming," 196–98; "Homecoming: Anse La Raye," 189, 190, 191; "The Liberator," 203; "The Light of the World," 181, 187,

Walcott, Derek (*continued*)
189–93, 210; "Mass Man," 259–60
(n. 6); *Midsummer*, 21, 182, 189, 194,
198, 199, 202, 204, 207, 260 (n. 11),
261 (n. 18), 262 (n. 22); "The Muse
of History," 202, 203, 242; *Omeros*,
181, 187, 194–97 passim, 210, 241,
259 (n. 2), 262 (n. 25); "Preparing for
Exile," 203; "Return to D'Ennery,"
187, 260 (n. 8); "Sainte Lucie,"
197; "Salsa," 203; "The Schooner
Flight," 19, 79, 181, 185–89, 194–95,
210, 259–60 (n. 6), 261 (n. 19);
Sea Grapes, 203; "Sea Grapes," 23,
209; "Signs," 199–200, 206; "The
Spoiler's Return," 185, 260 (n. 7);
The Star-Apple Kingdom, 263 (n. 31);
"The Star-Apple Kingdom," 189,
191, 208–10; "Summer Elegies,"
200; "Tales of the Islands," 181, 185;
Tiepolo's Hound, 178, 194, 261–62
(n. 21); "Tropic Zone," 189, 204–7,
262–63 (n. 28); *What the Twilight Says*,
19; "What the Twilight Says," 179,
260 (n. 11)
Whitman, Walt, ix, 174, 176, 188, 208,
226, 231
Wilbur, Richard, 6, 145
Williams, William Carlos, 6, 21, 64, 79,
226, 253 (n. 19), 264 (n. 9)
Wizard of Oz, The (Fleming), 115–16
Wolff, Janet, 7, 23
Wordsworth, William, 50, 60, 138
Wright, James, 145, 146
Wright, Jay, 264 (n. 7)
Writer's Digest, advice of, on "travel
poetry," 212, 213, 218, 220